32/95

D1416360

THE CASH FLOW PROBLEM SOLVER

CASH FLOW PROBLEM SOLVER

PROCEDURES AND RATIONALE FOR THE INDEPENDENT BUSINESSMAN

Bryan E. Milling

CHILTON BOOK COMPANY   RADNOR, PENNSYLVANIA

Copyright © 1981 by Bryan E. Milling
All Rights Reserved
Published in Radnor, Pennsylvania (19089), by Chilton Book Company
and simultaneously in Scarborough, Ontario, Canada,
by Nelson Canada Limited
Library of Congress Catalog Card No. 80-70388
ISBN 0-8019-6891-7

Designed by Jean Callan King/Visuality
Manufactured in the United States of America

Elements of Chapter 23 appeared in a different form in
Bryan E. Milling, *Handbook of Accounts Receivable Financing:
A Dynamic Approach to Cash Flow and Profits* (Englewood Cliffs,
N.J.: Institute for Business Planning, 1978).

4 5 6 7 8 9 0   0 9 8 7 6 5 4 3 2

To Annie
my personal cash flow problem

CONTENTS

ACKNOWLEDGMENTS

This book would not have been completed successfully without the editorial discipline enforced by Michael J. Strickland. Any positive elements contained in these pages stem largely from his talent and generosity.

I am also grateful to Frank Besnette, Gary Tallman, and Greg Neal. Their professional assistance, coupled with the facilities and atmosphere I enjoyed at Northern Arizona University, provided the resources necessary for any extended writing effort.

Finally, to my wife and family, whose patience and devotion were frequently tested during the writing of this book, I express my heartfelt thanks.

THE CASH FLOW PROBLEM SOLVER

INTRODUCTION

Cash flow management is essential to the success of every business. In fact, cash flow management is often more important to success than the ability to manufacture a product or generate a sale. You can lose a customer without irreparable damage. However, let a gap in your cash flow cause you to miss a payroll and you are out of business.

The *Cash Flow Problem Solver* is designed to help you avoid such crises in your business. It identifies the fundamental principles of cash flow management and helps you apply those principles to your business.

However, the *Cash Flow Problem Solver* isn't a textbook designed for professionals in finance and accounting. Instead, it is directed toward the businessman or woman whose background is marketing or manufacturing or engineering—the typical entrepreneur. Thus, the *Cash Flow Problem Solver* takes a profit-oriented approach to cash flow management. And it answers such questions as:

How does accelerating the accounts-receivable turnover benefit your bottom line?

What is the effect of idle assets on your cash flow and profits?

How do you combat a crimp in your cash flow that causes you to lose valuable trade discounts?

The *Cash Flow Problem Solver* not only answers these questions, but it gives realistic examples that illustrate the actual dollar cost of cash flow problems in a business, as well as the bottom-line benefits of effective cash flow management.

The emphasis on the bottom-line benefits of positive cash flow management is designed to hold your interest in a subject that many people find tedious. However, the *Cash Flow Problem Solver* doesn't stop there. The ideas illustrated in the book are crystallized in a set of numbered Cash Flow Concepts to encourage you to retain and utilize them. One Cash Flow Concept may identify a basic objective of accounts-receivable management. Another will provide a signal to help you avoid a dangerous gap in your cash flow. Still another may suggest a financing method that will increase your earnings. These Cash Flow Concepts have evolved from my experience with more than 1,500 businesses encountered during my career in commercial finance and banking.

Your situation is unique, but your cash flow problems are common to every business. If you understand the basic Cash Flow Concepts, you can adapt them to fit your special circumstance. Of course, not every Cash Flow Concept will be useful to you. However, if one idea serves as a reminder that helps you preserve the financial integrity of your business, or increase your earnings, then your effort in reading this book will be worthwhile.

Here are the first two Cash Flow Concepts:

1: Cash is essential for the survival, the growth, and the profitability of your business.

2: Cash flow management is essential to the success of your business.

For your business to survive, you must have cash to pay expenses and retire other liabilities on schedule. Although you can defer payment for some obligations because of a temporary cash shortage, pressing that privilege can lead to financial failure.

In addition, cash provides a necessary buffer to help absorb an unforeseen crisis or a managerial mistake. You can weather a wildcat strike or a severe drop in sales if you have the necessary cash reserve. Without that reserve, the same setback can be disastrous.

Also, cash is essential for growth. In fact, no matter how profitable your business, it cannot grow without an expanding cash flow, either from retained earnings or from a combination of earnings and cash obtained from external financing. As you will see in Chapter 13, cash is the limiting factor in the growth of any business.

Finally, cash is essential for achieving the profit potential of your business. A dollar held in the form of accounts receivable or inventory cannot be reinvested profitably until you convert it back into cash. Receivables and inventory are necessary parts of the cycle, but cash makes the cycle continuous.

Those facts make maximum cash generation the natural, primary objective of cash flow management.

The *Cash Flow Problem Solver* uses *maximum cash generation* as the guiding principle of cash flow management. Thus, in your cash flow management effort, you should seek the most rapid conversion of your receivables and inventory into cash. That doesn't mean that you should convert every asset into cash and close the doors. But it does recognize the crucial role that cash plays in achieving basic business objectives.

Of course, to be consistent, we should discuss the efficient use of cash as an asset similar to accounts receivable and inventory. An overinvestment in cash exacts an opportunity cost when you could employ that excess profitably elsewhere.

Nevertheless, don't look for a chapter on the profitable investment of excess cash. Instead, the book will concentrate on the factors that disrupt a firm's cash flow and reduce its earnings. After all, the lack of sufficient cash is always a problem. Seldom does excess cash lead to a serious business setback, and most businessmen can handle that problem without outside assistance.

The subject of cash isn't ignored entirely. We consider the proper working balances for a business when we discuss cash flow planning in Part Six. However, if your problem is *excess* cash, reading this book may be an educational experience for you, but I can't guarantee that it will be a profitable one.

The *Cash Flow Problem Solver's* approach to cash flow management invites you to take control of your cash flow—to exercise *positive cash flow management.* Positive cash flow management reduces the disruptions and maintains the smooth, continuous cash flow essential to the growth and profitability of your business. Although the best management effort will not provide absolute control of your cash flow, you can solve or avoid the common cash flow problems. Moreover, positive cash flow management can benefit your bottom line.

In Part One, the *Cash Flow Problem Solver* describes the cash flow process in "ideal" and in practical terms, and it emphasizes cash flow management as a profit center in your business.

In Parts Two and Three, the focus will be on two primary aspects of cash flow management: *component* management and *structural* management. Don't let these terms disturb you; there is no mystery to them. Component management concentrates on the specific assets in the cash flow process. Since we ignore cash as an independent asset, your accounts receivable and inventory become the subjects of our component management discussion. You seek the most profitable contribution from each component, apart from any relationship that component has with any other facet of your business.

The fundamentals of component management are not complicated in form, but often they are more difficult to implement than they appear. Structural management is more complicated. It concentrates on the interrelationship among the components in the cash flow process, or between those components and other aspects of the business's financial structure.

While structural management may be more complicated, it doesn't require financial wizardry. In most instances, your time and effort, coupled with a dash of common sense, provide the necessary ingredients for a profitable managerial effort. Indeed, the *Cash Flow Problem Solver's* approach is designed to simplify cash flow management as it increases your earnings.

Parts Four, Five, and Six concentrate on closely related considerations that contribute to positive cash flow management. In Part Four we consider the relationship between administrative practices and cash flow. You will find that proper paper flow is a necessary precedent for an efficient cash flow. Then we examine the effects of inflation on the cash flow process and some weapons that help combat those effects.

In Part Five, we turn our attention to leverage management—that is, the relationship between the cash flow process and the credit consideration available to a business. Certainly, few businesses prosper without external financing. Thus, the proper use of credit consideration becomes a natural element of positive cash flow management.

Finally, Part Six introduces the proper accounting tools necessary to implement positive cash flow management. The discussion culminates with the cash flow budget, the prudent manager's guiding light. Properly utilized, that budget heads off cash flow problems and increases earnings.

Before examining the fundamental principles of cash flow management, it is essential to establish a common framework for discussion. Part One provides that framework.

Chapter 1 introduces the schematic view of the cash flow process. You'll probably recognize that view, and you'll recognize that that idealized process rarely occurs in reality. Nevertheless, the ideal definition ensures that we start on the same wavelength.

Chapter 1 also presents a practical view of the cash flow process through a case history. This case history emphasizes the critical distinction between accrual and cash flow accounting. Failure to make that distinction leads to many of the cash flow problems that can afflict your business.

Chapter 2 focuses on the costs, direct and indirect, of cash flow problems and introduces the *Cash Flow Problem*

The Cash Flow Process

Solver's perspective on cash flow, namely that positive cash flow management is an important profit center in your business.

For many readers, Part One will be an elementary review, a synopsis of what they encounter every business day. Nevertheless, don't ignore these chapters: They provide the foundation for all that follows.

Cash Flow: A Practical View

The cash flow process is a circular system of asset transformation. In its simplest, schematic form, the system looks like this:

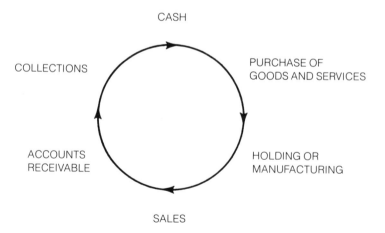

Thus, any business begins with cash. The purchase of goods and services, perhaps coupled with a manufacturing process, transforms that asset into inventory. Each sale transforms inventory into accounts receivable. Then, the collection process transforms accounts receivable back into cash. If the system works properly, the process repeats itself in a continuous cycle.

Of course, the system is more complicated than the schematic suggests. Trade credit, external financing, and retained earnings increase the total resources revolving in the cycle. Conversely, debt reduction, dividends, and operating losses shrink those resources. The periodic acquisition of fixed assets, which are not a part of the day-to-day cash flow cycle, further complicates the picture. However, when the process works smoothly, each asset—cash, inventory, accounts receivable—is pressed continuously toward the next phase in the cycle.

The cash flow schematic is simplistic in another respect, too. That is, it implies that the transformation process operates in a continuous, dynamic cycle. Unfortunately, the process seldom operates so smoothly. Instead, the cash flow in a business typically is erratic and subject to numerous disruptions.

For example, inventory sits as an idle asset until it is sold and delivered. Moreover, the seller must issue the proper invoices to transform sales into accounts receivable. A breakdown in any one of these tasks—the sale, the delivery, or the paperwork—interrupts the transformation process.

Similarly, until they are collected, accounts receivable serve only as evidence of the cash proceeds still due from sales. Failure to collect accounts as scheduled retards the transformation process. In fact, since collection of receivables provides the major source of cash from operations (excluding cash sales), slow-turning accounts can threaten the survival of a business.

Even cash itself—the asset that fuels the system—contributes little until the business converts it into marketable inventory. The unavailability of product (because of a snowstorm that disrupts delivery of a vital component, or a strike at a supplier's facility) leaves cash as an idle asset that is no more productive than unsold inventory or uncollected accounts receivable. Obviously, the whole transformation process must operate continuously if the business is to prosper.

These examples underline a basic fact of cash flow. That fact is summed up in Cash Flow Concept 3:

3: The cash flow process is an erratic system of asset transformation.

Just how erratic it can be is seen in the following case history. The experience of Drake Paper Company is a common, everyday one in the world of business. And it illustrates, too, that a growing, profitable business may be in the midst of a cash flow crisis. If you find that statement surprising, then you probably harbor a common misconception about the actual operation of cash flow in a business. That misconception underlies many of the problems faced by businesses, problems discussed throughout this book. Indeed, neither a rising sales volume nor a profitable operation spontaneously produces a positive cash flow.

THE ILLUSION OF PAPER PROFITS

Dan A. Drake, a dynamic salesman with limited financial expertise, founded Drake Paper in 1975. Although profits were slim, the business grew to a $100,000 monthly sales volume by the latter part of 1977.

In December of that year, Drake initiated an expansion program designed to produce a 50% increase in sales and place operations on a highly profitable basis.

The program produced immediate results. Sales increased from $100,000 in December to $150,000 in January of 1978. Moreover, as the firm's simplified income statement indicates, the higher volume generated $15,000 in earnings in the first month:

Income Statement 1/1/78–1/31/78	
Sales	$150,000
Cost of Sales	(105,000)
Operating Expenses	(30,000)
Earnings	$ 15,000

Unfortunately, Drake was unable to enjoy his success. Despite the company's profitability, the rapid sales increase led to a *$25,000 cash flow deficit.* Indeed, by the end of January, the firm was out of cash.

Before we illustrate the factors that led to Drake's cash shortage, we should emphasize two facts about that deficit.

First, the cash flow deficit was not the result of any extraordinary event. Rather, it followed naturally from the predictable relationships among the major elements in Drake's cash flow. Second, the deficit came as a complete surprise to Dan Drake. He erroneously assumed that a profitable operation automatically produces a positive cash flow. Indeed, he suffered from the "illusion of paper profits."

Drake forgot that the income statement is an *accrual* statement. That is, it records sales when they occur, not thirty days later, when the business collects the accounts receivable that proceed from the sales. This is a standard accounting procedure.

Similarly, a business accrues expenses as incurred, although the company may pay these obligations in some subsequent period. Some expenses, such as depreciation and amortization of prepaid items, represent prior cash disbursements, and these cloud the cash flow picture even further.

Accrual accounting is essential for financial management. It allows a business to measure performance—profit and loss—over a specific period by correctly matching revenues and expenses. However, sales do not coincide with cash inflow. Nor do expenses (or cost of sales) coincide with cash disbursements. Failure to recognize that distinction leads to the illusion of paper profits.

CASH ACCOUNTING

Cash accounting reflects the actual cash flow in a business, and we can use it to illustrate how Drake's actual cash flow in January left a $25,000 deficit despite a $15,000 financial profit. Here, we emphasize Cash Flow Concept 4:

4: Positive cash flow management requires a clear distinction between accrual accounting and cash flow accounting.

Cash accounting is an essential element of positive cash flow management. It recognizes the timing of the cash flow into a business from all sources, as well as the timing of the disbursements required to meet operating expenses and pay for purchases. A historical cash flow statement reflects actual past inflow and outflow. A projected statement, based on historical trends, predicts future cash flow.

Had Dan Drake recognized the significant difference between cash accounting and the illusory earnings implied by his income statement, the deficit cash flow would not have come as a surprise. His cash flow statement for January illustrates that point. That statement reflects the characteristics of the major elements in Drake's cash flow:

1. Accounts receivable, which are the company's only source of cash, turn in thirty days; Drake collects 100% of the prior month's sales.
2. Drake purchased $105,000 in inventory in December to meet January's forecasted sales volume; to maintain its credit rating, the company has always paid for every purchase within thirty days.
3. Drake pays all operating expenses as incurred; none is accrued for payment in the following month.

Based on these elements, Drake's projected (and actual) cash flow for January appeared as follows:

Cash Flow Statement 1/1/78–1/31/78	
Beginning Cash (in bank)	$ 10,000
Collections (December sales)	100,000
Operating Expenses	(30,000)
Payments (December purchases)	(105,000)
Cash Deficit	($ 25,000)

Thus, an apparent $15,000 profit is revealed as a predictable $25,000 cash flow deficit. The $40,000 difference emphasizes the significant difference between accrual and cash accounting.

Of course, Drake didn't actually experience a deficit cash flow. Instead, he deferred payment to some suppliers, absorbing modest injury to his payment record. Fortunately, his cash flow problem was not disastrous; nevertheless, it could have been avoided altogether. With sufficient foresight provided by a projected cash flow statement, Drake could have filled the gap with external financing, additional investment, or perhaps by accelerating the collection of his accounts receivable.

Drake's experience illustrates a primary tenet of cash flow management. That is, you must differentiate between accrued sales and expenses and carefully plan the cash flow associated with those transactions. Failure to do so can lead to the financial embarrassment of a sudden cash flow squeeze.

Of course, other accounting schedules add to the information provided by the basic income and cash flow statements. These are discussed as they apply to specific cases throughout the book. First, however, let's briefly review another financial statement that serves as a fundamental tool for cash flow management.

THE BALANCE SHEET

The balance sheet is another accrual financial statement. It provides a snapshot of the financial structure of a business at a particular time. That picture helps identify cash flow problems and orients solutions to those problems. Again, Drake Paper Company illustrates how valuable this financial tool can be.

Table 1–1 includes Drake's comparative balance sheets as of 12/31/77 and 1/31/78.

**TABLE 1–1 Comparative Balance Sheets:
Drake Paper Company**

	12/31/77	1/31/78
Cash	$ 10,000	—
Accounts Receivable	100,000	$150,000
Inventory	105,000	105,000
Other Assets	20,000	20,000
Total Assets	**$235,000**	**$275,000**
Accounts Payable	$105,000	$130,000
Other Liabilities	20,000	20,000
Total Liabilities	**$125,000**	**$150,000**
Stockholders' Equity	**$110,000**	**$125,000**
Liabilities and Equity	**$235,000**	**$275,000**

The earlier statement reflects the firm's financial structure as it appeared before the 50% sales increase. The latter statement shows how that increase altered the financial structure. Of course, this example first reiterates what we already know: That is, by 1/31/78, the firm had depleted its cash.

However, the balance sheet illustrates the effect of January's volume on the other elements in the structure. Accounts receivable increased from $100,000 to $150,000 in one month. That increase absorbed the firm's $15,000 profit, the beginning cash, and forced the increase in liabilities reflected in accounts payable; since the increase in sales is an accrued increase, and doesn't directly translate into cash until the following month, accounts payable increased without cash available for prompt payment. The firm must collect its accounts receivable (or use them as collateral for a short-term loan) to restore a satisfactory cash position.

Note another fact suggested by the balance sheets. Based on the detrimental effects of a 50% sales increase on Drake's cash flow and financial structure, further sales expansion is impossible. The growth in liabilities has already outpaced cash flow; another sales increase would be in accrued sales volume, not cash, and would exaggerate the fundamental problem. Indeed, a larger sales volume will lead to further deterioration in the firm's financial structure. Without external financing, accounts payable would fall so far behind payments that suppliers would cut the company off.

Moreover, neither analysis of the income statement, nor a review of the cash flow statement, demonstrates the effect of sales, revenues, and cash flow on the firm's financial structure. In fact, a business may have a positive cash flow and a profitable operation over the short term, while its financial structure develops faults that portend future problems—in Drake's case, an increase in accrued liabilities that outpaces the increase in cash.

Throughout the book, we will illustrate the value of the balance sheet in identifying and solving specific cash flow problems. Here, we only suggest that potential so that you will add the balance sheet to the income and cash flow statements as the fundamental tools for your cash flow management.

Incidentally, don't feel dismayed if you feel uncomfortable working with these financial tools. Certainly, most of the cash flow problems we discuss are more complex than Drake Paper's. However, none of the problems, or their solutions, requires more than an elementary understanding of the basic accounting process.

The Costs of Cash Flow Problems

To understand the benefits of positive cash flow management, you must understand that cash flow problems cost money. You may not be aware of the costs—or even of the problem. Nevertheless, the costs are real. Thus, Cash Flow Concept 5:

5: The cash flow process is a profit center in your business.

Solving your cash flow problems does more than help avoid financial embarrassment. It also increases your earnings. Higher earnings follow naturally each time you avoid the potential cost of a cash flow problem.

Every cash flow problem, however minor, hurts your bottom line. The injury isn't always serious. Often, it is not even apparent. But it is always real.

When you recognize these facts, the cash flow process becomes a profit center for you. And that perspective can lead to thousands of dollars in bottom-line benefits.

THE DIRECT COST OF A CASH FLOW PROBLEM

Most businessmen can calculate the direct cost of a cash flow problem, and you will see numerous calculations as we discuss specific problems throughout the book. Here we will look at the direct cost of a cash flow problem incurred by Kamco, Inc., a small wholesaler of rubber tubing products.

Jerry Shipp founded Kamco in 1971. The company has been profitable since its inception, and both sales and earnings increased steadily through 1976. However, earnings declined in 1977, despite an 11% rise in sales. As he reviewed his disappointing results in early 1978, Shipp centered his analysis on the financial data summarized in Table 2–1.

TABLE 2–1 Comparative Balance Sheets: Kamco, Inc.

	1976	1977
Sales	$1,800,000	$2,000,000
Earnings before Interest Expense	$ 90,000	$ 100,000
Interest Expense	$ 20,000	$ 33,000
Earnings after Interest Expense	**$ 70,000**	**$ 67,000**
Average Accounts Receivable	$ 200,000	$ 330,000
Average Bank Debt*	$ 200,000	$ 330,000

* Average interest rate is 10%.

Of course, Shipp quickly recognized that Kamco's higher interest costs in 1977 led directly to the decline in earnings. However, he also recognized this expense as only a symptom of the real problem.

Indeed, Shipp correctly concluded that the higher interest costs came from the debt necessary to support an extraordinary rise in Kamco's accounts receivable. In fact, receivables, bank debt, and interest costs all rose 65% in 1977. Retained earnings and trade credit supported the natural 11% rise in other assets. (If the relationship between asset growth and the bottom side of the balance sheet —liabilities and stockholders' equity—is unfamiliar, see Chapter 12.)

In Chapter 4 we illustrate how to measure an overinvestment in accounts receivable. Here, you need only recognize that a greater investment in accounts receivable requires a greater amount of borrowed money to avoid a cash flow deficit. An overinvestment ties up too much money in receivables, reducing earnings, restricting growth, and increasing interest charges from the external financing required to support the receivables. Shipp measured his overinvestment by comparing his average receivables in 1977 with the total appropriate, or "correct," for his sales growth—an 11% increase over the 1976 average:

Average Investment, 1977	$330,000
"Correct" Investment, 1977	222,000
Overinvestment	$108,000

In this instance, Shipp assumes that Kamco's average investment in receivables in 1976 is at the proper level. While further analysis might disprove that assumption, Kamco's overinvestment in 1977 is certainly no less than $108,000.

Moreover, the overinvestment reduced the firm's earnings in 1977 by $10,800. That reduction, which was the direct cost of this cash flow problem, came from the bank debt, at 10% interest, required to carry the excess in receivables. Indeed, had Shipp held his receivables investment in line with his sales growth, eliminating the need for the extra debt, Kamco would have had a respectable increase in earnings in 1977, instead of the actual decline.

Note that Kamco did not suffer a cash flow crisis—that is, a shortage of cash. The firm's borrowing power provided the cash to meet all obligations satisfactorily. Of course, that didn't solve the cash flow problem. Instead, it served only as an expensive method for avoiding a crisis. Indeed, Kamco's experience illustrates that a cash flow problem can be expensive without becoming an emergency.

Before we describe the practical line that distinguishes a cash flow problem from a cash flow crisis, let's use Kamco's experience to illustrate a less obvious cost of a cash flow problem.

THE INDIRECT COST OF A CASH FLOW PROBLEM

Kamco's experience shows that you should not ignore a cash flow problem simply because it doesn't develop into a crisis. In other words, you should not ignore a cash flow problem because you don't suffer a measurable *expense*. Indeed, the cost of a cash flow problem may not appear as an expense at all, but rather as profits foregone. To illustrate this, let's return to the example above. However, we will change one fact in the case.

Assume that Kamco has the same overinvestment in receivables, but that it carries the excess *without* the comparable increase in bank debt. Presumably, a strong equity base or lenient trade credit supports the overinvestment instead. Thus, Kamco eliminates the $10,800 in extra interest costs and enjoys an increase in earnings. Indeed, eliminating that expense leads to earnings of $77,800 in 1977, a respectable rise over the 1976 results.

Does that mean that the overinvestment in receivables has no effect on the company's bottom line? Indeed not! The overinvestment is still a cash flow problem, and that problem still hurts Kamco's earnings. Of course, the damage isn't visable in the form of higher interest costs. Instead, Kamco suffers an *opportunity cost.*

Opportunity cost measures the *indirect* cost of a cash flow problem. It represents *potential* earnings lost because of a cash flow problem: You make less than you should.

In this instance, Kamco loses the potential earnings available from $108,-000 in cash. Eliminating the overinvestment in receivables would generate that much cash for profitable use elsewhere. The firm could profit from expanding inventory, reducing other bank debt, or merely from the interest earned on a corporate savings account.

Those lost earnings, however calculated, measure the indirect cost of a cash flow problem. Of course, you won't find opportunity cost in an expense account, but the effect on your earnings is the same.

In later chapters, we will often refer to opportunity cost to measure the specific cost of a cash flow problem. To simplify the discussion, opportunity cost is measured in terms of the cost of borrowing. Thus, if you have a 10% cost of borrowing, a $100,000 overinvestment in receivables leads to at least a $10,000 (annualized) opportunity cost.

While the specific rate varies with time and circumstance, borrowing cost serves as a conservative criterion for measuring opportunity cost. In fact, as you will see later, you must earn more than your borrowing cost to justify incurring any debt at all.

Of course, you should recognize your own opportunity cost in any circumstance. It must be equal to or larger than your cost of borrowing. It cannot be less.

Now, let's add one more perspective to your view of the cash flow process.

CASH CAPABILITY

In the examples above, Kamco never suffers from a cash flow crisis. The firm had access to the cash necessary to meet all obligations promptly. In financial terminology, Kamco had sufficient *liquidity* for its operations.

Liquidity is an important concept for cash flow management. It indicates that a firm has the capacity to meet its obligations on time. However, "liquidity" has broad accounting connotations which aren't necessary for our discussion. To avoid jargon, and to narrow the subject so that we may concentrate on dollar flow, we require a different definition.

Thus, we measure liquidity in terms of a firm's *cash capability*. As defined here, cash capability measures the maximum cash available to a business at any point. We emphasize this with Cash Flow Concept 6:

6: A business can measure its cash capability as the sum of its cash reserves plus unutilized borrowing power.

In other words, cash capability measures the maximum cash available to support an increase in any other assets. It defines the practical limit on your cash flow. Exceeding your cash capability leads to an unacceptable cash flow deficit, or the failure to meet all obligations promptly. Indeed, exceeding your cash capability transforms a problem into a crisis.

Table 2–2 illustrates cash capability.

TABLE 2–2 Cash Capability

	Firm A	Firm B
Cash	$ 25,000	—
Accounts Receivable	50,000	$ 75,000
Inventory	50,000	75,000
Total Assets	**$125,000**	**$150,000**
Additional Borrowing Power	$ 25,000	

Firm A has $25,000 in cash and $100,000 in combined accounts receivable and inventory. The firm also has $25,000 in additional borrowing power from some external source, perhaps from a potential bank loan or additional supplier credit.

Whatever the source, that $25,000 borrowing power, coupled with the $25,000 cash on hand, gives the firm $50,000 in cash capability. It has that much cash available from internal and external sources to invest in other assets.

Firm B, on the other hand, has exhausted its cash capability. Without discussing the specific cause, it is apparent that the firm's higher investment in accounts receivable and inventory has absorbed all of its cash reserve and borrowing power. The business has reached the limit of its cash capability.

Cash capability is more than a catchy phrase. Because it defines the limits of the cash flow cycle in your business, it is an estimate of your protection against a cash flow crisis. You may not have a perfectly balanced cycle. Few businesses do. But you can operate successfully so long as you don't exhaust your cash capability. Moreover, the larger your cash capability, the less threat you suffer from any cash flow problem.

Kamco's experience proves that you can have a cash flow problem without having a crisis. In fact, unless you recognize the concept of opportunity cost, you can have a cash flow problem—such as an overinvestment in accounts receivable—without being aware of it. To solve the dilemma of invisible cash flow problems, you need a clearly defined objective to orient your cash flow management effort—namely, maximum cash flow generation. That is the principle underlying the management techniques discussed throughout the book.

Component management concentrates on accounts receivable and inventory as the two individual components in the cash flow process. Our discussion of each component involves several steps. First, we illustrate the specific relationship each component has to the cash flow process. The financial formulas that describe that relationship direct your component management effort. Next, we demonstrate how you can use the information derived from those formulas in a basic approach to component analysis. That analysis consists of identifying the proper investment in receivables and inventory for your business and, concurrently, the existence of any overinvestment.

Chapters 4 and 8 on component analysis also introduce some techniques that serve as the problem spotters. In other words, they help you identify cash flow problems in their incipient stages. Indeed, the earlier you identify and solve a problem, the less damage it will do to your bottom line. Certainly, this is the primary objective of your cash flow management effort.

We also develop the fundamental principles of component management by illustrating the specific factors that relate accounts receivable and inventory to the cash flow process, and include a look at the effect of their combined influence on your bottom line.

The latter consideration requires occasional deviation from maximum cash generation as the primary objective of cash flow management. Of course, you profit when you

PART TWO

Component Management

avoid or solve a cash flow problem. But often you can realize additional benefits by emphasizing earnings over cash generation.

Certainly, maximum cash generation is the principal objective of cash flow management. But you also should recognize the alternative of concentrating on maximum earnings. Indeed, you might exhaust your cash capability if the bottom-line benefits warrant.

Much of Part Two is directed toward the calculation processes essential for proper component management. Unfortunately, you might find some of these calculations a bit tedious. Nevertheless, remind yourself that the effort can be very profitable. Perhaps that will hold your interest.

Accounts Receivable in the Cash Flow Process

Accounts receivable represent the proceeds from sales. You trade your merchandise or service in exchange for your customer's promise to pay you in ten days or thirty days or perhaps even later. Then, the payment of those receivables becomes the primary source of operating cash. Indeed, too many broken promises to pay can leave your business without the funds to meet payroll, retire expenses, or service debt requirements.

Of course, most businessmen are aware of this, but not all can translate this awareness into successful, efficient cash flow management. Thus, this chapter illustrates the relationship between accounts receivable and the cash flow process.

COLLECTION PERIOD AND THE CASH FLOW PROCESS

Assuming a constant sales volume, a single concept, *collection period,* defines the relationship between accounts receivable and the cash flow process. Collection period is a critical factor: It measures the length of time your average sales dollar remains in the form of an account receivable.

7: Average collection period defines the relationship between accounts receivable and the cash flow process. The longer the collection period, the higher the investment in accounts receivable.

Of course, collection period alone doesn't determine the size of a firm's investment in receivables. Sales volume also has a direct influence: The larger the sales volume, the larger the investment in receivables.

The experience of Production Lumber, Inc. (PLI) demonstrates the relationship. PLI operates as a wholesale lumber broker. The company purchases lumber in carload lots from West Coast mills and ships it directly to its customers. PLI never takes possession of the lumber and, consequently, carries no inventory. Thus, the firm has a simple financial structure. In fact, as indicated in the 9/30/78 balance sheet (Table 3–1), PLI's only assets are cash and accounts receivable. Accounts payable make up the only liabilities.

TABLE 3–1 Production Lumber, Inc.

BALANCE SHEET		CASH FLOW	
	9/30/78		**9/1/78–9/30/78**
Cash	$ 10,000	Beginning Cash	$ 10,000
Accounts Receivable	$150,000	Collections (prior month's sales)	$150,000
Total Assets	**$160,000**	**Total Cash Available**	**$160,000**
Accounts Payable	$ 42,500	Payment for Purchases	$117,500
Stockholders' Equity	$117,500	Expenses	$ 32,500
Liabilities and Equity	**$160,000**	**Ending Cash**	**$ 10,000**

Table 3–1 reflects the following characteristics about the company's business:
1. PLI generates an average sales volume of $5,000 a day, or $150,000 per month.
2. All sales are made on thirty-day terms, and all customers pay within those terms.
3. Purchases average 85% of monthly sales volume; all suppliers require payment in ten days.

These characteristics leave PLI with an investment in receivables that holds constant at $150,000. At the same time, of course, that investment converts to cash at the rate of $5,000 a day, meaning that PLI's receivables have a thirty-day collection period.

Table 3–1, Column 2, shows that PLI's thirty-day collection period satisfies the firm's present cash flow requirements. Although the constant $10,000 beginning and ending monthly cash balance shows that the firm is operating only at a break-even level, neither making nor losing money, the thirty-day collection period meets the cash flow requirements for normal operations.

Now, assume that over the next six months PLI produces the same $150,-000 monthly sales volume. However, during that period, the average collection period stretches from thirty to sixty days. The company still has $5,000 a day in sales, but the average sales dollar remains as a receivable for sixty days.

Table 3–2 summarizes the effect that this longer collection period has on PLI's financial structure and cash flow.

TABLE 3–2 Production Lumber, Inc.

BALANCE SHEET		CASH FLOW	
	3/31/79		3/1/79–3/31/79
Cash	—	Beginning Cash	—
Accounts Receivable	$300,000	Collections	$150,000
Total Assets	**$300,000**	**Total Cash Available**	**$150,000**
Accounts Payable	$182,500	Payment for Purchases	$117,500
Stockholders' Equity	$117,500	Expenses	$ 32,500
Liabilities and Equity	**$300,000**	**Ending Cash**	**—**

Accounts receivable total $300,000. The firm has no beginning and ending monthly cash balance, and supplier credit stretches well beyond the normal industry allowance of ten days, as noted earlier in item 3. Yet nothing has changed in PLI's operation except the collection period. The firm still has $150,000 in monthly cash collections. But that cash is not sufficient to pay for the purchases required for the two-month sales volume. Indeed, receivables now convert to cash at only half the rate at which PLI generates sales. The inevitable result is a cash flow crisis.

CALCULATING COLLECTION PERIOD

Using Cash Flow Concept 7 requires two tasks. First, you must calculate the average collection period for your accounts receivable. Then, you must relate that period, and changes in that period, to your cash flow.

To calculate the average collection period:
1. Divide annual sales by 360 to determine your average daily sales volume
2. Divide that figure into the present balance of your accounts receivable
For example, if a business has $2 million in annual sales and $200,000 in accounts receivable, the calculation is:

1. Sales per Day $= \dfrac{\$2,000,000}{360} = \$5,555$

2. Average Collection Period $= \dfrac{\$200,000}{\$5,555} = 36$ days

Thus, each sale remains in the form of a receivable for an average of 36 days.

Generally, calculating collection period over the previous twelve months provides sufficient accuracy for the cash flow management effort. However, if you have had a recent fluctuation in sales, you should use a sales figure to reflect this fact. It can make a significant difference in the result.

For example, assume that $600,000 of the above sales volume came in the most recent quarter. To reflect that, the calculation is:

1. Sales per Day $= \dfrac{\$600,000}{90 \text{ Days}} = \$6,666$ in sales per day

2. Average Collection Period $= \dfrac{\$200,000}{\$6,666} = 30$ days

Thus, the collection period becomes significantly shorter. Naturally, that difference would influence any management decision affecting your investment in accounts receivable.

CASH FLOW AND COLLECTION PERIOD

To use the collection period calculation in your cash flow management effort, you must recognize how a change in the collection period affects your cash flow. Of course, we recognize the basic relationship: The longer the collection period, the higher the investment in accounts receivable. However, positive cash flow management requires a more precise measurement. Tables 3–3 and 3–4 help achieve that objective.

Table 3–3 details the effect different collection periods have on investment in accounts receivable over a range of daily sales rates from $1,000 to $5,000 a

TABLE 3–3 Effect of Collection Period on Investment in Accounts Receivable

Average Collection Period (days)	Sales per Day				
	$1,000	**$2,000**	**$3,000**	**$4,000**	**$5,000**
30	$30,000	60,000	90,000	120,000	150,000
35	35,000	70,000	105,000	140,000	175,000
40	40,000	80,000	120,000	160,000	200,000
45	45,000	90,000	135,000	180,000	225,000
50	50,000	100,000	150,000	200,000	250,000
55	55,000	110,000	165,000	220,000	275,000
60	60,000	120,000	180,000	240,000	300,000

Investment in Accounts Receivable

day. Use this table to measure the changes in collection period on your cash flow. For example, let's determine the cash generation potential from a modest reduction in collection period. Assume that

1. Your sales average $2,000 a day
2. Your average collection period is 45 days
3. You reduce your collection period to 40 days

From Table 3–3, you can see that the shorter collection period reduces your investment in receivables from $90,000 to $80,000. That reduction generates $10,000 in cash that you can invest profitably elsewhere, or you can add it to your reserves.

Table 3–4 simplifies the analytic process: It relates the number of days you reduce your collection period directly to the cash that reduction generates.

TABLE 3–4 Effect of a Reduction in Average Collection Period on Cash Flow

Reduction in Average Collection Period (days)	Sales per Day				
	$1,000	**$2,000**	**$3,000**	**$4,000**	**$5,000**
1	$ 1,000	2,000	3,000	4,000	5,000
3	3,000	6,000	9,000	12,000	15,000
5	5,000	10,000	15,000	20,000	25,000
7	7,000	14,000	21,000	28,000	35,000
10	10,000	20,000	30,000	40,000	50,000

Cash Generated

For example, if you have $2,000 a day in sales, you will generate $6,000 in cash from a three-day reduction in the average collection period. Viewed from another perspective, the lower collection period reduces your cash requirements by $6,000. This can provide a simple solution to many minor cash flow problems.

More important, of course, is the basic concept: Reducing the average collection period improves your cash flow because it shrinks your cash investment in accounts receivable.

ACCOUNTS-RECEIVABLE TURNOVER

Average collection period is a valuable management tool. However, traditional financial as well as cash flow management uses another tool. Although average collection period is a more appropriate measurement, you might encounter, or be more familiar with, a complementary calculation. That calculation measures the number of times a business *turns* (collects) its average investment in accounts receivable in the course of a year. The turnover rate comes from the calculation:

$$\text{Accounts-Receivable Turnover} = \frac{\text{Annual Sales}}{\text{Average Investment in Accounts Receivable}}$$

The data from the example above results in:

$$\text{A/R Turnover} = \frac{\$2,000,000}{\$200,000} = 10$$

That means that you turn (collect) your average investment in receivables ten times a year.

The calculation provides a number that becomes a yardstick with multiple uses. For example, turnover measures your efficiency in using the dollars you invest in accounts receivable. This efficiency rating has a direct effect on your cash flow and profitability.

Table 3–5 demonstrates that effect: It projects the average investment in receivables that results from different turnover rates, across sales volumes ranging from $1 million to $5 million per year.

Remind yourself that a lower investment in accounts receivable provides additional dollars for profitable investment elsewhere. In other words, Cash Flow Concept 8:

8: Increasing your accounts-receivable turnover rate improves your cash flow.

TABLE 3–5 Effect of Turnover Rate on Average Investment in Accounts Receivable

Turnover Rate	Annual Sales Volume				
	$1 million	$2 million	$3 million	$4 million	$5 million
6	$166,666	333,333	500,000	666,666	833,333
7	142,857	285,714	428,571	571,428	714,285
8	125,000	250,000	375,000	500,000	625,000
9	111,111	222,222	333,333	444,444	555,555
10	100,000	200,000	300,000	400,000	500,000
11	90,909	181,818	272,727	363,636	454,545
12	83,333	166,666	249,999	333,332	416,665

Average Investment in Accounts Receivable

For example, assume that you have the same $2 million sales volume, and you increase your receivable turnover rate from eight to nine times a year. From Table 3–5, you can see that this change reduces your investment in receivables from $250,000 to $222,222. This reduction generates almost $28,000 in cash, which you can use profitably elsewhere.

The collection period calculation and the accounts-receivable turnover calculation are the beginning tools for the cash flow management effort. Chapter 4 helps you use these tools as the fundamental bases for component analysis.

Component Analysis: Accounts Receivable

The collection period calculation determines how long it takes to convert your investment in accounts receivable into cash, but you must proceed beyond that calculation to determine the proper collection period for your business, as well as to identify any component problems that might cause an overinvestment in accounts receivable. This chapter reviews the fundamental tools for component analysis.

Component analysis begins with a straightforward comparison of your present collection period with your previous collection periods. Then, you complement that by looking at comparable competitor calculations.

Note, however, that as a subject for comparative analysis, average collection period suffers from an inherent weakness. The calculation is reasonably reliable only when it measures receivable activity over an extended term—such as ninety days or one year. Thus, by the time comparative analysis of your collection period identifies the existence of an accounts receivable problem, the associated overinvestment has already hurt your bottom line. Solving the problem immediately, which is unlikely, cannot repair the damage. Consequently, to identify component problems earlier, you must add another comparison to your analysis.

This comparison examines the ratio between your investment in accounts receivable and your monthly sales volume. As you will see, a significant change in that relationship can draw attention to a component problem before you feel it in your bank account.

Finally, this chapter reviews a familiar tool that also facilitates early identification of component problems. That tool, the aged analysis of accounts receivable, not only helps identify a component problem, but it pinpoints the specific accounts that threaten your cash flow. Indeed, a monthly aged analysis can help you diagnose and solve a component problem before it becomes costly.

COMPARATIVE ANALYSIS: AVERAGE COLLECTION PERIOD

The correct collection period translates into the proper investment in accounts receivable and becomes the natural target of your component management effort.

You can identify a component problem from your collection period calculation only with the aid of Cash Flow Concept 9:

9: Use comparative analysis to identify the correct collection period for your business.

To do a component analysis, compare your present average collection period with a previous collection period. To illustrate, assume that you have calculated your average collection period, as shown on p. 22, and found that your average sales dollar remains in the form of a receivable for 53 days. Then, using the collection period calculated at the end of the latest full year of operations as a point of comparison, you have the following figures:

	Current	Prior
Average Collection Period (Days)	53	42
Average A/R Investment (per $1,000 in daily sales)	$53,000	$42,000

Thus, measured against the previous collection period, you see an 11-day increase in your average collection period. As you now recognize, that difference produces an $11,000 dent in your cash capability for each $1,000 in daily sales.

However, using prior experience as the sole standard for comparison leaves a gap in your analysis. After all, it assumes that the previous average collection period is appropriate for your business: Or, what has been always should be. Unfortunately, you cannot rely on this assumption. Your average collection period last year does not necessarily define what is appropriate for your business now or in the future.

Consequently, you need another way to estimate the correct collection period for your business. You can do that by looking at comparable competitor calculations. Unless warranted by special circumstances, your collection period should approximate your competitors'. Indeed, mutual customers, credit terms, and credit policies should lead to common average collection periods.

Many businessmen are unaware of the availability of their competitors' financial data for comparative analysis. Of course, few closed corporations release financial information directly to competitors. However, while preserving anonymity, many firms provide that data to industry publications, which collate and publish comparative financial data regularly.

Assume that you find that your 53-day average collection period compares unfavorably with a 40-day average for your industry. That increases the probability that you have an overinvestment in accounts receivable. Alternatively, assume that the longer collection period actually approximates the industry average. That is, measured against competitive standards, this year's 53-day collection period apparently is correct for your business.

Does that mean that a longer collection period may be more profitable, even at the expense of your cash capability? Indeed, it does. And that apparent contradiction emphasizes the value of comparing your average collection period against both internal and external standards.

If comparative data from industry sources prove elusive, use the data provided by Dun and Bradstreet or Robert Morris Associates. These firms collect and publish a variety of financial data categorized by industry and sales volume. Most businesses will find representative data drawn from a number of similar firms. (Table 4–1 illustrates a page, with the associated disclaimer of limitations, from the annual *Statement Studies* compiled by RMA.)

Whatever the source of your data, don't overlook the value of comparative analysis.

COMPARATIVE ANALYSIS: THE RECEIVABLES/SALES RATIO

Comparative analysis of your collection period, either against internal or external data, may not identify a recent buildup in accounts receivable. Indeed, an expanding investment can become a problem before it results in a significant increase in your average collection period, particularly when measured over the previous twelve months.

Consequently, you must look at your monthly "accounts receivable to sales" ratio, which measures the relationship between your investment in receivables and your sales volume. This might reveal a component problem before it seriously impairs your cash flow or earnings.

The analytic process is straightforward. At the end of each month, you divide your current investment in accounts receivable by the sales generated during that month. For example, assume that on June 30, 1979, your investment in receivables totaled $150,000. During that month you generated $100,000 in sales. The calculation is:

$$\frac{\text{Accounts Receivable}}{\text{Sales}} = \frac{\$150,000}{\$100,000} = 1.5$$

TABLE 4-1

WHOLESALERS - ELECTRICAL SUPPLIES & APPARATUS
SIC# 5063

	Current Data						Comparative Historical Data			
	155(6/30-9/30/79)		304(10/1/79-3/31/80)				6/30/76-3/31/77	6/30/77-3/31/78	6/30/78-3/31/79	6/30/79-3/31/80
ASSET SIZE	0-250M	250M-1MM	1-10MM	10-50MM	ALL		ALL	ALL	ALL	ALL
NUMBER OF STATEMENTS	37	141	251	30	459		346	409	392	459
ASSETS	%	%	%	%	%	%	%	%	%	%
Cash & Equivalents	8.6	6.9	4.6	4.1	5.6		5.9	5.5	5.7	5.6
Accts. & Notes Rec. - Trade(net)	33.3	36.3	40.0	35.7	38.1		36.4	37.1	38.1	38.1
Inventory	30.5	38.8	38.5	36.7	37.8		40.2	39.9	38.1	37.8
All Other Current	1.6	1.1	1.2	3.3	1.3		1.6	1.4	1.8	1.3
Total Current	74.0	83.1	84.3	79.9	82.8		84.1	84.0	83.7	82.8
Fixed Assets (net)	18.1	12.0	10.2	11.7	11.5		10.8	10.6	11.4	11.5
Intangibles (net)	.3	.4	.4	1.1	.4		.6	.5	.4	.4
All Other Non-Current	7.6	4.4	5.1	7.3	5.2		4.5	4.9	4.4	5.2
Total	100.0	100.0	100.0	100.0	100.0		100.0	100.0	100.0	100.0
LIABILITIES										
Notes Payable-Short Term	13.9	9.0	11.8	11.7	11.1		9.9	10.0	10.6	11.1
Cur. Mat.-L/T/D	2.7	3.5	2.0	1.0	2.4		2.2	2.6	2.7	2.4
Accts. & Notes Payable - Trade	25.9	27.7	27.4	25.0	27.2		26.4	26.0	25.7	27.2
Accrued Expenses	5.0	7.2	6.6	6.3	6.6		5.5	5.9	6.4	6.6
All Other Current	5.6	4.7	4.3	2.9	4.5		4.0	4.2	4.3	4.5
Total Current	53.1	52.1	52.1	46.9	51.8		48.0	48.8	49.7	51.8
Long Term Debt	10.9	7.8	8.1	10.4	8.4		8.7	8.9	8.9	8.4
All Other Non-Current	6.0	1.4	1.1	3.0	1.7		1.1	1.8	1.3	1.7
Net Worth	30.0	38.7	38.7	39.7	38.1		42.1	40.4	40.0	38.1
Total Liabilities & Net Worth	100.0	100.0	100.0	100.0	100.0		100.0	100.0	100.0	100.0
INCOME DATA										
Net Sales	100.0	100.0	100.0	100.0	100.0		100.0	100.0	100.0	100.0
Cost Of Sales	63.3	72.1	77.5	76.5	74.6		75.3	75.7	75.2	74.6
Gross Profit	36.7	27.9	22.5	23.5	25.4		24.7	24.3	24.8	25.4
Operating Expenses	33.2	23.9	18.0	16.6	21.0		21.4	22.0	20.9	21.0
Operating Profit	3.5	4.0	4.4	6.8	4.4		3.3	2.3	3.9	4.4
All Other Expenses (net)	.1	.4	.9	.6	.6		.2	-.5	.4	.6
Profit Before Taxes	3.4	3.6	3.6	6.3	3.8		3.1	2.8	3.5	3.8
RATIOS										
Current	1.9	2.1	2.2	2.3	2.2		2.4	2.3	2.3	2.2
	1.5	1.6	1.6	1.7	1.6		1.8	1.8	1.8	1.6
	1.2	1.3	1.3	1.4	1.3		1.4	1.4	1.4	1.3
Quick	1.2	1.1	1.2	1.0	1.1		1.2	1.2	1.2	1.1
	.9	.9	.9	.9	.9		.9	.9	.9	.9
	.6	.6	.6	.7	.6		.7	.7	.7	.6
Sales/Receivables	**27** 13.5	**35** 10.3	**41** 8.9	**41** 8.9	**38** 9.5		* **36** 10.1	**37** 10.0	**38** 9.6	**38** 9.5
	44 8.3	**44** 8.3	**48** 7.6	**51** 7.2	**47** 7.7		* **45** 8.2	**46** 8.0	**46** 8.0	**47** 7.7
	60 6.1	**54** 6.7	**56** 6.5	**61** 6.0	**56** 6.5		* **56** 6.5	**58** 6.3	**55** 6.6	**56** 6.5
Cost of Sales/Inventory	**21** 17.5	**46** 8.0	**45** 8.2	**51** 7.1	**44** 8.3		**46** 8.0	**47** 7.7	**43** 8.4	**44** 8.3
	57 6.4	**64** 5.7	**61** 6.0	**70** 5.2	**62** 5.9		**69** 5.3	**66** 5.5	**62** 5.9	**62** 5.9
	99 3.7	**99** 3.7	**83** 4.4	**104** 3.5	**87** 4.2		**91** 4.0	**89** 4.1	**87** 4.2	**87** 4.2
Sales/Working Capital	7.3	6.5	6.3	5.7	6.3		5.6	5.6	6.0	6.3
	12.4	9.7	9.7	7.4	9.6		8.4	8.4	8.4	9.6
	42.6	15.8	16.9	9.5	16.9		12.2	12.9	12.6	16.9
EBIT/Interest	7.8	13.0	9.4	8.0	10.0		13.3	11.3	11.2	10.0
	(27) 4.4	(119) 5.5	(206) 4.3	(25) 5.2	(377) 4.6		(275) 5.1	(326) 4.9	(314) 4.7	(377) 4.6
	2.3	2.1	2.3	2.8	2.3		2.2	2.3	2.4	2.3
Cash Flow/Cur. Mat. L/T/D		5.7	8.7	38.4	8.6		6.9	8.1	8.7	8.6
	(67) 3.6	(152) 4.6	(19) 8.7	(245) 4.2			(169) 2.9	(199) 3.0	(217) 3.6	(245) 4.2
	.9	2.4	4.3	1.9			1.1	1.4	1.8	1.9
Fixed/Worth	.2	.1	.1	.1	.1		.1	.1	.1	.1
	.4	.2	.2	.3	.2		.2	.2	.2	.2
	1.2	.5	.5	.4	.5		.4	.4	.5	.5
Debt/Worth	1.1	.8	.9	1.0	.9		.8	.8	.8	.9
	1.8	1.4	1.7	1.3	1.6		1.4	1.6	1.4	1.6
	7.8	3.1	3.1	3.0	3.1		2.4	2.9	3.1	3.1
% Profit Before Taxes/Tangible Net Worth	63.4	44.2	36.6	45.4	40.4		28.3	33.1	37.4	40.4
	(33) 25.0	(137) 23.1	(249) 23.8	28.9	(449) 25.0		(337) 18.0	(399) 20.5	(384) 23.9	(449) 25.0
	10.5	11.7	14.7	25.3	14.2		8.7	10.4	12.9	14.2
% Profit Before Taxes/Total Assets	16.0	16.2	14.6	18.1	15.6		13.5	13.7	14.8	15.6
	9.7	8.9	8.5	11.7	9.0		7.1	7.7	8.6	9.0
	1.5	4.6	5.1	7.3	5.1		2.8	3.3	4.4	5.1
Sales/Net Fixed Assets	72.7	70.3	76.6	59.1	72.2		81.2	81.8	79.9	72.2
	30.0	42.8	39.6	24.4	38.0		43.3	39.9	37.1	38.0
	13.0	19.2	18.4	12.7	18.1		18.0	17.8	17.9	18.1
Sales/Total Assets	3.6	3.5	3.5	3.2	3.5		3.5	3.5	3.5	3.5
	3.2	3.0	3.0	2.6	3.0		2.9	2.9	2.9	3.0
	2.3	2.4	2.5	1.6	2.4		2.4	2.3	2.4	2.4
% Depr., Dep., Amort./Sales	.7	.4	.3	.2	.4		.3	.3	.3	.4
	(34) 1.4	(131) .6	(229) .5	(26) .5	(420) .6		(310) .5	(367) .5	(366) .5	(420) .6
	1.9	1.0	.8	1.0	.9		.8	.9	.9	.9
% Lease & Rental Exp/Sales	1.2	.6	.5	.2	.5		.5	.5	.4	.5
	(28) 1.7	(90) 1.2	(142) .7	(12) .4	(272) .9		(211) .9	(254) .8	(230) .9	(272) .9
	2.9	2.0	1.1	.9	1.5		1.5	1.5	1.6	1.5
% Officers' Comp/Sales	4.2	2.8	1.5		1.9		2.1	2.1	2.0	1.9
	(20) 6.9	(70) 3.8	(106) 2.5		(204) 3.2		(177) 3.6	(211) 3.7	(189) 3.2	(204) 3.2
	14.7	6.0	4.1		5.2		5.4	4.8	5.2	5.2
Net Sales ($)	17135M	253595M	2149868M	1304455M	3725053M		1969447M	2483102M	2701236M	3725053M
Total Assets ($)	5869M	84116M	733799M	560546M	1384330M		721401M	919087M	956389M	1384330M

©Robert Morris Associates 1980

M = $thousand   MM = $million
See Pages 1 through 10 for Explanation of Ratios and Data

* The boldface figures represent the upper quartile, the median, and the lower quartile average collection period among all firms included in this sample.

Standing alone, of course, that ratio tells you only that your receivables at the end of June were 150% of sales for the month. However, the ratio has more potential as a problem spotter when you compare it to calculations from previous months. In fact, a change in the ratio can serve as a harbinger of an impending change in the prevailing trend of your cash flow.

To illustrate, assume that your sales for July 1979 increase to $110,000. At the end of the month, your investment in accounts receivable totals $190,000. Of course, a higher sales volume naturally leads to a larger investment in accounts receivable. However, repeating the ratio calculation, you find:

$$\frac{\text{Accounts Receivable}}{\text{Sales}} = \frac{\$190,000}{\$110,000} = 1.7$$

The higher ratio of receivables to sales means your investment in A/R grew more rapidly than sales. This change in the relationship between your investment in receivables and your sales volume is often the first sign of a component problem: Your collection turnover rate is decreasing, and your average collection period is increasing. Receivables and sales volume are two critical elements of the cash flow process. Thus, the monthly calculation of the receivables to sales ratio allows you to keep track of any developing problem.

INTERPRETATION OF STATEMENT STUDIES FIGURES

RMA recommends that Statement Studies data be regarded only as general guidelines and not as absolute industry norms. There are several reasons why the data may not be fully representative of a given industry:

(1) The financial statements used in the *Statement Studies* are not selected by any random or statistically reliable method. RMA member banks voluntarily submit the raw data they have available each year, with these being the only constraints: (a) The fiscal year-ends of the companies reported may not be from April 1 through June 29, and (b) their total assets must be less than $50 million.

(2) Many companies have varied product lines; however, the *Statement Studies* categorize them by their primary product Standard Industrial Classification (SIC) number only.

(3) Some of our industry samples are rather small in relation to the total number of firms in a given industry. A relatively small sample can increase the chances that some of our composites do not fully represent an industry.

(4) There is the chance that an extreme statement can be present in a sample, causing a disproportionate influence on the industry composite. This is particularly true in a relatively small sample.

(5) Companies within the same industry may differ in their method of operations which in turn can directly influence their financial statements. Since they are included in our sample, too, these statements can significantly affect our composite calculations.

(6) Other considerations that can result in variations among different companies engaged in the same general line of business are different labor markets; geographical location; different accounting methods; quality of products handled; sources and methods of financing; and terms of sale.

For these reasons, RMA does not recommend the Statement Studies figures be considered as absolute norms for a given industry. Rather the figures should be used only as general guidelines and in addition to the other methods of financial analysis. RMA makes no claim as to the representativeness of the figures printed in this book.

Robert Morris Associates, Philadelphia National Bank Building, Philadelphia, PA 19107

© 1980 by Robert Morris Associates

All rights reserved. No part of this book may be reproduced or utilized in any form or by any means, electronic or mechanical, including photocopying, recording or by any information storage and retrieval system, without permission in writing from Robert Morris Associates.

Of course, you might dispense with the actual calculation each month and rely on an *estimate* of the relationship between your sales volume and your investment in accounts receivable. However, actually going through the calculation each month helps reduce the potential errors inherent in such estimates. Indeed, that simple calculation, when compared with the calculations from previous months, can draw attention to a component problem long before it develops into a crisis.

Incidentally, if your business is seasonal and a major portion of your sales occur in a particular part of the year, adjust your receivables to sales ratio analysis accordingly. That is, compare your monthly ratio against that for the same month for the previous year. This will prevent the distortions that inevitably arise from seasonal fluctuations in sales and collections.

THE LIMITS OF COMPARATIVE ANALYSIS

While comparative analysis contributes to your component management effort, it has some natural limitations.

As the first step in problem recognition, it enables you to identify a potential overinvestment (or underinvestment) in accounts receivable. However, you must proceed further to find the specific cause of any deviation from the norm.

Moreover, comparative analysis does not account for the unique characteristics in a business that can justify a collection period or a receivables-to-sales ratio that differs significantly from the standards. For example, if you boost sales with the aid of a more lenient credit policy, your collection period naturally will exceed that of your more conservative competitors.

Alternatively, if you are undercapitalized, you may need a shorter collection period to generate the cash necessary for survival. Your averages will fall below the industry norms. Certainly, special circumstance colors any analysis.

Let's review one more tool for component analysis that enables you to spot problems in their early stages and, in this instance, also helps identify the specific source of the problems.

THE AGED ANALYSIS OF ACCOUNTS RECEIVABLE

Cash Flow Concept 10 should become a primary tool for positive cash flow management.

10: Complete component analysis requires a monthly aging of your accounts receivable.

Table 4–2 demonstrates the potential in that tool. It is an aging analysis drawn from a firm that sells on net thirty-day terms, meaning that payment is expected thirty days from the date of the sale. The analysis is normally constructed as of the last day of the month. Table 4–2 follows the standard format:

1. Column 1 includes the total debt due from each customer.
2. Column 2 summarizes the accounts due for sales made during the month just ended; that is, current amounts not yet due and payable.
3. Column 3 isolates those receivables still due for sales made in the previous month; those amounts are one to 30 days past due.
4. Column 4 identifies amounts that remain unpaid for sales made two months previously; those receivables are 31 to 60 days past due.
5. Column 5 pinpoints any account more than 60 days past due.

TABLE 4–2 Sample Aged Analysis of Accounts Receivable

Customer	Total A/R Debt	Current	1–30 Past Due	31–60 Past Due	61–90 Past Due
Page Distributing	$ 12,000	$ 2,000	$ 4,000	$4,000	$2,000
Jones Manufacturing	27,000	27,000	—	—	—
Sales, Inc.	9,000	9,000	—	—	—
Houston Wire	15,000	—	15,000	—	—
American Wholesale	17,000	10,000	4,000	3,000	—
Woodwork, Inc.	3,000	—	3,000	—	—
MFI	5,000	5,000	—	—	—
Continental Supply	12,000	12,000	—	—	—
Total	**$100,000**	**$65,000**	**$26,000**	**$7,000**	**$2,000**

Of course, you should design your aging analysis to suit your own circumstance. For example, a grocery wholesaler typically sells on seven-day terms. Consequently, he uses a weekly aging analysis that separates accounts due according to his special terms. Similarly, a firm allowing sixty days for payment would adjust the format in Table 4–2.

Regardless of the specific form, however, observe the benefits that you can derive from an aged analysis of your accounts receivable.

First, that analysis identifies the specific accounts within the total component that make up an overinvestment. (An overinvestment is narrowly defined here as any account not paid within original terms. You may recall that in Part One, current receivables were included in the overinvestment picture; however, in terms of aging analysis, an account not yet past due cannot be defined as an overinvestment.) Referring to Table 4–2, you can easily see the receivables that lengthen the firm's average collection period beyond thirty days.

Also, the aging analysis can provide a picture of any recent change in the makeup of a firm's receivables. Table 4–2 reflects a typical mix of current and past-due accounts. Certainly, every business carries some customers that do not pay promptly. However, if the pattern of past-due accounts changes (by comparison with aging analysis from previous months), you will see the deviation almost immediately. Thus, an aging analysis allows you to spot the early development of a potential A/R problem.

The accounts in the third column (indicating payments are one to thirty days past due) may not portend a problem. However, as you see an increase in such accounts from one month to the next, you should begin to recognize a trend. Unless you respond to the trend, it will lead to a longer average collection period and a higher, more costly investment in accounts receivable.

Of course, management of the accounts receivable component includes more considerations than proper recognition of past-due accounts. As we will discuss later, you may find slower paying accounts to be profitable for your business. However, that doesn't negate the value of a monthly aged analysis of your accounts receivable as an essential element of component analysis.

Analysis of accounts receivable is a necessary element in your management effort because it enables you to see where you stand.

Component Management: Selling Terms

Selling terms set a time limit on each customer's promise to pay for a purchase. Thus, when he purchases your product or service, the customer understands that you expect payment in ten days or thirty days or whatever length of time you establish as your standard requirement. You agree to "carry" the customer's account for the designated period.

If every customer pays in accordance with the designated terms, then those terms define your collection period. Of course, that perfect coincidence rarely occurs. Almost every business has customers who take longer to pay. Nevertheless, your designated selling terms exert a significant influence on your customer's paying habits. And your selling terms directly affect the cash flow process in your business. The effect of selling terms on your cash flow is the subject of this chapter.

First, we transform the obvious principle—a longer selling term increases your collection period—into a form that relates to your cash flow and earnings. To do that, we must rely on the unrealistic assumption that sales volume remains constant, whatever selling terms a business designates.

Second, we recognize that while selling terms affect the cash flow in a business, they also affect sales volume. Certainly, that consideration carries significant weight in your management effort.

Third, we examine a final element in this phase of component management: How allowing discounts for early payment influences a firm's cash flow and earnings. Industry practice or competitive pressure may force you to offer such discounts, and you should recognize how they affect your bottom line.

35

SELLING TERMS AND THE CASH FLOW PROCESS

Our initial view of the relationship between your selling terms and the cash flow process ignores the influence those terms exert on sales volume. That restriction allows us to concentrate on the fundamental relationship, as stated in Cash Flow Concept 11.

11: Selling terms have a direct influence on cash flow and earnings.

As an example, we will look at the Hillsboro Ceramics Company, a manufacturer of high grade industrial ceramics for sale to the pharmaceutical industry. Hillsboro occupies a unique position: Demand for its product exceeds supply. Consequently, the company sells all of its $5,000 daily production on a continuous basis. Moreover, taking advantage of this demand-supply relationship, Hillsboro presently has the shortest sales terms possible. The company requires cash payment at the time of purchase, and it still sells 100% of its production.

At the same time, management recognizes the volatility of the marketplace. They want to retain their customers when competition increases or demand subsides. Consequently, they decide to offer "reasonable" terms for payment and absorb the cost associated with carrying an investment in accounts receivable in exchange for a loyal customer base in the future.

Before adopting this policy, John Thompson, Hillsboro's controller, analyzed the effects the primary alternative selling terms would have on the firm's cash flow and earnings. Thompson's analysis began with the following assumptions:

1. Regardless of the terms offered, Hillsboro will maintain the same $5,000 average daily sales volume; production already equals capacity.
2. The company will incur a 10% per annum cost—financial or opportunity— from carrying an investment in accounts receivable.
3. All customers will pay strictly in accordance with whatever terms the firm designates.

The results of Thompson's analysis show that longer selling terms lead to a higher investment in accounts receivable. Thus, they exert a detrimental effect on earnings. Table 5–1 illustrates the investment in receivables (and the cost of car-

TABLE 5–1 Effect of Selling Terms on Investment in Accounts Receivable and Earnings

Selling Terms	Investment in Accounts Receivable	Accounts-Receivable Carrying Costs 10% per Year
Net 10 Days	$ 50,000	$ 5,000
Net 30 Days	$150,000	$15,000
Net 60 Days	$300,000	$30,000

rying that investment) that results from allowing ten, thirty, or sixty days for payment. In this instance, we assume that the carrying costs translate directly into a reduction in Hillsboro's earnings.

Allowing ten days for payment reduces Hillsboro's annual earnings by $5,000, compared to its profits from making all sales for cash. This reduction comes from the cost of carrying the $50,000 average investment in receivables that naturally accrues from ten-day selling terms. Increasing those terms to thirty days reduces earnings by $15,000, while sixty-day terms assess a $30,000 penalty on Hillsboro's bottom line.

It is also important to note how the alternative selling terms affect Hillsboro's cash flow. Thus, ten-day terms absorb $50,000 of the firm's cash capability: Hillsboro must reduce its cash reserve by that much, or it must have a like amount of borrowing power. Longer terms naturally increase that drain. Indeed, allowing sixty days for payment absorbs $300,000 of Hillsboro's cash capability. This is a substantial consideration, even for a large firm.

Using Thompson's analysis, Hillsboro's management decided to absorb the least expense possible in their effort to build customer loyalty. Thus, they selected ten-day selling terms as the standard corporate policy.

Of course, few firms occupy Hillsboro's enviable position. Demand seldom exceeds supply on a continuous basis. At the same time, if you can exercise some liberty in selecting your selling terms, recognize how that decision will affect your cash flow and earnings.

Don't exaggerate the significance of the influence selling terms have on your cash flow and require cash payment for all purchases. The cost of carrying a reasonable investment in accounts receivable is a normal business expense. In fact, you often will find that your selling terms have a greater effect on earnings than your prices do. For example, Hillsboro might increase its prices by 10% to offset the cost of carrying the investment in receivables that comes with its new selling terms. The price increase would probably be viewed by Hillsboro's customers as a negligible price to pay for the more flexible sales policy.

Of course, selling terms exert another influence: They also affect a firm's sales volume. You must consider that influence when you select the selling terms for your business.

SELLING TERMS, SALES VOLUME, AND CASH CAPABILITY

Most businesses have a large number of competitors who offer similar products and services. Selling terms inevitably become an important part of that competition. Thus, a business might lengthen its selling terms because it will increase sales. Other competitive factors remaining equal, longer selling terms allow customers to retain their cash longer without violating the terms. In other words, it expands their cash capability.

Of course, the firm that offers longer selling terms suffers an opportunity cost, because longer terms lead naturally to a larger, more costly investment in accounts receivable. Thus, the decision to offer more liberal terms requires a fair estimate of the trade-off between the cost of a larger investment in accounts receivable and the bottom-line benefits of a higher sales volume. Remember this as Cash Flow Concept 12:

12: Longer selling terms can increase earnings, but at the expense of a firm's cash capability.

The case of ABC Distributing Company illustrates one approach to analyzing that trade-off. ABC is a regional distributor of small electric motors. Operating in a highly competitive market, the firm can gain no significant advantage from price structure, product quality, or service capability. Consequently, ABC's management explored the potential bottom-line benefits that might come from allowing longer terms for payment. The analysis began with a review of the relevant factors in the firm's current operations:

1. ABC now generates $50,000 per month in sales; in line with industry practice, all sales are made on thirty-day terms. Since all customers observe those terms, ABC carries a $50,000 investment in accounts receivable.
2. ABC earns a 20% gross margin on sales; that is, after covering product and sales costs, twenty cents out of each dollar remains to cover the firm's fixed costs of $7,500 per month. In addition, that gross margin must cover ABC's 1% *monthly* cost of carrying its investment in accounts receivable.
3. After covering the above costs, ABC's present sales volume nets $2,000 in monthly earnings.

Marketing surveys suggest that ABC indeed can increase sales by offering longer selling terms. In fact, each thirty-day increase in ABC's designated payment terms will lead to a $10,000 increase in monthly sales. Table 5–2 considers the effects the higher volume will have on the firm's earnings and its investment in accounts receivable.

First, note that the analysis assumes that all of ABC's customers will observe the longer terms allowed for payment. This is a valid assumption, since no business should pay sooner than necessary.

TABLE 5–2 Effect of Longer Selling Terms on Sales, Cash Flow, and Earnings

	Selling Terms (days)		
	30	60	90
Sales Volume (monthly)	$50,000	$ 60,000	$ 70,000
Average A/R	50,000	120,000	210,000
Gross Margin (20% of sales)	10,000	12,000	14,000
Fixed Costs	(7,500)	(7,500)	(7,500)
A/R Carrying Cost (1% per month)	(500)	(1,200)	(2,100)
Net Monthly Earnings	**$ 2,000**	**$ 3,300**	**$ 4,400**

Nevertheless, each projected increase in selling terms leads to higher earnings, even after considering the cost of carrying a larger investment in accounts receivable. Indeed, the $10,000 sales increase that comes from lengthening payment terms from thirty to sixty days ultimately translates into a $1,300 rise in monthly earnings. This is a $15,600 annual bottom-line benefit. Then, increasing selling terms from sixty to ninety days adds another $10,000 to ABC's monthly volume, and provides another $1,100 in monthly earnings.

Of course, every business won't duplicate ABC's experience. But Table 5-2 illustrates the benefits a business may derive from more lengthy selling terms. Of course, practical limits exist on that potential. For example, longer selling terms absorb a firm's cash capability. Increasing ABC's payment terms from thirty to sixty days raised its investment in receivables from $50,000 to $120,000. That increase uses $70,000 of ABC's cash capability. The firm must draw that amount from its cash reserves or borrowing power to carry the increase in assets.

Also, this analysis ignores another cost inevitably associated with longer payment terms: Longer selling terms increase the loss a business suffers from bad-debt write-offs. The new customers you gain with more lenient terms tend to be financially weaker, perhaps unable to comply with the shorter time allowed for payment by your competitors. Note that the expense exists, and that our example overstates ABC's real increase in profits. Also note that, even if you possess unlimited cash capability, the potential gain from longer selling terms isn't infinite. At some point, the cost of carrying a gigantic investment in receivables will offset the incremental gain from higher sales. Nevertheless, within practical limits, the potential profits from extended selling terms can be significant.

Finally, we must add one additional qualification. If you operate in a highly competitive environment, as ABC does, you may realize only temporary gains from extending your payment terms. Competitors may emulate your actions as soon as they recognize your gains. In such instances, your sales may soon return to a lower level, while the extended payment period remains constant. You end up with the same sales volume, but with a higher investment in accounts receivable. A short-term gain turns into a long-term reduction in earnings.

Consider that potential result before you lengthen your selling terms. Certainly, that complicates the decision process, and, unfortunately, it isn't subject to objective analysis.

TRADE DISCOUNTS IN THE CASH FLOW PROCESS

Many businesses allow discounts off the original sales price if a customer pays for a purchase within a short, specified time after shipment. For example, a business might allow a 1% or 2% discount if a customer pays for a purchase within ten days, whereas it requires full payment if the buyer takes thirty days to pay.

Before you decide to offer trade discounts, you must estimate the costs and benefits that will result. You can begin your analysis by measuring the benefits. When a customer pays in accordance with the discount terms, it shortens your average collection period and accelerates your cash flow. Simultaneously, of course, your investment in receivables is reduced, as are the costs associated with carrying that investment.

However, allowing discounts for early payment also exerts some detrimental effects on your bottom line. The basic circumstances of the ABC Distributing Company illustrate how to weigh those negative effects against the benefits.

We will consider the effect on ABC's cash flow and earnings from offering any one of three alternative selling terms to its customers:

1. Net 30 days
2. 1% 10, net 30 days
3. 2% 10, net 30 days

We assume that ABC's sales will remain a constant $50,000 a month regardless of the selling terms offered.

However, customer payment habits will vary in response to the different terms. Naturally, if ABC offers no discounts, all customers will take the full thirty days to pay. (And of course in reality, some will take longer to pay.) At the other extreme, every customer will pay within ten days in exchange for a 2% discount. This incentive for early payment is too large for any customer to ignore.

However, there are mixed results from offering a 1% discount for payment in ten days. Indeed, projections indicate that only half of the firm's customers will take advantage of the smaller discount. The other half will pay the full price in thirty days.

Table 5–3 summarizes the effects these alternative selling terms have on ABC's cash flow and earnings. The summary again assumes that the firm incurs a 12% annual cost for carrying its investment in accounts receivable. This cost, added to any discounts allowed, measures the total expenses associated with each of the alternative selling terms.

TABLE 5–3 Effects of Early-Payment Discounts on Cash Flow and Earnings

ABC DISTRIBUTING

Selling Terms	% Taking Discount	Average A/R	Annual Carrying Cost (12%)	Annual Cost Discount Allowed	Effect on Earnings
Net 30 Days	N/A	$50,000	$6,000	—	($ 6,000)
1% 10, Net 30 Days	50%	33,333	3,999	3,000	(6,999)
2% 10, Net 30 Days	100%	16,666	1,999	12,000	(13,999)

Note that ABC suffers the least cost when it offers no discounts for early payment. While that policy leads to a $50,000 investment in receivables, the firm's annual cost of carrying that investment totals $6,000.

Now, note how allowing discounts for early payment affects earnings. Offering a 1% discount reduces ABC's earnings by $6,999, compared to the $6,000 reduction effected by the net thirty-day terms. The savings gained from reducing the size of the firm's investment in receivables is more than offset by the cost of the discounts.

Allowing 2% discounts is even more expensive. Not only is the discount larger, but every customer takes it. Indeed, that policy leads to a $13,999 reduction in ABC's earnings.

Again, using Table 5–3, observe from a different perspective the relationship between ABC's payment terms and its investment in accounts receivable.

If no discounts are included in the selling terms, ABC must carry the $50,000 investment in accounts receivable: It must commit that much cash capability to its investment in that single asset.

While that investment level is the most profitable, a limited cash capability may force ABC to offer discounts. A 1% discount reduces the drain on that capability to $33,333, while the 2% discount further reduces the investment in receivables to $16,666.

Thus, note that Table 5–3 elucidates Cash Flow Concept 13:

13: Trade discounts help your cash flow at the expense of your earnings.

Of course, if you can reinvest the accelerated cash flow rapidly and profitably, the earnings you lose from today's discounts may return more to you in the future. However, that still doesn't eliminate the implications of Cash Flow Concept 13.

A FINANCIAL VIEW OF TRADE DISCOUNTS

Before you add a discount to your selling terms, consider the discount as a cost of borrowing. When you allow a discount for payment in ten days instead of thirty, you actually *pay* your customer for the use of his cash. This means that you use the cash for the twenty days you otherwise would have to wait for the full payment.

However, you pay dearly for that privilege, as Table 5–4 illustrates. It de-

TABLE 5–4 Effective Cost of Early-Payment Discounts

Discounts Allowed for Payment in Ten Days	Annualized Cost to Seller
1/2%	9%
1%	18%
2%	36%

tails the effective annual interest you would have to pay a lender for borrowed funds to equal the actual cost in dollars—the difference between the full price and the discounted price—of allowing the discounts.

Thus, assuming that your customers take the discount, the expense you absorb from allowing a 2% discount translates into a 36% annual borrowing cost. That reiterates why you profit from eliminating discounts from your payment terms. In fact, you can profit from eliminating discounts even if you have to use your borrowing power to carry the resulting higher investment in accounts receivable.

Table 5–4 also indicates the different response customers have to a 1% versus a 2% discount. A customer will take a 2% discount, even if it leaves him in a cash flow bind, because losing that discount is equivalent to paying a 36% annual borrowing cost. His cost from missing the discount is the same as your cost for allowing it. Of course, a customer also suffers a cost when he misses a 1% discount. But the penalty is less severe. Indeed, a customer is more likely to pass up the smaller discount as an alternative to straining his cash capability.

Although eliminating discounts from your payment terms can increase your earnings, this should not prompt you into any rash action. Other factors deserve fair consideration. For example, industry custom may dictate your designated terms. If your customers expect trade discounts, eliminating them will drive them to your competitors. In such instances, discounts become a normal business expense recognized in your price structure.

Moreover, don't overlook the effect eliminating discounts will have on your cash flow. Increasing your investment in receivables from $50,000 to $150,000, for example, is a significant drain on the cash capability of a small business. Indeed, it absorbs the cash reserves and borrowing power that may be essential for its survival. So, exchanging discounts for survival is a fair trade.

Component Management: Credit Policy

In Chapter 5 we generally assumed that every customer pays in accordance with the seller's designated terms. Of course, rarely does this occur. In some instances, clerical error or honest oversight delays payment. In other instances, customers defer payment to protest some real or imagined problem with a product or service.

However, most customers who fail to pay within a firm's designated terms simply suffer from their own cash flow problems. They lack the capability to generate or borrow the cash to honor their obligations promptly.

Certainly, you could refuse to sell to anyone who failed to pay within your designated terms. However, that restriction might prove to be expensive. Many businesses increase their earnings from sales to slow-paying customers, although at the expense of their cash capability.

At the same time, you don't want to have too many slow-paying customers or customers who never pay. Either can have a devastating effect on your cash flow and earnings.

The need to balance your allowance for slow-paying customers against your cash flow requirements calls for a well-designed credit policy that satisfies your earnings objectives, while it operates within the limits of your cash capability. The credit policy should include guidelines that identify which prospective customers deserve credit. This chapter shows how a *change* in your present credit policy will affect your investment in accounts receivable. Of course, you can alter your credit policy in only two fundamental ways. You can make it more restrictive or less restrictive: That is, you can tighten it or loosen it.

The specific steps that alter your credit policy are less important than the effects the alteration will have on your sales, cash flow, and earnings.

This chapter also introduces the concept of *cash insurance,* which employs a credit insurance policy to protect a business against the cash drain caused by uncollectible accounts receivable. Such protection reduces the risk a business normally accepts when it carries a significant investment in receivables. That benefit, in turn, often helps to overcome a major psychological obstacle many businessmen confront when contemplating a larger sales volume, whether from an expanded marketing effort or from a more liberal credit policy. Overcoming that obstacle can be very profitable.

CREDIT POLICY AND CASH FLOW

We will use Chem-Etch, Inc., to illustrate Cash Flow Concept 14:

14: Credit policy has a direct effect on the cash flow and earnings in a business.

Chem-Etch operates as a regional manufacturer of printed circuit boards for sale to the electronics industry. In one sense, the firm enjoys an enviable position. It sells its maximum plant capacity of $3,000 daily for a monthly volume of $90,000.

However, the company attained that position only after a struggle to achieve industry acceptance for its products. To earn that acceptance, Chem-Etch adopted a credit policy that encouraged sales at the expense of its cash capability. In fact, it willingly sold to customers who clearly lacked the financial ability to pay in accordance with the thirty-day selling terms.

While that policy helped push up the firm's sales volume, it finally led to a cash flow problem. Indeed, at 9/30/79, Chem-Etch's average collection period reached 75 days, and its investment in accounts receivable rose to $225,000. On the same day, as illustrated in Table 6–1, the firm reached the natural limit set by its cash capability. Chem-Etch was out of cash, an experience that is common among young, growing businesses. Sales volume becomes the singular objective, and often a young business thinks that justifies a liberal credit policy.

Naturally, Chem-Etch's cash flow problem put an end to that policy. Indeed, since the firm was operating at capacity—and turning down new orders daily—the need to induce sales with such a liberal policy no longer existed. Consequently, the company adopted a more restrictive credit policy that soon reduced its average collection period to sixty days, still thirty days beyond the firm's designated terms.

Table 6–1 illustrates the predictable effect of that more restrictive policy. By 12/31/79, Chem-Etch's investment in accounts receivable dropped to $180,000, providing the company with a healthy $45,000 cash reserve. (We ignore the cash flow from earnings in this example.)

TABLE 6-1 Effect of Credit Policy on Cash Flow

CHEM-ETCH, INC.

	9/30/79	12/31/79	3/31/80
Daily Sales	$ 3,000	$ 3,000	$ 3,000
Collection Period (days)	(75)	(60)	(45)
A/R Investment	225,000	180,000	135,000
Cash	-0-	45,000	90,000
A/R Carrying Cost (at 10% a year)	22,500	18,000	13,500
Reduction in Carrying Cost	—	4,500	9,000

In addition to relieving the cash flow bind, the more restrictive credit policy provided Chem-Etch with another benefit: It reduced the costs associated with carrying a large investment in accounts receivable. Indeed, the new policy gave the firm a $4,500 (annualized) bottom-line benefit.

When the more restrictive credit policy had no effect on sales, Chem-Etch tightened the credit reins again. Thus, management set a 45-day payment period as an objective. Over the following three months, the firm's receivables dropped to $135,000, cash reserves rose to $90,000, and Chem-Etch began to feel the benefits of a $9,000 reduction in annual carrying costs.

Of course, no credit policy ensures that you will maintain a predetermined average collection period on a continuous basis. But at the same time, a designated collection period should serve as a target for that policy.

CREDIT POLICY AND SALES VOLUME

Your credit policy affects sales volume in the same manner as your designated selling terms: A liberal credit policy contributes to higher sales, while a more restrictive policy tends to reduce sales. This should come as no surprise. After all, whatever your designated selling terms, your credit policy defines your *implied* terms.

Your implied terms reflect the average time you actually allow customers to pay for their purchases. For example, assume that you designate thirty days as your standard selling terms, but your credit policy approves sales to customers who habitually pay in sixty days. Inevitably, you will attract customers who are precluded from buying elsewhere because of more restrictive credit requirements. The longer implied terms encourage an increase in sales.

To understand the relationship between implied terms and your cash flow and earnings, look again at Table 5-2 on page 38.

The same principles apply to both implied and designated selling terms. Increasing those terms from ten to either thirty or sixty days will increase your sales volume. Also, the earnings on that additional volume typically will outpace the rising cost of carrying a larger investment in accounts receivable. In either instance, longer terms increase both sales and profits at the expense of your cash capability.

Again, you can't control your implied terms precisely, but you should recognize the relationship between your sales volume and the implied terms set by your credit policy.

CREDIT POLICY RULES

A tighter credit policy, one that reduces the length of your implied selling terms and shortens your average collection period, accelerates collections and reduces your investment in accounts receivable. In other words, it improves your cash flow. At the same time, a more restrictive credit policy tends to reduce sales. You can predict that result logically.

As you tighten your credit standards, prospective customers must demonstrate more financial strength and have a better payment history to qualify for credit consideration. Those who fail to meet your standards must buy elsewhere. That reduces the number of prospective customers available to you, and inevitably it reduces your sales volume.

Of course, if the demand for your products or services exceeds your present capacity, a tighter credit policy may not affect your sales (as in Chem-Etch's experience). Normally, however, when you consider tightening your credit reins, you should weigh the benefits of a better cash flow against the lower earnings from a reduced sales volume.

Obviously, you get the opposite effect from loosening your credit reins. Thus, a more liberal credit policy leads to a longer average collection period and a larger investment in accounts receivable. Of course, that simultaneously absorbs some of your cash capability and hurts your cash flow. A less restrictive policy, which lengthens the implied term allowed for payment, also encourages a boost in sales because it expands the pool of potential customers.

Moreover, as suggested in Table 5–2, those longer implied terms ultimately can increase your earnings. You gain that benefit so long as the profits on the higher volume offset the rising costs that come from carrying a larger investment in accounts receivable.

Of course, practical limits exist on the benefits you can derive from a more lenient credit policy. And you should recognize those limits before you open your credit lines to any customer who walks in the door.

On the other hand, never make payment within your designated terms a moral issue. It is less important that a customer pays within a certain term than it is that you realize the maximum bottom-line benefits from his purchase. Indeed, many businessmen lose sales and earnings because they refuse to allow customers to delay payments beyond the designated due dates. In any event, so long as it doesn't strain your cash capability, profits take precedence over prompt payment.

THE LIMITS ON A LIBERAL CREDIT POLICY

Longer selling terms, whether designated or implied, can increase your earnings. You gain that benefit when the profit margin on sales induced by those terms exceeds the cost of carrying a larger investment in accounts receivable. We illustrated that potential with the case of the ABC Distributing Company in Chapter 5. However, higher earnings from a more liberal credit policy are not automatic. Indeed, the profit potential from changing your credit policy depends on some key factors that were not emphasized in ABC's experience.

The profit margin you realize on each additional sales dollar stands as the key factor that determines the benefits that might flow from a more liberal credit policy. In the case of ABC, a healthy 10% margin on new sales easily offset the modest 1% per month cost of carrying the firm's investment in accounts receivable. Obviously, a business that operates with a narrower margin will not enjoy the same benefits. Nor will the business that suffers an unusually high cost from carrying its investment in receivables realize similar gains. Those costs often rise more rapidly than a firm's investment in receivables.

Another factor not considered in ABC's experience also exerts a significant influence on the profits you generate with a more liberal credit policy: your bad-debt experience. Of course, every business suffers some loss from customers who ultimately fail to pay for their purchases. However, the business that adopts a less restrictive credit policy inevitably will watch the loss rate rise.

Again, you can predict the result logically. A number of the customers you attract with your liberal policy lack the capacity to pay within normal industry terms. They have cash flow problems. Moreover, as you increase the time you allow a customer to pay for a purchase, you increase the chances that his problem will develop into your disaster. That inevitably contributes to a higher bad-debt expense.

Below, you will see how that higher expense can offset the benefits of a higher sales volume. In fact, a small increase in bad-debt experience (as a percentage of total sales) can make a big dent in your earnings. You can't predict the size of that dent accurately, but you can be certain that it will appear. Thus, it becomes a factor in your estimate of the benefits from a more liberal credit policy.

Don't forget that when you allow longer terms for payment, you must have the cash capability to absorb the associated increase in your accounts receivable. In fact, if a more liberal credit policy would stretch that capability, you might be more comfortable with lower earnings from your present credit policy. You won't earn as much, but you will sleep better at night: You won't increase the risk of having a cash flow problem.

Let's take an example that recognizes the limits on the benefits that can be derived from a more liberal credit policy. That example moves us closer to a real business environment, and it serves as a model for analyzing your own situation.

The East Texas Service Corporation (ETSC) is a direct competitor of the ABC Distributing Company. Recognizing the sales increase garnered by ABC's longer selling terms, ETSC decided to adopt a similar policy. However, the policy had two important differences.

First, rather than extending its selling terms, ETSC adopted a more liberal credit policy, gradually lengthening its implied terms. That approach presumably encouraged the firm's existing customers to pay in accordance with the designated thirty-day terms, while it still allowed sales to businesses that lacked that capability.

Also, ETSC's analysis included a fair assessment of the effect longer implied terms would have on the firm's bad-debt expense.

Recognizing these differences, the firm's analysis was based on the following assumptions:

1. Each ten-day increase in average collection period that ETSC allows will increase sales by $300 per day, or $108,000 per year.
2. ETSC earns 9% on sales before deducting any loss from bad debts, or the cost of carrying the firm's investment in accounts receivable.
3. The company incurs a 12% annual cost from carrying its average investment in receivables.
4. The firm's present thirty-day terms result in bad-debt write-offs that amount to 1% of ETSC's annual sales volume.

   Estimates indicate that each ten-day increase in the average collection period will increase that loss rate by one-quarter of 1%: i.e., a forty-day collection period will increase the loss from bad debts to 1.25% of total sales.

Table 6–2 summarizes the results of ETSC's analysis.

TABLE 6–2 Limits on a Liberal Credit Policy

EAST TEXAS SERVICE CORPORATION

	Implied Terms (days)				
	30	40	50	60	70
Daily Sales	$ 2,100	$ 2,400	$ 2,700	$ 3,000	$ 3,300
Annual Sales	756,000	864,000	972,000	1,080,000	$1,188,000
Average A/R	63,000	96,000	135,000	180,000	231,000
EBCC[1] at 9%	68,040	77,760	87,480	97,200	106,920
ARCC[2] at 12%	(7,560)	(11,520)	(16,200)	(21,600)	(27,720)
Bad Debt (and percent of annual sales)	(7,560) (1%)	(10,800) (1.25%)	(14,580) (1.5%)	(18,900) (1.75%)	(23,760) (2%)
Net Earnings	**$ 52,920**	**55,440**	**56,700**	**56,700**	**55,440**

[1] Earnings Before Carrying Costs
[2] Accounts Receivable Carrying Costs

As anticipated, the sales gained by increasing the firm's average collection period from thirty to forty days lead to higher earnings. While the $2,520 gain is modest, it does represent the earnings foregone with a more restrictive credit policy.

By allowing the average collection period to increase to fifty days, ETSC gains an additional $1,260 in earnings, and total profits rise to $56,700 per year. However, that marks the limit on the company's gains from a more liberal credit policy.

Increasing the collection period from fifty to sixty days provides no addition to earnings, despite another $108,000 increase in sales. Any further increase in collection period allowed by even more liberal credit guidelines actually reduces earnings.

Let's review the facts that limited the benefits ETSC derives from lengthening its implied terms.

The firm's profit margin (before deducting carrying costs and bad-debt expense) is a full percentage point below that enjoyed by ABC Distributing Company. That small difference becomes significant when applied to the total sales volume in a business. Indeed, it translates into a $10,000 reduction in earnings on each $1 million in sales volume.

In addition, ETSC incurs a higher cost from carrying its investment in accounts receivable. Again, that difference becomes significant when measured against a larger investment carried for a full year.

Finally, the rising bad-debt expense naturally associated with a more liberal credit policy completes the detrimental effect on the gains anticipated from the higher sales volume. As implied terms increase, so do bad debts. No realistic analysis can ignore that fact.

Of course, how these factors affect your business depends on your special circumstance. Also, you must decide if your cash capability will allow you to carry the accounts receivable. Then, you can determine whether or not longer implied terms can be profitable for you.

CREDIT POLICY AND SALES PRICE

We've seen that a business inevitably incurs an increase in carrying costs and bad-debt losses whenever it uses a liberal credit policy to induce a higher sales volume. Carrying costs increase as a longer average collection period leads to a larger investment in accounts receivable. At the same time, a business absorbs higher losses from bad debts. In both instances, the more liberal the credit policy, the larger the increase in costs. Of course, that can limit the benefits a business can derive from a more liberal credit policy.

However, a business with sufficient cash capability can adopt another policy that overcomes that limit: It can adjust prices, thus applying Cash Flow Concept 15:

15: An upward price adjustment can offset the cost of selling to slow-paying customers.

Even a modest price adjustment can offset the higher costs associated with a more liberal credit policy.

To illustrate the potential of that policy, let's examine the results that come from a two-tiered price structure tied to customer payment habits. In this instance, we assume that a supplier sets a $10 per unit price for customers who observe his designated thirty-day terms for payment. Customers who take sixty days to pay must absorb a 10% premium. Product costs in either instance hold constant at $7 per unit.

Table 6–3 compares the results that come from selling 1,000-unit lots to both kinds of customers.

TABLE 6–3 Credit Policy and Sales Price

(A)

	30 Days Payment Price ($10.00)	60 Days Payment Price ($11.00)
Units	1,000	1,000
Monthly Sales Volume	$10,000	$11,000
Average A/R Investment	$10,000	$22,000

(B)

Gross Earnings Calculation

Sales	$10,000	$11,000
Product Costs at $7 per Unit	(7,000)	(7,000)
Monthly A/R Carrying Cost (1% per month)	(100)	(200)
Bad-Debt Losses	(100[1])	(200[2])
Gross Earnings	**$ 2,800**	**$ 3,600**

[1] 1% bad-debt losses
[2] 2% bad-debt losses

Column 1 measures the gross earnings from the sales to customers who observe the thirty-day payment terms. Deductions for accounts-receivable carrying costs and a bad-debt reserve leave the supplier with $2,800 in gross earnings. Of course, the business has to cover operating expenses out of that margin. But the gross margin calculation is sufficient for the comparison here.

Now, examine Column 2, showing the results that come from that 10% price adjustment applied to the same unit volume of sales to customers who take sixty days to pay.

Of course, the firm suffers two cost increases from that policy. The seller's investment in receivables rises. The $11,000 monthly volume translates into a $22,000 higher average investment in receivables. Also, bad-debt losses increase from 1% to 2% of the monthly sales volume. That naturally follows from sales to slow-paying customers.

However, the 10% price differential easily offsets both the higher accounts-receivable carrying costs and the increase in losses from bad debts. Moreover, the price adjustment produces an $800 net increment in earnings. That measures the benefit the seller derives from contributing his cash capability to a slow-paying customer for an extra thirty days.

In fact, only a 5% price differential would produce a slight increase in earnings for the supplier. This emphasizes that only a small differential can easily offset the cost that comes from selling to slow-paying customers. Of course, you must have the cash capability to carry the investment in receivables that results from those sales. But if you have the capability, adjusting your prices upward can increase your earnings.

Incidentally, the customer who pays slowly seldom complains about a modest price differential. He is more interested in liberal credit consideration that eases the strain on his own cash flow. Typically, he is willing to pay for that consideration.

CREDIT INSURANCE

Despite its long, successful history as a cash management tool, credit insurance remains an obscure concept to many businessmen. Indeed, the businessman who insures his buildings, equipment, and vehicles against common perils overlooks protecting an asset that is often more critical for the survival of his business—his accounts receivable. Here we emphasize Cash Flow Concept 16:

16: Credit insurance provides protection against the cash drain caused by uncollectible accounts receivable.

Certainly, a vehicle theft or a warehouse fire can disrupt a business. But the inability to collect a large receivable can cut off the cash flow critical for survival.

The value of credit protection will become apparent as we review the basic concept and operation of credit insurance. Not only can that protection prevent a cash flow crisis, but it can also lead to higher earnings.

The Indemnification Principle

A business that adopts a more liberal credit policy to increase sales accepts the risk—indeed, the inevitability—of higher bad-debt write-offs.

Certainly, you can offset those losses by adopting a complementary policy that adjusts prices upward to slow-paying customers. However, that still does not remove the risk. In fact, you must recognize that bad-debt losses seldom occur in a systematic proportion to sales. You may accurately project an average loss rate over an extended period, but each loss actually occurs on an individual, random basis.

For example, a business might realistically anticipate $100,000 in total bad-debt losses for the next ten years. However, the precise timing of the write-offs belies prediction. Thus, the business might lose $10,000 each year for ten years, or it might suffer a $100,000 loss in one year, but none in the other nine.

A $10,000 annual loss from bad debts might not impose a serious strain on your cash flow. However, taking a $100,000 loss from uncollectible accounts in one year may threaten your survival.

Recognizing that fact, credit insurance indemnifies a business against the catastrophic loss in cash that might occur when a large receivable becomes uncollectible because of (1) debtor bankruptcy, (2) debtor composition (reorganization of debt by creditors), or (3) any other proceeding that reflects a debtor's insolvency. In such events, the insurance company replaces much of the cash flow that otherwise would be lost in a bad-debt write-off. Of course, the insurance policy sets the basic terms of reimbursement.

The Credit Insurance Policy

The credit insurance policy establishes the principles of the relationship between a business and a credit insurance company. (American Credit Indemnity, a subsidiary of Control Data Corporation, is the nation's largest credit insurance company.) The contract, or policy, identifies the specific risks that will shift from the business to the insurer.

Usually, a policy provides coverage for losses suffered from any of a firm's accounts receivable that become uncollectible. However, that coverage is subject to two practical limits.

First, the insurance company applies a deductible amount to each loss. For example, if a $10,000 account proves uncollectible under terms of the policy, the business receives a $7,500 cash reimbursement from the insurer and absorbs the $2,500 loss. The specific deductible amount is set by the terms of the contract.

The deductible provision encourages the business to maintain prudent credit and collection policies. That interest might wane if the firm received 100% protection against any loss. Credit insurance protects against catastrophe, not recklessness.

Second, the insurance company limits the maximum coverage for each debtor. Typically, those limits are tied to ratings established by national credit agencies, such as Dun and Bradstreet. For example, a company with a D&B rating of BB1 might automatically qualify for a maximum $25,000 in coverage under the terms of the credit insurance policy. A business with a higher rating qualifies for more coverage, and one with a lower rating receives less.

In the absence of ratings, special endorsements specify the amount of risk acceptable to the insurer. Of course, the business can extend credit consideration in excess of the coverage limits. However, it must accept the full risk of loss associated with that excess.

Obviously, credit insurance isn't free. While premiums vary, the coverage may cost 1/4% to 1/2% of annual sales. That may be a small price to pay for survival. Moreover, credit insurance can encourage management policies that pay the cost of the coverage and increase earnings.

Confident Credit Policy

A business can use a more liberal credit policy to encourage a higher sales volume that increases earnings. Credit insurance contributes an element of confidence to the businessman who adopts that policy.

Credit insurance doesn't provide the cash capability to carry the increased investment in receivables that results from that policy. A business must obtain that capability from other sources. At the same time, credit insurance can give a businessman confidence in lengthening his implied selling terms. When he recognizes that he suffers a reduced risk from an erroneous credit decision, he can concentrate on sales rather than on credit and collections.

Of course, credit insurance doesn't cover imprudence, but it adds an element of confidence to a more liberal credit policy. The loss from a mistake will be tangible, but it won't be terminal.

Don't overlook the value of credit insurance. If your business has the cash capability, you can enjoy higher profits without the threat of uncollectible accounts. Indeed, such protection may ensure the profitability of a more liberal credit policy.

In this chapter we have ignored the cost of your credit and collection effort. While you certainly should recognize that cost, it usually remains fairly constant over any reasonable range of sales volumes.

From another perspective, you can consider the credit and collection effort as a normal part of your cost of sales. You assume that the cost of checking credit and following past-due accounts for payment absorbs a predetermined portion of each sales dollar. That allows proper consideration for the effect those expenses have on the earnings that come from a fluctuating sales volume.

7

Inventory in the Cash Flow Process

To meet customer demand as it arises, most businesses invest in some quantity of merchandise. That merchandise investment measures the size of a company's inventory. Since a business typically pays for its inventory at the time of purchase, or within thirty days thereafter, the size of its investment in inventory exerts an important influence on its cash flow. We illustrate that influence in this chapter, beginning with some fundamental characteristics that distinguish inventory from accounts receivable as components in the cash flow process.

INVENTORY AND ACCOUNTS RECEIVABLE

Inventory has the same relationship to the cash flow process as accounts receivable. However, some important differences between the two components make inventory management more challenging.

For example, accounts receivable are *self-liquidating* assets. Once a sale is made, a receivable converts naturally into cash when collected. Inventory is a less accommodating asset. Indeed, you have to push it through the cash flow cycle. It sits idle until you generate the sale that converts it into cash or accounts receivable.

Moreover, apart from the purchase cost, it usually is more expensive to carry an investment in inventory than in accounts receivable. Of course, the financial or opportunity cost of carrying either investment is the same. Additionally, an investment in receivables requires a reasonable expenditure for a credit and col-

54

lection effort. However, these costs seldom match the expense associated with carrying inventory.

Most significantly, you must warehouse your stock. You must buy or lease a facility that enables you to store and maintain your investment in a salable condition. And, the larger your total inventory, the larger your warehouse expense.

An investment in inventory also requires unavoidable handling costs, such as personnel, equipment, and processing. You incur those costs each time you take delivery of a new purchase or generate a sale. Naturally, your handling costs increase proportionately with your sales volume. Moreover, you must insure your inventory against the threat of fire, theft, and other perils. The larger and more perishable your inventory, the higher your insurance expense. While you also can insure accounts receivable against losses from bad debts, the costs are not nearly comparable to those associated with your physical inventory.

Finally, most types of inventory have a limited shelf life. For several reasons, that investment can lose value while you hold it for sale. For example, a grocer must discard unsold vegetables after only a day or two. A chemical distributor suffers the same fate with some compounds that lose potency a week or a month after production.

Even nonperishable inventory can lose value as it sits in your warehouse. In some instances, it may become obsolete, made unsalable by technological innovation or merely by a change in customer preference. Indeed, a minor improvement in a competitor's product can transform your leading source of revenue into a back-shelf item.

In other instances, competitive price pressure can reduce the value of your investment. Your inventory inevitably loses some salability anytime your competitors lower prices to attract sales. While you can view that as an opportunity cost— you end up with a smaller profit margin rather than higher expenses—the effect on your earnings is the same. Thus, you incur another cost from carrying an investment in inventory.

At the same time, the cost of carrying inventory should be kept in perspective. You should measure the actual or potential costs of carrying inventory against the benefits you stand to gain from that investment. Again, you can recognize that gain best by comparing it with your investment in receivables.

Accounts receivable, once generated from sales, become sterile assets: They contribute nothing until they are converted into cash through collection.

In contrast, any item in your inventory promises additional profits to your business. Moreover, that item can contribute a much larger return than any other investment you normally make.

For example, if you generate a $10 sale from an item that costs $7, you gain a $3 contribution to your operating costs and profits. That gain represents a 42% return on your investment. Moreover, should you repeat that sale, or turn that inventory item, four times a year, the cumulative annual return on your investment becomes 168%. That potential return justifies the higher carrying costs inevitably associated with your investment in inventory.

Of course, the potential profits from any inventory shouldn't encourage you to carry a quantity that could exhaust your cash capability. But you should balance the potential profits against the cost of carrying the investment.

Finally, you also should recognize one important similarity between accounts receivable and inventory. That is, you can't reduce your investment in either asset below some minimum level without hurting your sales and profits.

Thus, if you shorten your designated or implied selling terms too much, you will lose sales to your more liberal competitors. You will reduce your investment in accounts receivable, but chances are good that you also will reduce your earnings. Lower revenue generally translates into lower profits.

You suffer a similar fate when you seek to lower your investment in inventory too far. That is, you begin to lose sales to your better stocked competitors. You suffer *stock-out* costs, which you must absorb anytime you do not have an item on hand to meet customer demand.

Stock-out cost is another opportunity cost. However, it is more difficult to measure than one resulting from an overinvestment in accounts receivable or inventory. As a minimum measure of the expense, you can estimate your stock-out cost in terms of a customer's dissatisfaction that arises from having to wait for the particular item he wants. That dissatisfaction naturally makes him more susceptible to your competitors.

At the next level, the stock-out cost increases when your customer actually does acquire the product elsewhere. You incur the maximum opportunity cost because you ultimately may lose all of his future business to a better stocked competitor. If you do regain his business in the future, the potential profit from the single lost sale measures your stock-out or opportunity cost.

Consequently, when you determine your proper investment level in inventory, you must weigh the stock-out costs that come from having too little inventory against the costs of carrying a larger investment.

AVERAGE INVESTMENT PERIOD

Here, we will illustrate Cash Flow Concept 17:

17: Average investment period defines the relationship between your inventory and the cash flow process.

Similar to the collection period calculation in Chapter 3, average investment period measures the length of time each dollar invested in inventory remains in that form before a sale converts it into cash or into an account receivable.

The data to illustrate this concept come from the case of Tire Distributors, Inc., a wholesaler located in a large southwestern state. In summary form, TDI generated the following results in its fiscal year ending 8/31/79:

Sales	$2,400,000
Cost of Goods Sold	(1,920,000)
Operating Cost	(390,000)
Earnings	$ 90,000

However, as you might anticipate, TDI's profitable operation did not preclude a costly cash flow problem.

Table 7–1 presents a picture of the problem with a look at the firm's 8/31/79 balance sheet. The balance sheet reflects the following facts about the company's operation:

1. TDI's $300,000 investment in accounts receivable comes from a 45-day collection period and a $200,000 monthly sales volume
2. At 8/31/79 TDI was carrying a $480,000 investment in inventory
3. The company presently purchases $160,000 per month from its suppliers, an amount equal to TDI's monthly cost of sales
4. The firm's suppliers allow a 2% discount for payment within ten days after a purchase, and expect payment within 30 days

TABLE 7–1 Tire Distributors, Inc.
Balance Sheet 8/31/79

Cash	$ 10,000
Accounts Receivable	300,000
Inventory	480,000
Total Assets	**$790,000**
Accounts Payable	$240,000
Bank Loan	250,000
Total Liabilities	**$490,000**
Stockholders' Equity	$300,000
Equity and Liabilities	**$790,000**

It is easy to see that with purchases of $160,000 per month and accounts payable of $240,000 per month, TDI is violating its suppliers' payment requirements. Even with the aid of a $250,000 bank loan, the firm is paying suppliers 45 days after purchase, rather than within the expected 30 days.

In spite of their designated terms, at 8/31/79 TDI's suppliers obviously tolerated the firm's payment practices. Indeed, the suppliers apparently were seeking sales more avidly than prompt payment.

At the same time, TDI's payment practices cost the firm dearly. In fact, the inability to pay for purchases within ten days cost TDI $3,200 in lost discounts each month ($160,000 × 2%). Moreover, that doesn't consider the financial or opportunity cost associated with the potential overinvestment.

Recognizing the expensive cost of a cash flow problem, TDI's management searched for a way to take advantage of the lost discounts. As a first step in that search, they found that the firm needed $187,000 in cash to take supplier discounts.

That total comes from the difference between TDI's actual accounts payable at 8/31/79 and the amount that would be due if the company took all available discounts. Thus, if TDI took all discounts on $160,000 in monthly purchases, accounts payable could not exceed the average purchase amount for any ten-day period: that is, one-third of $160,000, or $53,333. Based on the $240,000 in accounts payable due, then, TDI needed $187,000.

Management then began to look for a source for the cash necessary to take the supplier discounts. Immediately, that search ran into two roadblocks.

First, TDI's banker refused to increase its loan above the $250,000 total outstanding at 8/31/79. Certainly, the required $187,000 increase would exceed even a liberal banker's limit.

Second, management analyzed the potential benefits that might come from a reduction in TDI's average collection period. However, they found that since the existing 45-day collection period approximated the industry average, any significant reduction imposed by shorter selling terms or a tighter credit policy would injure sales. Generating cash by reducing the firm's investment in accounts receivable was not a realistic alternative.

Finally, TDI's management examined the one remaining potential solution to its problem: the cash that might come from a reduction in the firm's investment in inventory. That analysis began with the calculation of the average investment period.

Calculating the average investment period for any business is done in two steps:

1. Divide cost of goods sold by 360 to obtain the average daily cost of goods sold

2. Divide that total into the firm's present investment in inventory to find the average investment period

Thus, TDI's calculation becomes:

1. $\text{Average Daily Cost of Goods Sold} = \dfrac{\$1,920,000}{360} = \$5,333$

2. $\text{Average Investment Period} = \dfrac{\$480,000}{\$5,333} = 90 \text{ Days}$

At 8/31/79, each dollar TDI invested in inventory remained in that form for ninety days.

How TDI uses that information to solve its cash flow problem is illustrated below. Here, you should recognize that average investment period is analogous to average collection period. By reducing average investment period, TDI cured its cash flow problem and added thousands of dollars to its bottom line.

USING AVERAGE INVESTMENT PERIOD

Average investment period relates your daily cost of goods sold to your total investment in inventory. It measures the average number of days' sales you maintain in stock. To use that information, you must recognize how a change in that investment period affects your cash flow.

We return to TDI's experience. The average investment period calculation indicated that the firm had inventory sufficient for ninety days' sales at 8/31/79. Of course, that calculation averages the investment periods for all of the items that make up the firm's total inventory. That is, TDI's inventory of some tire sizes was sufficient for only sixty days' sales, while other sizes on hand would satisfy normal customer demand for six months or more.

Additional research into supplier shipping habits indicated that TDI seldom had to wait more than thirty days for delivery of any order placed with any supplier. Indeed, most suppliers shipped major orders in even less time.

Combining these facts led to a solution of TDI's cash flow problem. Management correctly concluded that it was unnecessary to maintain inventory on hand to satisfy ninety days' sales, when any item in that inventory could be restocked in thirty days or less.

Thus, they decided to reduce the average investment period from ninety to fifty days. This objective would leave the firm with inventory adequate to service most customer requirements promptly. Moreover, TDI would still carry inventory necessary for twenty days' sales beyond the normal restocking period. That cushion was designed to satisfy extraordinary customer demand or unavoidable delays in shipping by suppliers.

Significantly, the lower investment in inventory generated $213,320 in cash for TDI: Inventory dropped from $480,000 to $266,680. Table 7–2 illustrates the effect the lower investment had on the firm's financial structure. Note two important facts about that new structure.

First, the cash enabled TDI to reduce accounts payable to the level necessary to earn the firm the 2% discounts allowed for payment within ten days. TDI's

TABLE 7–2 Tire Distributors, Inc.
Balance Sheet 12/31/79

Cash	$ 36,653
Accounts Receivable	300,000
Inventory	266,680
Total Assets	**$603,333**
Accounts Payable	$ 53,333
Bank Loan	250,000
Total Liabilities	**$303,333**
Stockholders' Equity	$300,000
Equity and Liabilities	**$603,333**

monthly bottom-line benefit of $3,200 translates into a $38,400 annual increase in earnings. That's significant in any business league.

Second, the reduction in inventory also added more than $26,000 to the firm's cash reserves. As the lower investment improved earnings, it also enhanced TDI's cash position.

You can easily estimate the potential cash you can generate from a reduction in inventory. Merely measure your average investment period against that actually required to satisfy the real needs of your business. Interrelate your sales projections with each supplier's ability to deliver his products on time. You may find, as in TDI's circumstance, that you can reduce you inventory substantially without hurting your sales volume.

Of course, you won't reduce your inventory to a level that would increase your stock-out costs. But recognize that excess inventory is not only costly to carry but also absorbs your limited cash capability. Thus, eliminating any excess inventory improves your cash flow and increases your earnings.

Table 7–3 illustrates the direct relationship between average investment period and cash flow. Thus, if your cost of goods sold averages $2,000 per day, then a ten-day reduction in average investment period contributes $20,000 to your cash flow. If you can effect that reduction without an increase in stock-out costs, you will generate that much cash for permanent, profitable investment elsewhere.

TABLE 7–3 Effect of Investment Period on Average Total Inventory

| Average Investment Period Days | Cost of Goods Sold per Day | | | | |
	$1,000	$2,000	$3,000	$4,000	$5,000
30	30,000	60,000	90,000	120,000	150,000
35	35,000	70,000	105,000	140,000	175,000
40	40,000	80,000	120,000	160,000	200,000
45	45,000	90,000	135,000	180,000	225,000
50	50,000	100,000	150,000	210,000	250,000
55	55,000	110,000	165,000	220,000	275,000
60	60,000	120,000	180,000	240,000	300,000

Total Inventory

(We don't illustrate the direct dollar benefit you derive from a reduction in average investment period here. Conceptually, the relationship is analogous to that demonstrated with accounts receivable in Chapter 3.)

At the same time, however, recognize that reducing your investment in inventory provides a larger bottom-line benefit than a comparable reduction in accounts receivable. After all, not only do you reduce the financial (or opportunity) cost of carrying an excess investment, you also reduce the physical costs. The total benefit can be substantial.

Let's consider that same relationship from a different point of view.

ANNUAL TURNOVER RATE

You add perspective to your component management effort by calculating your annual inventory turnover rate. That calculation measures the number of times a business sells, or *turns,* its average investment in inventory in the course of a year. It is an activity indicator that relates your investment in inventory directly to your sales volume, and it is crystallized in Cash Flow Concept 18:

18: Turning your inventory more rapidly improves your cash flow and earnings.

To find your inventory turnover rate, divide the annual cost of goods sold in your business by your average investment in inventory. Explicitly, the formula is:

$$\text{Inventory Turnover Rate} = \frac{\text{Annual Cost of Goods Sold}}{\text{Average Inventory}}$$

Using the data from TDI's original circumstance, we find:

$$\text{Inventory Turnover Rate} = \frac{\$1,920,000}{\$480,000} = 4$$

Thus, on the average, TDI converts each item in its inventory into a sale four times a year. Of course, that was before the firm effected the reduction in its inventory.

The turnover rate calculation is significant because of its direct relationship to your cash flow and profits. Thus, if you increase your turnover rate—that is, turn your inventory more rapidly—you lower your average investment in inventory and improve your cash flow.

Most businessmen apply turnover rate more often to inventory than to accounts receivable. Even the most haphazard manager senses that moving merchandise more rapidly is an underlying key to profitability. However, he less frequently attaches the same importance to turning his accounts receivable.

Table 7–4 clarifies the relationship between turnover rate and investment in inventory.

TABLE 7-4 Effect of Turnover Rate on Average Investment in Inventory

Annual Turnover Rate	Annual Cost of Goods Sold				
	$700,000	$1,400,000	$2,100,000	$2,800,000	$3,500,000
2	350,000	700,000	1,050,000	1,400,000	1,750,000
3	233,333	466,666	700,000	933,333	1,166,667
4	175,000	350,000	525,000	700,000	875,000
5	140,000	280,000	420,000	560,000	700,000
6	116,666	233,333	350,000	466,666	538,333
7	100,000	200,000	300,000	400,000	500,000
8	87,500	175,000	262,500	350,000	437,500

Average Investment in Inventory

Assume that a business has a $700,000 annual cost of goods sold (70% of a $1 million sales volume). If that business turns its inventory only twice a year, its average investment in inventory will total $350,000.

Now, consider the benefit that comes from increasing that turnover rate from two to three times a year. With the same sales volume, the higher turnover rate reduces the firm's average investment in inventory by more than $116,000. The more rapid turnover in assets generates that much cash for use elsewhere.

Obviously, the larger your sales volume, or the more you increase your inventory turnover rate, the greater the benefits to your business.

Of course, your ultimate objective is to hold the average investment in inventory that contributes the most earnings to your business and increases your cash flow.

Component Analysis: Inventory

The financial formulas introduced in Chapter 7 provide useful insight into the relationship between inventory and the cash flow process. However, you must proceed beyond those basic calculations to identify any overinvestment in inventory, as well as to isolate the underlying problem that precipitates that overinvestment. This chapter facilitates those objectives by reviewing the basic tools for analyzing inventory in the cash flow process.

First, we discuss the fundamentals of comparative analysis. In Chapter 4 we illustrated how comparative analysis applies to your investment in accounts receivable. But you apply the same concepts to analyze your investment in inventory. Then, we look at the analytic tools designed specifically for inventory. Of course, the periodic physical count remains the starting point for analysis, but you can't rely on that count alone. Indeed, you must complement it with specific item analysis.

COMPARATIVE ANALYSIS: AVERAGE INVESTMENT PERIOD

Component management emphasizes the most efficient, profitable investment in accounts receivable and inventory in the cash flow process. That emphasis recognizes that you can have a cash flow adequate for normal operations but still carry an excess investment in either component.

Indeed, to recognize an overinvestment in either accounts receivable or inventory, you must do a comparative analysis. Regarding inventory, that translates into Cash Flow Concept 19:

19: Comparative analysis helps identify the correct average investment period for your inventory.

Using comparative internal analysis, if your average investment period exceeds that experienced by your business in prior periods, you may have an overinvestment in inventory. Further analysis might contradict that view, but any discrepancy from past performance invites a deeper look.

Similarly, if your investment period is longer than that of your competitors (perhaps using the comparative data available from Dun and Bradstreet or Robert Morris Associates), an excess investment in inventory may be exerting a subtle, detrimental effect on your bottom line.

At the same time, remember also that a significant difference in either instance doesn't prove the existence of a component problem. Special circumstances—a special sale or an extraordinary purchase opportunity, for example—may justify a temporary overinvestment in inventory measured by normal standards. But, deviations from the norm do call for explanation.

Certainly, this reaffirms the important benefit you derive from comparative analysis. It draws attention to the extraordinary, the problem that needs correction, or the circumstance that at least deserves explanation.

The correct investment period translates into the proper investment level in inventory, and it becomes the target for your component management effort.

COMPARATIVE ANALYSIS: THE INVENTORY/SALES RATIO

Continuing the analogy with the comparative analysis of your accounts receivable, you can use a regular examination of your *inventory-to-sales ratio* to identify a potential overinvestment in inventory: The ratio compares your investment in inventory to your monthly sales total.

For example, if your inventory last month totaled $300,000, and sales for the same month reached $150,000, the ratio calculation is:

$$\frac{\text{Inventory}}{\text{Sales}} = \frac{\$300,000}{\$150,000} = 2$$

Thus, your investment in inventory was twice your sales volume for the month. Certainly, the ratio provides a straightforward summary of the relationship between those two critical elements.

Now, assume that that ratio is appropriate for your business: Your normal operation requires an investment in inventory that doubles your monthly sales volume. The ratio then becomes the standard against which you compare the results of your operations every month.

If any monthly calculation results in a higher inventory-to-sales ratio—that is, above 2 to 1—you can assume that you have a potential component problem. Of course, the ratio rises in response to both an increase in inventory or a drop in sales. Consequently, the actual problem may not lie in component management. Indeed, it may be a problem associated with your sales effort, or perhaps with a general decline in the economy.

Alternatively, should the ratio between inventory and sales fall below 2 to 1, or whatever standard is appropriate for your business, then you may deserve a compliment for managing your inventory efficiently. After all, that result comes from either a higher sales volume relative to your investment in inventory or a lower inventory level relative to sales. Over the short term, either circumstance is desirable.

Of course, you also should recognize the other possible implication of a lower inventory-to-sales ratio. That is, as you increase sales relative to any investment in inventory, you also increase the risk of incurring stock-out costs. The benefits from a better cash flow may be offset by the opportunity costs associated with lost sales.

In any instance, of course, the inventory/sales ratio serves the same function as any other tool for comparative analysis—to draw attention to a potential overinvestment in inventory. But you must look further to locate the specific source of that problem.

PHYSICAL COUNT AND ITEM ANALYSIS

A periodic count of every item in stock is the first, fundamental principle of sound inventory management. The physical count serves two primary objectives.

First, it enables you to verify the accuracy of your accounting procedures that keep track of your investment in inventory. As you verify the exact amount of each item in stock, you confirm the value of your investment.

Second, and even more important, the physical count provides the basic data necessary to perform an item analysis of your inventory. Keep in mind Cash Flow Concept 20:

20: Item analysis identifies the specific source of an overinvestment in inventory.

Item analysis becomes the fundamental tool that enables you to control your investment in inventory.

Remember, average investment period defines the relationship between your inventory and the cash flow process. However, there is a limitation inherent in the information provided by that calculation. That is, as the term implies, it defines an "average" relationship, assuming that every item you stock turns at exactly the same rate. Thus, a sixty-day average investment period asserts that each product that makes up your total investment in inventory moves from purchase to resale in exactly two months. It also implies that your stock of every item in inventory is sufficient for two months' sales.

Those are valid assumptions if your inventory includes only one product. However, with a few exceptions, most businesses carry a wide variety of different products. Inevitably, some products turn more rapidly than others. Indeed, whatever your average investment period, when you consider specific items within your inventory, you may have an overinvestment in some, the correct investment in others, and insufficient investment in still others. Consequently, complete component analysis requires that you go beyond the average investment period calculation and examine your investment in each product that you carry: That is, you must perform item analysis.

Item analysis measures the amount of your investment in each item in stock against the amount actually required, based on your recent sales experience. To illustrate this, we return to the case of Tire Distributors, Inc., as discussed in Chapter 7.

TDI solved its cash flow problem by reducing its average investment in inventory from a level appropriate for ninety days' sales to a level still sufficient for fifty days' sales. Of course, that reduction didn't occur spontaneously.

Instead, the firm used item analysis to identify the specific tire sizes that made up the overinvestment in inventory. That analysis proceeded on the following assumptions:

1. TDI had no need to stock a quantity of any tire above that necessary to satisfy two months' sales
2. TDI measured that standard by looking at the actual sales activity over the previous sixty days for each tire in stock
3. As a starting point for analysis, TDI conducted a physical count of its inventory that included a breakdown of the number of each tire size in stock

Let's review some of the relevant results of TDI's analysis, as illustrated in Table 8–1.

TDI found 420 tires, Stock 100, on hand at 8/31/79, although only 140 had been sold during the last sixty days. Indeed, the stock on hand of that single tire

TABLE 8–1 Item Analysis: 8/31/79

TIRE DISTRIBUTORS, INC.

Tire Stock Number	Number in Stock	Number Sold Last 60 Days	Days Sale in Inventory	Action
100	420	140	180	Reduce
101	300	300	60	Satisfactory
102	270	540	30	Increase
103	850	170	300	Reduce
104	90	30	180	Reduce
105	63	9	420	Eliminate

size was sufficient for normal demand over the next six months. TDI could carry one-third the inventory of that item without the serious risk of incurring any stock-out costs.

Analysis of Stock 101 showed that the amount in stock was exactly right for sixty days' sales. TDI's investment in that item was appropriate for its sales volume.

Now, look at the results of Stock 102. Although the firm sold 540 units over the previous two-month period, only 270 were on hand for sale at 8/31/79. Perhaps TDI was awaiting delivery of 270 units to bring that stock item up to the proper 540 level necessary to meet normal demand. If not, the firm was confronting the possibility of stock-out costs because of a deficient inventory of a rapidly selling tire.

TDI's Investments in Stock 103 and 104 also were excessive. Thus, those items became candidates for the firm's reduction program. We find the same result from Stock 105. However, that item, a relatively small part of TDI's total inventory, produced the sale of only 9 units over the sample sales period. That suggests probable product obsolescence, and it should encourage the elimination of that item altogether from the investment in inventory.

Of course, TDI may carry that item to meet the sporadic demands of a customer who buys a significant number of other tire sizes. If not, that item becomes excess inventory: It doesn't generate enough sales to justify carrying it at all.

Now, let's review the primary benefits of item inventory analysis.

Item analysis enables you to identify the specific items in stock that make up an overinvestment in inventory. Eliminating that excess reduces the size of your average investment in inventory and improves your cash flow. Also, it is an early-warning problem spotter, analogous to the aging analysis of accounts receivable.

An overinvestment in inventory seldom develops suddenly. The build-up occurs slowly: One item moves more slowly than average, then another. As you identify these slower-moving products on a regular basis, you can make the appropriate adjustments before the cumulative effects hurt your cash flow or earnings.

Of course, your response might be to lower your inventory level or increase your sales effort for those particular items. In either circumstance, item analysis provides the signal for action. Used properly, this problem spotter can add significant earnings to your bottom line.

Inventory management is a complex process. Indeed, maintaining the proper investment in inventory involves a consideration of purchasing costs, customer demands, and delivery time, as well as carrying costs.

Component Management: Quantity Control

Effective quantity control is the key to successful inventory management. You want to maintain an inventory level adequate for anticipated sales requirements, while avoiding an overinvestment that exerts a detrimental effect on your cash flow and earnings. This chapter introduces some cash flow concepts that help achieve those objectives.

First, we review the elements that make up the proper inventory level in a business. Then, we demonstrate a practical approach that relates inventory requirements to projected sales volume. Properly estimating that requirement obviously is a critical factor in effective quantity control. Indeed, it becomes the target inventory level you seek to achieve and maintain.

Of course, no objective inventory level should exceed the natural limits set by your cash capability. Thus, we expand our illustration to demonstrate the interrelationships among your projected sales and inventory requirements and the cash flow process. Certainly, no well-managed business can ignore those interrelationships.

Then, we alter our perspective, assuming that an effective cash flow is less important than the most profitable investment in inventory. We will discuss the quantity control methods that help achieve that investment. Although that investment may not provide the most efficient cash flow, you often may find it worthwhile to exchange some of your cash capability for higher earnings.

THE ELEMENTS OF INVENTORY INVESTMENT

The proper investment in inventory generates the maximum earnings for a business without stretching the limits of its cash capability. Of course, no business maintains that investment continuously. But that objective serves as the natural target of the quantity control effort. The stock necessary to satisfy normal day-to-day sales requirements makes up the core of that target. And the equation for measuring your inventory requirements is summarized in Cash Flow Concept 21:

21: Normal stock plus safety stock plus growth stock equals the target investment in inventory.

For example, assume that an office supply firm sells an average of 10 boxes of carbon paper per day, or 300 boxes per month. If the firm buys carbon paper only once a month, then each order should call for no fewer than 300 boxes. This is the minimum necessary to satisfy the firm's normal sales requirements.

Of course, customer demand fluctuates. Over any short-term period, sales of any particular item can exceed normal requirements. Consequently, an investment in inventory properly includes some *safety stock.*

Safety stock describes that part of your inventory that satisfies a modest, unanticipated increase in customer demand. It provides a measure of protection against stock-out costs. For example, the office supply firm might begin each month with an inventory of 330 boxes of carbon paper. While that total exceeds normal requirements, the 30 extra boxes provide a cushion to satisfy an unanticipated increase in demand. The cost of carrying the safety stock should be less than the opportunity cost incurred from the loss of those potential sales.

Safety stock also helps to offset shortages that might result from erratic supplier shipments. An unforeseen strike, snowstorm, or material shortage can delay shipment of any order. Safety stock helps defer the decrease in sales caused by such disruptions.

Growth stock is the final element in a firm's target investment in inventory. It satisfies the demand created by a projected increase in sales volume. Certainly, no effort to increase sales makes sense unless you carry the stock necessary to supply the higher volume.

For example, assume that the office supply firm adds a salesman in an effort to expand its market. At the same time, the firm must increase its inventory of carbon paper, as well as all other items, to satisfy the anticipated increase in sales. If the higher volume does not follow, the firm will find itself with a temporary overinvestment in inventory. However, that is a necessary risk inherent in any push to increase sales.

Of course, the investment in inventory must be properly allocated among the different products that make up the total. Moreover, that total should not exceed the firm's cash capability, a point we will return to later in the chapter.

ESTIMATING INVENTORY REQUIREMENTS

A realistic sales projection, based on Cash Flow Concept 21, is a necessary precedent to estimating your inventory requirements. We will examine one approach that relates inventory requirements to a particular sales projection, using the experience of Atlas Belts, Inc., a small distributor of power transmission belts.

Atlas presently generates $200,000 per month in sales. However, over the next twelve months, the firm expects that volume to increase steadily to $400,000 per month. Specifically, the firm expects sales for the next four quarters as follows:

	Quarter			
	1	2	3	4
Projected Sales	$750,000	$900,000	$1,050,000	$1,200,000
Monthly Average	250,000	300,000	350,000	400,000

Beginning with these projections, Atlas developed its inventory requirements for each quarter based on its operational characteristics:
1. Product costs average 75% of sales
2. Unacceptable stock-out costs are incurred whenever inventory drops below the level necessary to satisfy two months' sales volume
3. Inventory necessary for projected sales must be on hand at the beginning of each quarter

Atlas can project its inventory requirements in a straightforward manner. The first step merely multiplies the anticipated monthly volume by 75%, the average cost of sales. Multiplying that total by two provides the inventory level necessary to satisfy the projected sales volume while avoiding stock-out costs.

For example, the inventory necessary to begin the firm's first quarter comes from the following calculation:

Projected Monthly Sales		Cost of Sales		Two Months' Requirements	
$250,000	×	75%	×	2	= $375,000

Of course, that calculation provides an estimate of the company's total inventory requirements. Atlas must complement that estimate with item analysis, perhaps coupled with specific product-sales projections, to achieve the correct inventory mix.

Also, Atlas must relate the estimated inventory requirements to its cash capability. From our perspective, that is the most important part of the projections.

PROJECTED INVENTORY AND THE CASH FLOW PROCESS

Estimating the inventory requirements necessary to achieve any projected sales volume is an essential step in cash flow management. However, should the inventory requirements exceed the limits set by your cash capability, you must reduce your ambitions, or risk the embarrassment of a cash flow problem. Keep in mind Cash Flow Concept 22:

22: Estimated inventory requirements must recognize the limits set by the cash capability in a business.

The eventual result of the projections developed by Atlas Belts indicated a cash flow deficit. That result, summarized in Table 9–1, reflects additional facts about the firm's operations:

1. Atlas will begin the projected year with a $100,000 cash reserve, as indicated in Column 1

2. The firm's credit and collection policies produce a constant thirty-day average collection period from its accounts receivable

3. All of the firm's suppliers require payment for all purchases within thirty days

TABLE 9–1 Projected End-of-Quarter Balance Sheets

ATLAS BELTS, INC.

	Beginning Fiscal Year	1	2	3	4
Cash	$100,000	$ 50,000	$ 7,500	($27,500)	($65,000)
Accounts Receivable	200,000	250,000	300,000	350,000	400,000
Inventory	300,000	375,000	450,000	525,000	600,000
Total Assets	**$600,000**	**$675,000**	**$757,500**	**$847,500**	**$945,000**
Accounts Payable	$150,000	$187,500	$225,000	$262,500	$300,000
Bank Loan	200,000	200,000	200,000	200,000	200,000
Total Liabilities	**$350,000**	**$387,500**	**$425,000**	**$462,500**	**$500,000**
Stockholders' Equity	$250,000	$287,500	$332,500	$385,000	$445,000
Liabilities and Equity	**$600,000**	**$675,000**	**$757,500**	**$847,500**	**$945,000**

While they offer no discounts for early payment, suppliers quickly eliminate slow-paying customers from credit consideration

4. Atlas earns 5% on all sales.

We also assume that Atlas anticipates no increase in the $200,000 bank loan outstanding at the beginning of the projected year (Column 1). Now, observe what happens to the firm's cash position as it presumably achieves the sales projected for each quarter in the upcoming year.

Since to meet supplier requirements Atlas must maintain accounts payable on a thirty-day basis, the increase in receivables and inventory naturally associated with the higher sales volume absorbs the firm's cash reserves. In fact, by the end of the third quarter, the projections indicate an unavoidable, but unacceptable, deficit cash position (Column 4).

That deficit grows as the projected sales increase further in the fourth quarter. Moreover, the problem becomes more serious despite the firm's profitable operations and efficient accounts-receivable management.

Thus, Atlas must reduce its projected sales volume for the upcoming year, or obtain additional cash from another source to supplement its cash reserves. Otherwise, the inventory requirement would exceed the firm's cash capability, resulting in a serious cash flow problem.

MANAGING FOR PROFITS

Relating inventory requirements to cash capability is an important element of positive cash flow management. However, if you have adequate cash capability, you may find it profitable to change your management emphasis. Instead of seeking the most efficient cash flow, you can direct your management efforts toward producing the largest bottom-line benefits for your business.

Of course, seeking maximum profits is a natural business objective. However, the most profitable investment in inventory often exceeds the limits set by a firm's cash capability. The experience of Atlas Belts proved that.

We presume here that cash capability doesn't stand as an obstacle to profitability. In that happy event, the component management effort changes its orientation. Indeed, that effort seeks the most profitable inventory investment level. To find that level, you must achieve the proper balance between two contradictory categories of costs.

One category, inventory carrying costs (as discussed in Chapter 7), increases as a business expands its investment in inventory. The second category, acquisition costs, exhibits the opposite reaction. That is, these costs tend to fall as a firm's average inventory investment level rises.

We will demonstrate the technique that enables you to minimize these costs and ultimately maximize your bottom-line benefits.

Acquisition Costs

Every businessman recognizes the direct cost of acquiring inventory: the purchase price of the merchandise. However, many overlook other acquistion

costs, which increase the actual cost of any particular order, and the inverse relationship they have to the size of the average investment in inventory.

Cash Flow Concept 23 emphasizes the importance of acquisition costs:

23: Inventory acquisition costs rise as a business increases the number of orders entered per year.

A business can measure its acquisition costs as the total of the following:
1. The actual cost of the merchandise acquired
2. The administrative costs that arise from scheduling, entering, and receiving an order
3. The labor costs associated with receiving, inspecting, and shelving each order
4. The cost of accounting and paying for the order

Two facts concerning these costs become relevant here. First, the administrative, accounting, and labor costs associated with any order are more significant than many businessmen realize. Indeed, the cumulative acquisition costs
from numerous orders can exert a significant downward effect on your earnings.
Second, the cumulative acquisition costs hold relatively constant regardless of
the size of the order involved. Indeed, apart from the cost of the merchandise, it
costs little more to order and receive 1,000 units for stock than it does for 100
units.

Thus, you can reasonably conclude that as you increase the size of each
order, you reduce the total number of orders you enter each year. And as you
reduce the number of purchase orders, you reduce your annual acquisition costs.

To illustrate how reducing these costs can benefit the bottom-line in a business, we will use the experience of the Southwest Light Company, a regional bulb
distributor. For the upcoming year, Southwest projects sales of 24,000 units (four
to a package) of its standard 100-watt bulbs. Beginning with that projection, the
firm analyzed its acquisition costs based on the following assumptions:
1. Southwest's supplier of 100-watt bulbs requires a minimum order of 4,000
units; however, Southwest can order any amount above that minimum.
2. The company has the warehouse capacity to store the 24,000 units required
for the full year's projected sales.
3. Southwest's cumulative acquisition costs total $600 for each order entered.
In this instance, we also assume that Southwest's unit purchase price remains
constant regardless of the size of the order entered with its supplier.

Table 9–2 illustrates the anticipated results of the firm's analysis. Thus, as
Southwest reduces the number of orders entered during the year—that is, increasing the size of each order—the company reduces its annual acquisition
costs.

In fact, by including the firm's total annual requirement for 24,000 units in
one order, Southwest reduces its acquisition costs for the year to only $600. That
is $3,000 less than the costs the firm would incur by purchasing the same stock in
six minimum-order lots.

TABLE 9–2 Annual Acquisition Cost Analysis

SOUTHWEST LIGHT COMPANY

Order Size (units)	4,000	6,000	8,000	12,000	24,000
Number of Orders	6	4	3	2	1
Annual Acquisition Costs ($600 per order)	$3,600	$2,400	$1,800	$1,200	$600

Thus, using a single order to obtain your total annual requirement for every item you stock reduces acquisition costs to a minimum. Of course, as acquisition costs drop, your average investment in inventory increases. That, in turn, increases your carrying costs associated with that investment.

Carrying Costs

We will demonstrate how you trade off acquisition costs and carrying costs to obtain the most profitable investment in inventory. Keep in mind Cash Flow Concept 24:

24: Annual inventory carrying costs rise as the average size of that investment increases.

From our perspective, you can presume that the financial or opportunity costs also increase in exact proportion to the size of that investment. However, other carrying costs also increase, although the proportions are less precise. Thus, as you increase your investment in inventory, you increase your warehouse costs. You need more space to store more inventory. As your investment grows, you also will see rising insurance and maintenance costs, as well as an increase in the expenses that come from deterioration or obsolescence.

Indeed, it is easy to surmise that the cumulative increase in carrying costs easily can offset the gain you realize from reducing your acquisition costs to a minimum. A two-step analysis supports this assertion. First, let's examine the effect ordering frequency has on the size of a firm's average investment in inventory. We use some simplified assumptions to illustrate that effect:

1. A business sells its stock at a constant, predictable rate
2. A business receives each new order on the same day that it sells the last item from the previous order
3. However determined, all orders for each item are exactly the same size
4. A business has no need to carry any safety stock

Beginning with these assumptions, we can calculate the average investment for each item a business stocks, using the order quantity as follows:

$$\text{Average Inventory} = \frac{\text{Size of Each Order}}{2}$$

While the calculation may not provide a precise average, it is sufficiently accurate for most business circumstances.

Table 9–3 uses the calculation to estimate Southwest Light's average investment in inventory that would result using the order sizes in Table 9–2. As you might suspect, the firm's average investment in 100-watt light bulbs increases as Southwest reduces the number of orders entered per year.

TABLE 9–3 Average Investment Analysis

SOUTHWEST LIGHT COMPANY

Order Size (units)	4,000	6,000	8,000	12,000	24,000
Average Units in Stock	2,000	3,000	4,000	6,000	12,000
Average Investment at $1.50 Per Unit	$3,000	$4,500	$6,000	$9,000	$18,000
Carrying Cost at 15% of Average Investment	$ 450	$ 675	$ 900	$1,350	$ 2,700

Table 9–3 also measures the annual carrying costs that the firm can anticipate from the alternative ordering frequencies. The analysis first translates the firm's investment into financial terms using $1.50 per unit as a constant purchase cost. Then, it assumes that carrying costs average 15% of the average investment.

Presumably, that 15% cost includes Southwest's financial or opportunity costs, as well as the warehouse, maintenance, insurance, and any other costs that are necessary to support an investment in inventory.

Note what happens to Southwest Light's annual inventory carrying costs as it reduces the number of times it orders 100-watt bulbs in a year. As the number of orders decrease, the firm's average investment in inventory rises rapidly. So, too, do the associated carrying costs. Indeed, if Southwest enters only one order for the year, those carrying costs rise to $2,700. Thus, as you reduce acquisition costs by ordering less frequently, you see a rise in the cost of carrying your inventory.

THE MOST PROFITABLE BALANCE

You achieve the maximum bottom-line benefits when your average investment in inventory reduces the total of your acquisition and carrying costs to a minimum. You can identify that investment level in one of two ways.

You can perform a tabular comparison of the costs that come from various acquisition alternatives. Table 9–4 illustrates that approach, again using the

Southwest Light Company data. The table totals the acquisition and carrying costs for each purchase quantity considered. The minimum total identifies the order size—and ultimately the average inventory investment—that is most profitable (least costly) for the firm.

TABLE 9–4 Total Inventory Cost Analysis

SOUTHWEST LIGHT COMPANY

Order Size (units)	4,000	6,000	8,000	12,000	24,000
Annual Procurement Costs	$3,600	$2,400	$1,800	$1,200	$ 600
Annual Carrying Costs	450	675	900	1,350	2,700
Total Costs	**$4,050**	**$3,075**	**$2,700**	**$2,550**	**$3,300**

You can see that Southwest incurs the least cost by ordering 12,000 units twice a year. We emphasize that fact in Cash Flow Concept 25:

25: Profitable quantity control requires purchasing major inventory items in the most economic quantities.

As an alternative to the tabular analysis, you can use the Economic Ordering Quantity (EOQ) formula.

The EOQ Calculation

A tabular analysis can become tedious and time-consuming. Fortunately, you can identify the most economic ordering quantity for an item with the aid of an electronic calculator and the formula:

$$EOQ = \sqrt{\frac{2CS}{I}}$$

Don't be intimidated by this approach. Simply figure the data as follows:
1. C = Acquisition costs associated with each order
2. S = Sales for the product projected for the year
3. I = Cost of carrying each unit for a year

To illustrate the calculation process, we use the data from Southwest Light, where

C = $600

S = 24,000 units

I = $ .225 (15% × $1.50 per unit cost)

The calculation becomes:

$$EOQ = \sqrt{\frac{2 \times \$600 \times 24,000}{.225}}$$

$$EOQ = 11,313 \text{ units}$$

Thus, Southwest Light's most profitable order quantity is 11,313 units, rather than the 12,000 units indicated in the tabular comparison. While the difference may have little effect on that firm's bottom line, don't miss the point of this illustration: If you can isolate your anticipated sales volume, acquisition costs, and carrying costs, you can use the EOQ formula to determine the most profitable purchase quantities for the major items that make up your investment in inventory.

Achieving the objective set forth in Cash Flow Concept 25 leads naturally to the most profitable investment in inventory for your business.

Quantity Discounts in EOQ Analysis

We have presumed that Southwest Light's purchase price for 100-watt bulbs held constant regardless of the number of units included in any order. Presumably, the firm paid $1.50 per unit for a 4,000-unit order or a 24,000-unit order.

That is an unrealistic assumption. Many businesses allow discounts off of the list unit price for larger quantity purchases. Justification for quantity discounts proceeds from the same logic that underlies the EOQ analysis. That is, it costs little more to ship a large order than a small order. Thus, a business reduces its total shipping costs by filling fewer, larger orders. The potential benefits from quantity discounts are significant, so remember Cash Flow Concept 26:

26: EOQ analysis should include consideration of any available quantity discounts.

Selling in larger quantities also provides other savings for a business. Typically, the firm will carry a lower average investment in stock and enjoy a higher inventory turnover rate. That translates directly into lower carrying costs.

Indeed, the cumulative benefits from these reduced costs easily become significant enough to justify quantity discounts to encourage larger orders. Should they become available, you must alter your EOQ analysis to weigh the effect those discounts might have on your most profitable ordering quantity.

Table 9–5 demonstrates one approach to that analysis. Again utilizing the experience of the Southwest Light Company, we now assume that larger quantity purchases earn the firm quantity discounts.

Thus, the supplier's pricing structure begins with a $1.50 unit price for quantities ordered in lots fewer than 8,000. At 8,000 units, the price drops to $1.40, at 12,000 to $1.30, and finally to a low of $1.20 for 24,000 units.

Notice how those discounts affect Southwest Light's EOQ analysis. Thus, despite the higher carrying costs, the firm's most profitable ordering quantity

TABLE 9–5 Effect of Quantity Discounts on EOQ Analysis

SOUTHWEST LIGHT COMPANY

Order Size	4,000	8,000	12,000	24,000
Cost (units)	$ 1.50	$ 1.40	$ 1.30	$ 1.20
Annual Cost (24,000 units)	36,000	33,600	31,200	28,800
Annual Procurement Cost	3,600	1,800	1,200	600
Annual Carrying Cost	$ 450	$ 900	$ 1,350	$ 2,700
Total Annual Costs	**$40,050**	**$36,300**	**$33,750**	**$32,100**

rises from 12,000 to 24,000 units. The quantity discounts offset the higher carrying costs and contribute to Southwest Light's earnings.

You should take advantage of every bit of profit potential that can come from your component management effort. But although economic ordering quantity analysis can be a valuable component management tool, you also should consider some inherent limitations as you weigh the benefits that analysis offers.

First, remind yourself of the natural limits set by the cash capability in your business. You can't enjoy the benefits of large quantity purchases if they lead to cash flow crises. Certainly, a limited cash capability restricts your purchase options, whatever profit potential you lose.

Also, EOQ analysis ignores inflation as an element in inventory management. Anticipatory buying to beat impending price increases has become a focal point of practical inventory management. As prices rise more rapidly, you may find profitable justification to buy as much as your cash capability will allow, regardless of the decision criteria that come from your EOQ analysis.

Of course, neither qualification negates the value of EOQ analysis. In any circumstance, that analysis orients your component management view in the direction of quantity control. That is the key to successful, profitable component management.

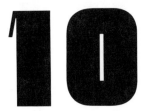

Component Management: Accounting Methods

Inventory is a unique component in the cash flow cycle. Indeed, it is the *only* component that changes in value according to which accounting principle you apply to keep track of it. The principles you use to value your inventory affect both the earnings and cash flow in your business. Illustrating the effects the major inventory accounting principles have on a business requires a departure from our previous view of the cash flow process.

EARNINGS AS CASH FLOW

Until now, we have concentrated on factors that affect the day-to-day cash flow cycle. We alter that approach here and note the relationship between earnings and the cash flow process. This relationship can be defined in Cash Flow Concept 27:

27: Earnings represent an addition to the cash flow in a business.

We will use as an example the unusual circumstance of Autrey Sports, Inc., a wholesale sporting goods operation. Autrey recently completed two consecutive fiscal year-ends with exactly the same investment in accounts receivable and inventory. Moreover, the firm maintained the same total accounts payable to suppliers while incurring no other debt.

However, in the interim bounded by the two fiscal year-end statements, Autrey Sports generated $100,000 in earnings. Table 10–1 demonstrates how those results affected the firm's financial structure.

Since all other assets and liabilities remained constant, the earnings translated directly into a $100,000 increase in Autrey's cash balance. As each dollar increased the firm's net worth, it also expanded its cash reserves.

Autrey's experience suggests a different definition of cash flow in a business: It describes the cash a business generates from operations in the course of a year, or the *annual* cash flow.

Here, we isolate the contribution that comes from earnings, a contribution that easily can become an important management consideration. After all, earnings make up another source of cash that can be used to increase assets or decrease liabilities. Or, from Autrey's example, you can use that contribution to increase your cash reserves.

Of course, cash flows into a business incrementally throughout the year. However, a better perspective is gained by considering it on an annual basis because it recognizes the impact of the contribution.

Note that throughout most of the book, we ignore the income-tax obligations that naturally arise in a profitable operation. In most instances, tax considerations have no effect on the major cash flow concepts that we discuss. However, we make an exception here to illustrate the effects two major inventory accounting alternatives have on the cash flow that proceeds from earnings in a business.

FIFO VS. LIFO INVENTORY ACCOUNTING

A business can value its fiscal year-end inventory in accordance with one of two major accounting principles.

FIFO accounting, or *first-in–first-out,* is based on the assumption that a

TABLE 10–1 Comparative Fiscal Year-End Balance Sheets

AUTREY SPORTS, INC.

	7/31/78	7/31/79
Cash	$ 50,000	$150,000
Accounts Receivable	200,000	200,000
Inventory	300,000	300,000
Total Assets	**$550,000**	**$650,000**
Accounts Payable	$150,000	$150,000
Stockholders' Equity	400,000	500,000
Liabilities and Equity	**$550,000**	**$650,000**

business sells its inventory in the order it is acquired. Presumably, the first item purchased from a supplier becomes the first product sold to a customer. All subsequent purchases are then sold sequentially. At the end of the fiscal year, FIFO accounting values the ending inventory, or unsold inventory still on hand, using the actual dollar cost of the items most recently acquired.

LIFO accounting, or *last-in–first-out,* assumes that a business sells its inventory in the reverse order in which it was acquired. In other words, the business sells its latest purchase from a supplier before any like item already in stock. Then, at year's end, the business values its unsold inventory using the costs from the earliest purchases.

We will use the case of the Odd-Ball Bearing Company to illustrate these principles. Then, we will measure the effect each alternative has on Odd-Ball's earnings and cash flow.

Odd-Ball Bearing Company, a wholesale distributor of industrial bearings, recently completed its first year in business. Table 10–2 summarizes the firm's inventory activity during that year. The summary measures the movement of inventory in terms of the number of units, or boxes of bearings, purchased and sold, as well as in terms of the actual dollar costs associated with those units.

Thus, Odd-Ball began operations with 1,500 units in stock, each having an average unit price of $2.00. Consequently, the firm's opening-day inventory carried a value of $3,000.

During the first six months in business, Odd-Ball purchased 7,500 additional units for inventory. However, persistent inflation in the bearing business increased the average cost per unit during that period to $3.00. The 3,750 units purchased in the third quarter cost $3.50 each, while the average price rose to $4.50 per unit for the last 3,750 units purchased during the year.

TABLE 10–2 Annual Inventory Activity

ODD-BALL BEARING COMPANY

	Units	Cost per Unit	Actual Cost
Beginning Inventory	1,500	$2.00	$ 3,000
Purchases:			
1st Quarter	3,500	$3.00	$10,500
2nd Quarter	4,000	3.00	12,000
3rd Quarter	3,750	3.50	13,125
4th Quarter	3,750	4.50	16,875
Total Inventory Available for Sale	16,500	—	$55,500
Ending Inventory	5,250	—	*

* Varies according to which accounting principle is used.

Measured in terms of actual dollar cost, Odd-Ball's purchases for inventory in its first year of operation totaled $55,500. This is the total cost of the actual inventory on hand at the end of the year, coupled with what was sold during the year.

Using the information in Table 10–2, Odd-Ball's accountant calculated the fiscal year-end inventory value in accordance with each of the two major accounting alternatives.

Using FIFO accounting for the 5,250 units on hand at the end of Odd-Ball's fiscal year, the accountant calculated the following inventory value:

3,750 units × $4.50	=	$16,875
1,500 units × $3.50	=	$ 5,250
Ending Inventory Value	=	$22,125
(5,250 units)		

Presumably, all 3,750 units purchased during Odd-Ball's fourth quarter remain unsold at year's end. Also, 1,500 units acquired during the third quarter remain in stock. Using the prices for the actual purchases within each quarter results in a $22,125 FIFO value for Odd-Ball's fiscal year-end inventory.

The accountant then valued the firm's inventory using the alternative principle, LIFO accounting. This method leads to the following valuation for the 5,250 units Odd-Ball had on hand at the end of its fiscal year:

1,500 units × $2.00	=	$3,000
3,750 units × $3.00	=	$11,250
Ending Inventory Value	=	$14,250
(5,250 units)		

Thus, LIFO accounting assumes that the firm's year-end inventory includes the original 1,500 units on hand when the year began, plus the first 3,750 units acquired during the first six months of operation. The logic of LIFO asserts that all sales came from the stock purchased after the first 5,250 units, all of which remain unsold at the end of the year. That logic leads to a $14,250 final value for Odd-Ball's inventory, $7,875 less than that measured by FIFO accounting.

Now, let's see how the alternative inventory values affect Odd-Ball's cash flow.

INVENTORY VALUATION AND CASH FLOW FROM EARNINGS

The FIFO and LIFO accounting principles exert different influences on a firm's earnings calculation. Certainly, actual sales remain the same, and actual inventory purchase costs do not change. However, different ending-inventory

values lead to different earnings results. That affects a firm's income-tax obligation, which does influence annual cash flow. To keep both principles in perspective, remember Cash Flow Concept 28:

28: LIFO inventory accounting usually leads to a better annual cash flow than FIFO accounting.

A two-step process illustrates the difference that results from the two accounting principles.

First, we examine the effect the different year-end inventory values have on
the cost-of-goods-sold total used to calculate earnings. Then, we look at the effect
that calculation has on a firm's income-tax obligation.

Again, Odd-Ball's experience helps to simplify the illustration. Table 10–3
summarizes the first step in that process with the comparative cost-of-goods-sold
calculations that come from FIFO and LIFO inventory valuations.

Both alternatives begin with Odd-Ball's opening-day $3,000 inventory. (The
basic procedure would be the same whether or not the firm was just beginning
operations.) To that total, both calculations add the actual purchase price of the
inventory acquired during the year to obtain the total cost of the inventory available for sale. To determine the cost of goods sold, each calculation subtracts the
alternative ending-inventory values from the total cost of the inventory available
for sale.

We already know that LIFO accounting produces a lower ending-inventory
value than does FIFO accounting. Here, that difference leads to a $7,875 higher
cost of goods sold total.

Up to this point, neither accounting alternative has had any effect on Odd-
Ball's daily or annual cash flow. Sales revenue remains constant in either circumstance. And the actual purchase costs for the firm's inventory remain the same.
Indeed, the only difference comes from the different methods of valuing the inventory Odd-Ball had on hand at the end of the fiscal year.

Table 10–4 illustrates where that difference becomes relevant. It compares

**TABLE 10–3 Comparative Effects of FIFO and
LIFO Accounting on the Cost-of-Goods-Sold
Calculation**

ODD-BALL BEARING COMPANY

	FIFO	LIFO
Beginning Inventory	$ 3,000	$ 3,000
Purchases (actual cost)	52,500	52,500
Total Inventory Available for Sale	55,500	55,500
Less: Ending Inventory	(22,125)	(14,250)
Cost of Goods Sold	**$33,375**	**$41,250**

TABLE 10–4 Effect of FIFO and LIFO Accounting on Earnings

ODD-BALL BEARING COMPANY

	FIFO	LIFO
Sales	$60,000	$60,000
Cost of Goods Sold	(33,375)	(41,250)
Operating Expenses	(10,000)	(10,000)
Pre-tax Earnings	$16,625	$ 8,750
Taxes at 40%	(6,650)	(3,500)
After-Tax Earnings	**$ 9,975**	**$ 5,250**

Odd-Ball's earnings calculations using the cost-of-goods-sold totals derived from the alternative accounting principles.

Thus, FIFO accounting, with the lower cost of goods sold, leads to pre-tax earnings $7,875 above those calculated using the LIFO accounting data. Again, up to this point, neither alternative has any effect on Odd-Ball's cash flow. However, the next step in the calculation applies a 40% tax rate to the firm's pre-tax earnings. Now the difference tells.

Thus, FIFO accounting leaves Odd-Ball with a $6,650 tax obligation, compared to the $3,500 liability that comes from LIFO accounting. Viewed from another perspective, FIFO accounting increases the firm's cash income-tax obligation (local, state, and federal) $3,150 above that calculated with the LIFO method.

This difference becomes more explicit by comparing the annual cash flows that come from the two accounting alternatives.

COMPARATIVE CASH FLOWS

To emphasize the different results that come from FIFO and LIFO accounting, we will review the actual annual cash flow that Odd-Ball Bearing will experience in either circumstance. This review relies on the following simplified assumptions:

1. Odd-Ball offers no credit terms; all sales are made in exchange for cash at the time of purchase.
2. Also, the firm pays cash for all purchases and operating expenses; Odd-Ball defers no obligation in the form of accounts payable of accrued liabilities.
3. The company has cash reserves sufficient to handle all business on a cash basis.

Table 10–5 compares the annual cash required to fund Odd-Ball's operation, using both accounting alternatives. We ignore cash flow into the business

**TABLE 10–5 Effect of FIFO and LIFO
Accounting on Cash Flow**

ODD-BALL BEARING COMPANY

	FIFO	LIFO
Beginning Inventory	$ 3,000	$ 3,000
Purchases	52,500	52,500
Operating Expenses	10,000	10,000
Taxes	6,650	3,500
Total Cash Requirements	**$72,150**	**$69,000**

from sales in this illustration, presuming that it is an element of the cash flow "sufficient" for operations. Confirming our earlier analysis, LIFO accounting reduces the cash expenditures required for Odd-Ball's first year in business by $3,150.

Of course, you may not find the difference in cash flow in Odd-Ball's circumstance particularly exciting. However, remember that Odd-Ball is a very small business. Increase its volume from $60,000 to $600,000 for the year, and the cash benefit from LIFO accounting rises proportionately to $37,200.

INVENTORY VALUATION AND FINANCIAL STRUCTURE

We will again use Odd-Ball to illustrate the different effects LIFO and FIFO accounting have on the financial structure in a business: that is, the balance sheet. Now, to amplify the effects LIFO and FIFO have on the balance sheet, we add Odd-Ball's opening-day balance sheet, as illustrated in Table 10–6, Column 1.

On opening day, the company had only $3,000 in inventory and $25,000 in

**TABLE 10–6 Effect of FIFO and LIFO Accounting on
Balance Sheets**

ODD-BALL BEARING COMPANY

	Beginning Balance Sheet	End of Year FIFO	End of Year LIFO
Cash	$25,000	$15,850	$19,000
Inventory	3,000	22,125	14,250
Total Assets	**$28,000**	**$37,975**	**$33,250**
Stockholders' Equity	**$28,000**	**$37,975**	**$33,250**

cash. This is a simple but healthy financial structure for almost any new business. Now, examine the comparative financial structures that exist at the end of Odd-Ball's first year using the two accounting principles.

As you would suspect, LIFO accounting leaves the firm with $3,150 more cash on hand than FIFO accounting. That benefit accrues despite the lower earnings that apparently result from the LIFO calculation. Of course, the year-end balance sheet also reflects the lower inventory valuation that comes from LIFO accounting. That difference translates ultimately into a lower total for the stockholders' equity account than with FIFO accounting.

Thus, the positive effect LIFO accounting exerts on Odd-Ball's cash flow is, psychologically, at least, partially offset by an understatement in the firm's inventory value and a lower net worth. That lower net worth can become an argument against LIFO accounting. At the same time, recognize that the difference reflects the accounting principles, not the actual value. Concentrate on the additional cash that a business can gain with the aid of LIFO accounting.

THE LOGIC AND LIMITS OF LIFO ACCOUNTING

Because a business sells most of its inventory sequentially as purchased, it is impossible to justify LIFO accounting in physical terms. The sequence may not be precise, but the approximate order generally holds true. Nevertheless, LIFO accounting, which assumes a business sells its inventory in reverse of the order acquired, is more logical than you might suspect. And, indeed, it is easy to justify it in our modern economic environment.

That logic argues that a business should relate its current sales to its current costs. Thus, in an inflationary environment, where prices rise constantly, using the most recent costs for the cost-of-goods-sold calculation makes more sense than the use of older, lower costs that are no longer realistic.

While LIFO accounting lowers a firm's apparent earnings, it also provides a valuable cash contribution to help offset the higher cost of replacement inventory. In fact, LIFO accounting becomes a necessary weapon in the battle against inflation.

Along with this logic, you also should recognize the limits on LIFO accounting.

First, the principle exerts a positive influence on cash flow *only* in an inflationary environment. In the unlikely event that your industry experiences a year of declining prices, LIFO accounting will lead to higher earnings and a smaller annual cash flow than FIFO accounting.

Of course, the modern economic environment leaves little room for declining prices. Trends undoubtedly will proceed steadily upward. However, should we miraculously move into a deflationary era, recognize that LIFO accounting would have a detrimental effect on your cash flow.

Also, LIFO accounting understates the true financial strength in a business because it lowers the inventory valuation, earnings, and net worth. To the extent that the lower values lead to a critical view of creditworthiness, LIFO accounting becomes detrimental to a business.

Certainly, most creditors understand LIFO accounting, at least conceptually. However, they often find it difficult to translate LIFO accounting into a higher credit line for their businesses. Of course, these limitations don't negate the cash benefits you derive from LIFO accounting. After all, that should always be your primary objective.

Because all aspects of a business are interrelated, positive cash flow management should seek an individually selected and financially correct balance among the assets and liabilities that make up the financial structure in a business. Part Three reviews the concepts that orient structural management—that is, the management of assets, liabilities, and equity.

Chapter 11 demonstrates the direct relationship between the cash flow and the financial structure in a business. In Chapter 12, we expand upon the requirements set by the cash flow cycle to better orient your structural management effort. Chapter 13 concentrates on the particular cash flow problems associated with rapid growth in a business. Cash flow sets an upper limit on the rate of expansion any firm can achieve, so recognizing that limit is an important element in structural management.

Chapter 14 considers the relationship between a firm's investment in fixed assets and the annual cash flow that comes from operations. We generally ignore these assets in our discussion of specific concepts, since they are not part of the day-to-day cash flow cycle. However, as fixed assets become a significant part of the financial structure in a business, they inevitably

PART THREE

Structural Management

exert a larger influence on the annual cash flow.

Finally, we add an operational perspective to structural management by looking at the fundamentals of break-even analysis. Most businessmen recognize the basic concept: That some minimum sales volume must be generated to avoid suffering a loss. But few businessmen utilize cash-flow break-even analysis, a complementary view of the break-even volume in a business. Chapter 15 demonstrates the importance of using both forms of break-even analysis as a management tool.

Financial Structure and the Cash Flow Process

Even the most proficient component management effort does not preclude cash flow problems. Indeed, a satisfactory cash flow requires financially sound interrelationships among all of the elements that appear on your balance sheet. At the same time, the cash flow cycle ultimately becomes the controlling factor in that interrelationship.

In this chapter, we examine the minimum cash investment required for a business, exclusive of any potential assistance from creditors. Certainly, few enterprises prosper without financial assistance, but the restriction illustrates a fundamental tenet of structural management.

We build on that conceptual foundation to illustrate the position creditors hold in your financial structure. Creditors can provide a valuable addition to your cash capability. In fact, that contribution may provide the boost you need to achieve a profitable sales volume.

REQUIREMENTS OF THE CASH FLOW CYCLE

The natural cash flow cycle converts cash into inventory into accounts receivable and back into cash. An efficient management of your receivables and inventory improves cash flow and contributes to higher earnings. However, whether your sales volume is large or small, your financial structure must provide necessary cash capability. We emphasize this with Cash Flow Concept 29:

29: A balanced financial structure provides the cash capability necessary to support the natural cash flow cycle.

We will use the Bayline Bolt Corporation as an illustration of this concept. Bayline, a stud-bolt wholesaler, was founded recently by Glen Mayes, a salesman with years of experience in the industry.

Before beginning operations, Mayes projected his initial cash requirements, based on the following assumptions:

1. Bayline would generate $1,000 per day, or $30,000 per month, in sales from inception.

2. The 45-day collection period standard in the industry will translate that volume into a $45,000 average investment in accounts receivable.

3. Achieving that sales objective will require a $48,000 average investment in inventory; any investment below that level will lead to excessive stock-out problems.

4. Bayline's cost of goods will be 80% of the retail price, resulting in a gross profit margin of 20%, exclusive of operating expenses.

5. Bayline's monthly operating costs, exclusive of inventory purchases, will average $6,000.

6. Presumably, the initial sales volume will provide break-even operating results; the firm will neither make nor lose any money.

Mayes's projections also recognized a common constraint that is confronted by any new business venture: He could not count on trade credit consideration; all suppliers would require cash payment for all purchases upon delivery.

Beginning with these assumptions, Mayes found that the cash flow cycle set by the anticipated operating characteristics determined the cash investment required to initiate operations. That investment had to be sufficient to support the firm's anticipated investment in accounts receivable and inventory, plus provide the $7,000 Mayes believed was the minimum necessary for operating cash. Indeed, the investment had to fund the components in the cash flow cycle.

Table 11–1 compares three of Bayline's balance sheets.

Prior to initiating operations, Mayes invested $100,000 in cash in the business. The firm has at this point no other assets or liabilities. Since Bayline lacks access to any external credit consideration, the $100,000 also represents the firm's total cash capability.

By opening day, Bayline had purchased (for cash) the $48,000 in inventory necessary to achieve the $1,000 daily sales volume. After opening day, the firm purchased inventory on a daily basis (again for cash) to replace what was sold. Remember that Bayline has to maintain that minimum investment to achieve the projected sales volume.

Forty-five days after beginning operations, while maintaining the $48,000 investment in inventory, Bayline has a $45,000 investment in accounts receivable. Of course, the remainder of Mayes's original investment rests in his operating account: That is, the minimum he deems necessary for normal contingencies.

Column 3 reflects the financial structure that evolves naturally from Bay-

TABLE 11–1 Relationship Between Financial Structure and Cash Flow Cycle

BAYLINE BOLT CORPORATION

Comparative Balance Sheets

	Prior to Opening Business	Opening Day	Forty-Five Days after Opening
Cash	$100,000	$ 52,000	$ 7,000
Accounts Receivable	—	—	45,000
Inventory	—	48,000	48,000
Total Assets	**$100,000**	**$100,000**	**$100,000**
Liabilities	—	—	—
Stockholders' Equity	**$100,000**	**$100,000**	**$100,000**

line's cash expenditures during the first forty-five days in business. We can summarize those expenditures as follows:

Beginning Cash	$100,000
Initial Inventory Purchase	(48,000)
Replacement Inventory Purchases (80% of selling price)	(36,000)
Operating Expenses (45 days at $6,000 per month)	(9,000)
Cash Reserve	$ 7,000

Note two important implications suggested by Bayline's cash flow and financial structure.

First, the gross profit on sales (accrued in the form of 20% of the firm's investment in receivables) exactly offsets the $9,000 in operating expenses. As anticipated, the $1,000 daily sales volume does result in a break-even operation.

Second, with the $1,000 daily sales volume and the other operating characteristics, Bayline's investment in accounts receivable and inventory cannot be less than $93,000.

Thus, a lower inventory level would preclude the daily sales volume necessary to prevent a loss. So, too, would any attempt to reduce the firm's average collection period below the industry average. Enforcing a shorter period would steer customers toward Bayline's more lenient competitors.

Indeed, the cash flow cycle set by the firm's operating characteristics dictates the initial investment, and the resulting figures in the financial structure, necessary for a break-even sales volume. Any investment less than $100,000 would lead to unavoidable losses.

Figure 11–1 provides a conceptual view that should help clarify the relationship. Note two additional facts about Bayline's circumstance forty-five days after opening.

First, so long as Bayline continues to generate $1,000 a day in sales, the company's financial structure will remain unchanged. Each day's new sales will be exactly offset by an equal collection of accounts receivable from previous sales. Similarly, operating expenses will continue to equal Bayline's gross profit margin from those sales.

Second, without additional cash capability, Bayline cannot increase sales to a profitable level. After all, any increase in sales would require a pro rata increase in accounts receivable and inventory that would quickly exhaust the firm's minimal cash reserves. Indeed, an increase in sales would lead to a cash flow problem.

For example, assume Mayes decided to increase Bayline's daily sales volume to $1,250 a day, or $37,500 a month without increasing the cash investment.

Table 11–2 shows the effects of the higher sales volume on Bayline's financial structure. Based on the original operating assumptions, that volume would

FIGURE 11–1 Conceptual View of the Relationship Between Financial Structure and the Cash Flow Cycle

Bayline Bolt Corporation

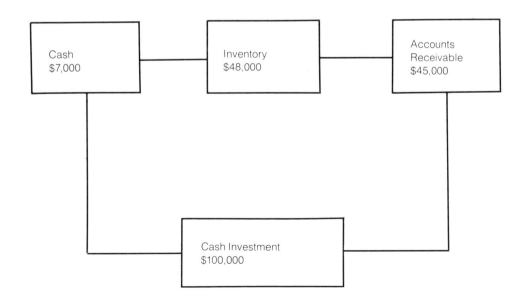

**TABLE 11–2 Effect of Higher
Volume on Financial Structure**

BAYLINE BOLT CORPORATION

Cash	($16,250)
Accounts Receivable	56,250
Inventory	60,000
Total Assets	**$100,000**
Stockholders' Equity	$100,000

require a $60,000 investment in inventory—that is, an amount sufficient for sixty-days' sales—and a $56,250 investment in accounts receivable.

Naturally, Bayline would never reach the $16,250 deficit cash position. The firm's suppliers, still requiring cash payment on delivery, would cease shipments as soon as the firm exhausted its cash capability. Indeed, the higher volume would produce an unacceptable, unbalanced financial structure.

Thus Cash Flow Concept 29 presumes that a business can control the size of its investment in accounts receivable and inventory. Obviously, an overinvestment in either component that differs from the original assumptions increases the cash capability required for a firm's financial structure.

Also, it is apparent from Bayline's experience that a balanced financial structure does not guarantee profitable operations. Indeed, a smooth cash flow may produce only break-even results, while a deficit cash flow naturally leads to problems.

THE CREDITOR'S CONTRIBUTION TO CASH CAPABILITY

Glen Mayes quickly recognized that he could not increase his sales volume above the break-even level without expanding his cash capability. Lacking the resources to increase his cash investment in Bayline, Mayes pursued a logical alternative: He negotiated more reasonable payment terms from his suppliers. We can formulate that alternative as Cash Flow Concept 30:

30: Credit consideration increases the cash capability in a business.

Bayline's suppliers agreed to allow thirty-day payment terms for all purchases. This was a reasonable response to a customer who paid cash for $24,000 in purchases each month for several months in a row.

Taking advantage of the cash capability supplied by the more liberal payment terms, Mayes quickly pushed Bayline's sales up to $1,250 per day. This volume produced two significant changes in the firm's financial circumstances.

TABLE 11–3 Creditor's Contribution to the Financial Structure and Cash Flow Cycle

BAYLINE BOLT CORPORATION

Cash	$ 7,750
Accounts Receivable	56,250
Inventory	60,000
Total Assets	**$124,000**
Accounts Payable	$ 24,000
Stockholders' Equity	100,000
Liabilities and Equity	**$124,000**

First, the higher volume made Bayline a profitable operation. Since Mayes held Bayline's fixed costs constant, the firm began generating monthly earnings as follows:

Sales	$37,750
Cost of Sales (80%)	(30,000)
Fixed Costs	(6,000)
Monthly Earnings	$ 1,500

FIGURE 11–2 The Creditor's Contribution to the Financial Structure and Cash Flow Cycle

Bayline Bolt Corporation

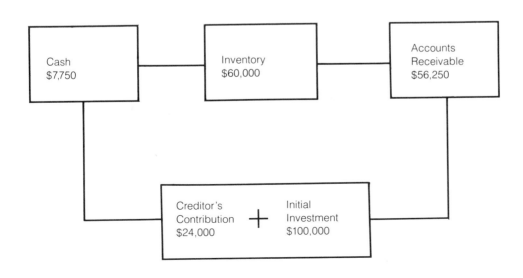

Second, Bayline generated the higher volume without straining its cash capability. Table 11–3 reflects the creditor's contribution. (To simplify the illustration, we ignore the profits that come from Bayline's higher volume.) The $30,000 in supplier credit enables Bayline to carry the higher investment in inventory and receivables that came with the sales increase.

The creditor's contribution enables a business to increase the total asset investment revolving in the cash flow cycle. Thus, it expands the potential for profits. Figure 11–2 provides a conceptual view of the contribution the $24,000 in credit consideration made to Bayline's cash flow and financial structure.

Also, a business gains the same benefit regardless of the source of the contribution. For example, had Mayes obtained a $24,000 bank loan while continuing to pay cash for all purchases, the financial results would have been the same. Of course, borrowing costs would have lowered earnings slightly.

Also, to reiterate Cash Flow Concept 29, the need for the creditor's contribution to Bayline's cash capability arose from the requirements set by the firm's cash flow cycle. Had industry standards allowed a cash flow cycle with a lower investment in inventory and receivables—relative to sales volume—the firm might have prospered without external financing.

Structural Management: A Matter of Balance

A fundamental accounting principle, interrelated with the concept of cash capability, must underlie your management effort: Your assets must equal your liabilities plus stockholders' equity. Although there is no perfect financial structure to suit every business, the fundamental relationship of financial structure and cash flow always holds true.

In this chapter, we will apply this principle so that you will be able to anticipate the effects of any financial decision on the cash flow process in your business. We also consider the effects that earnings and losses have on a business's financial structure and cash capability.

THE BALANCE SHEET EQUATION

Managing your financial structure and cash flow requires that you use a basic accounting equation:

$$\text{Total Assets} = \text{Total Liabilities} + \text{Stockholders' Equity}$$

This principle can be stated succinctly in Cash Flow Concept 31:

31: A balance sheet must balance.

Unfortunately, many businessmen overlook this fundamental requirement in their cash flow management. Often they commit themselves to expanding assets without estimating the effects this expansion will have on their firms' financial structure and the cash flow process.

Yet, as indicated in the equation, a $50,000 increase in liabilities or stockholders' equity (or some combination of the two) must accompany a $50,000 increase in *total* assets. Moreover, both increases in the balance sheet must observe the demands set by the cash flow cycle.

Of course, you can increase your inventory or accounts receivable without affecting liabilities or stockholders' equity. However, any such increase that uses your cash reserves still recognizes the balance in the equation.

CASH CAPABILITY AND FINANCIAL STRUCTURE

Cash capability describes the total resources a firm has available to finance an increase in the assets revolving in the cash flow cycle: that is, accounts receivable and inventory. The total cash capability in a business is measured as the sum of its cash reserves plus any unused credit consideration.

However, employing cash capability as a management concept can be complicated. When you commit some portion of that capability, you must recognize how that decision affects your financial structure and cash flow cycle. Moreover, you must anticipate both the immediate and future effects of those decisions. Certainly, failure to estimate carefully the results of any major financial decision can lead to a cash flow crisis.

We illustrate this in Table 12–1, which shows the comparative balance sheets of a small wholesaler, Priority Products, Inc. (PPI). Column 1 represents PPI's financial structure, with a $100,000 monthly sales volume, and it reflects the characteristics of the business:

1. All customers observe PPI's thirty-day selling terms; the firm collects $100,-000 in cash each month from the previous month's sales.
2. PPI purchases $75,000 per month from its suppliers on thirty-day terms; a

TABLE 12–1 Structural Management and Cash Capability

PRIORITY PRODUCTS, INC.

Cash	$ 25,000	$ 25,000	—
Accounts Receivable	100,000	100,000	125,000
Inventory	100,000	125,000	125,000
Total Assets	**$225,000**	**$250,000**	**$250,000**
Liabilities	$ 75,000	$100,000	$100,000
Stockholders' Equity	**$150,000**	**$150,000**	**$150,000**
Liabilities and Equity	**$225,000**	**$250,000**	**$250,000**

strict management policy requires payment in strict accordance with those terms.

3. Fixed cash expenses average $25,000 per month.

These characteristics leave PPI with a break-even operation: Income equals expenses, and cash collected each month equals cash expended.

Now, consider the results of PPI's decision to increase sales above the break-even level. We assume that the firm already has $50,000 in additional cash capability to finance an increase in sales. In addition to the $25,000 in cash reserves, it also has $25,000 in unused credit consideration.

Recognizing that potential, PPI's management decides to increase the firm's investment in inventory from $100,000 to $125,000. Projections suggest that the higher investment will help increase sales to $125,000 per month and lead to profitable operations.

The increase in inventory must use $25,000 out of PPI's cash capability. Either an increase in liabilities or a decrease in cash reserves must supply the funds for the new inventory. Of course, some combination of cash reserves and liabilities that total $25,000 also would provide the cash capability necessary for the inventory. However, assume that management can exercise only one alternative or the other, and not some combination.

Column 2 recognizes management's logical option to use the creditor's consideration to finance the expansion in inventory. Thus, PPI's inventory, total assets, and liabilities all rise by $25,000. And, following Cash Flow Concept 31, the financial structure remains balanced.

However, the changes indicated in PPI's financial structure represent only the initial effects of the decision to increase inventory. Positive cash flow management also requires proper consideration of the future alterations in that structure should the sales projections prove accurate.

Column 3 visualizes that future when PPI achieves the higher sales volume of $125,000 per month, while it also maintains the increased investment in inventory.

Thus, the successful sales effort leads PPI directly into a cash flow problem. As sales increased, so did the firm's investment in accounts receivable. As that rise absorbed the rest of the firm's excess cash capability, cash reserves dropped to zero. PPI is out of cash.

The critical point illustrated by PPI's experience is that any decision to increase your investment in any asset in the cash flow cycle, other than cash, absorbs some of your cash capability. It effects a change in your financial structure represented by an increase in liabilities or a decrease in cash. In any instance, you must have the appropriate capability to absorb the increase or decrease.

Moreover, you must look beyond the present and anticipate the future consequences of your decisions. The cash flow cycle imposes demands that must be met by the cash capability held in your financial structure, or in the form of additional external credit consideration.

When any doubts exist about the potential effects of any decision on your financial structure, turn to Cash Flow Concept 31: A balance sheet must balance.

Then measure the effects your decision has on your financial structure and cash flow cycle. That effort may preclude a cash flow problem.

LOSSES: A DRAIN ON CASH CAPABILITY

In the case of Priority Products, we assumed that the equity account was constant in order to orient our primary concern—day-to-day cash flow management. Now, adopting a slightly different perspective, we examine the effects profits and losses have on the financial structure and cash capability in a business, considering the detrimental effects of a loss and the positive contribution from earnings. The effect of a loss can be summarized in Cash Flow Concept 32:

32: An operating loss drains an equivalent amount of cash capability from a business.

We will go back to Priority Product's 12/31/78 balance sheet. However, we will now presume that PPI holds its investment in accounts receivable and inventory constant from one year to the next.

Assume that PPI suffers a $25,000 loss for the year marked by the 12/31/78 and 12/31/79 balance sheets. Table 12–2 demonstrates the two extreme results of that loss on PPI's financial structure. In either instance, the loss translates into a reduction in PPI's equity account: From $150,000 to $125,000.

Of course, all elements of a firm's financial structure are affected simultaneously. The balance sheet always balances. Since we are holding PPI's investment in accounts receivable and inventory constant, we can anticipate the potential effects of the loss on the other elements in the firm's financial structure.

As one extreme, PPI's total liabilities might increase by $25,000. Table 12–2, Column 2, demonstrates that potential result. Of course, any increase in liabilities absorbs an equivalent amount of cash capability.

TABLE 12–2 Effect of a Loss on Financial Structure

PRIORITY PRODUCTS, INC.

	12/31/78	12/31/79	12/31/79
Cash	$ 25,000	$ 25,000	—
Accounts Receivable	100,000	100,000	$100,000
Inventory	100,000	100,000	100,000
Total Assets	**$225,000**	**$225,000**	**$200,000**
Liabilities	$ 75,000	$100,000	$ 75,000
Stockholders' Equity	$150,000	$125,000	$125,000
Liabilities and Equity	**$225,000**	**$225,000**	**$200,000**

At the other extreme, PPI might hold its liabilities constant at the expense of its cash reserves. Of course, that policy, reflected in Column 3, leaves the business in a desperate cash position. Indeed, those reserves dwindle down to nothing.

Of course, PPI's management logically would seek some reasonable balance between the two extremes, but that would not change the point of this illustration. Also, the loss could be offset by additional cash investments by stockholders, or perhaps by negotiating larger lines of credit. However, in the absence of those options, you should foresee the inevitable penalty a loss exacts on cash capability.

Now, we will examine the positive side of the picture.

PROFITS: A CONTRIBUTION TO CASH CAPABILITY

Logically, an operating profit has the opposite effect from a loss. In this case, keep in mind Cash Flow Concept 33:

33: Earnings provide an equivalent increase in the cash capability in a business.

Table 12–3 shows that that logic is sound. Again we use PPI's 12/31/78 financial statement and assume that accounts receivable and inventory remain constant, and that PPI generates $25,000 in earnings during the interim between the two year-ends.

Note the effects those profits have on the firm's financial structure.

Of course, in any event, PPI's equity account increases by an amount equal to the earnings. Profits translate directly into an increase in the net worth of a business. However, as that occurs, other changes must also occur in the firm's financial structure.

TABLE 12–3 Effect of a Profit on Financial Structure

PRIORITY PRODUCTS, INC.

	12/31/78	12/31/79	12/31/79
Cash	$ 25,000	$ 25,000	$ 50,000
Accounts Receivable	100,000	100,000	100,000
Inventory	100,000	100,000	100,000
Total Assets	**$225,000**	**$225,000**	**$250,000**
Liabilities	$ 75,000	$ 50,000	$ 75,000
Stockholders' Equity	$150,000	$175,000	$175,000
Liabilities and Equity	**$225,000**	**$225,000**	**$250,000**

Considering the extremes, the $25,000 increase in equity must be balanced by either a matching reduction in total liabilities or by an equivalent increase in cash. Table 12–3, Columns 2 and 3, illustrates these results.

The positive cash flow manager might select some balance between the two extremes. In any circumstance, however, the earnings contribute $25,000 to PPI's cash capability as they reduce liabilities or increase cash reserves.

Unfortunately, many businessmen fail to control their investments in accounts receivable and inventory properly, even though they operate profitably. As those investments increase, they absorb the cash capability from earnings.

Your management perspective now should include a clear understanding of the natural balance enforced by the accounting principle held in Cash Flow Concept 31. If you adhere to that principle, you will be able to identify the specific source of any cash capability committed for any business purpose. The identification of the source is a necessary precedent to the commitment of any cash capability. Without that source, you have a cash flow problem.

Although our illustration centered on the cumulative effects of a full year's operations, obviously profits and losses, except in extraordinary circumstances, occur incrementally throughout the year.

In PPI's experience, for example, we can assume that the firm's $25,000 in earnings increased the firm's equity and cash capability at an average rate of about $2,100 per month. From this, you should be able to anticipate the potential benefits held in earnings and the detrimental effects that will follow a loss. You can do that because most businesses accrue profits in the form of uncollected accounts receivable. The actual cash flows into the business only when the customers pay.

Similarly, an operating loss usually appears in the form of accrued expenses or accounts payable. A loss this month doesn't drain cash from the business until next month.

Of course, the only way you can anticipate either result is to devise an income statement and balance sheet for your business promptly at the end of each month. That information will let you offset the effects of a loss or take advantage of the cash capability that will flow in from a profit.

13

Structural Management: Growth Control

In Chapter 1, the experience of the Drake Paper Company demonstrated the crucial difference between accrual and cash flow accounting. Drake's rapid increase in sales produced higher earnings but left the firm with a cash flow problem. The earnings rested in the form of uncollected accounts receivable, while payments to suppliers and operating expenses exhausted Drake's cash reserves.

Based on the discussion in Chapters 11 and 12, you now can view Drake's problem as a structural one. Indeed, the characteristics of the firm's cash flow cycle made the problem both predictable and inevitable.

Moreover, Drake's experience is a common occurrence among growing businesses. Success often leads to cash flow problems. Even a business that is expanding at a relatively modest rate can outpace its cash capability.

This chapter concentrates on a common aspect of cash flow management associated with many successful businesses: the problems that stem from growth. Growth control is a special consideration in structural management. To some extent, of course, our discussion merely reiterates the basic cash flow concepts that underlie structural management. At the same time, however, that discussion provides the opportunity to emphasize the critical concept that limits the growth rate in any business: available financing.

We will also illustrate some of the growth potential held in positive cash flow management.

103

THE GROWTH SYNDROME

Most businessmen seek growth as a natural business objective. They press constantly to increase sales this month over last month, and this year over last year. This pressure comes from two primary sources.

First, the desire for growth is an instinctive drive. Failure to satisfy that drive, however measured, ultimately leads to frustration. In the business environment, that drive translates into a constant push for higher sales.

Moreover, the expansion rate in a business becomes a measure of relative achievement. Presumably, a 20% growth rate represents a larger achievement than a 10% growth rate. Thus, growth rate stands as a gauge for comparison among businessmen.

Second, the desire for growth is a natural financial requirement. The business that doesn't grow stagnates financially, even though it may operate profitably. Certainly, when inflation proceeds at a 10% annual rate, a business earning 5% on a constant sales volume inevitably falls behind. The higher earnings that usually accompany increasing sales become a financial requirement.

We illustrate that point in Chapter 17 in our discussion of the effects of inflation on cash flow. Here, we suggest that those effects act as natural spurs that encourage business expansion. Of course, the financial structure in a business imposes a limit on the rate at which it can expand without creating a cash flow problem.

THE STRUCTURAL LIMITS ON GROWTH

Chapters 11 and 12 emphasized that, in any circumstance, a firm's cash flow cycle dictates the financial structure and cash capability necessary to avoid a cash flow problem. We examine the same concept here from a different perspective, one that helps to define the limits on the growth rate in a business. This can be encapsulated in Cash Flow Concept 34:

34: Financing requirements place a structural limit on the growth rate in a business.

As an example, we will use the Energy Window Company, a manufacturer of thermal glass windows. Since the firm's product improves insulation, demand is now sufficient to allow Energy Window to double its present $200,000 monthly volume.

However, before yielding to that demand by increasing production, Herb Elliot, Energy Window's controller, measured the effect rapid growth would have on the firm's financial structure. He found that the realistic limit on the prospective growth rate fell well below 100%.

Elliot's analysis began with a review of Energy Window's relevant characteristics:

1. A sixty-day average collection period translates the present volume into a
$400,000 investment in accounts receivable; that collection period is con-
sistent with the industry average.
2. Material costs average 75% of sales, or $150,000 per month; experience
indicates that the firm must maintain an inventory sufficient for two month's
sales on hand in order to achieve any projected volume.
3. Suppliers typically allow thirty days for payment. Company policy requires
strict observance of those terms: Accounts payable cannot exceed one
month's purchases or 50% of the inventory in stock.
4. The firm maintains a minimum $50,000 cash balance (to satisfy bank re-
quirements).
5. Any increase in sales requires a proportionate increase in cash, accounts
receivable, and inventory.
These characteristics translate into the financial structure in Table 13–1.

**TABLE 13–1 Energy
Window Company**

BALANCE SHEET 8/31/79

Cash	$ 50,000
Accounts Receivable	400,000
Inventory	300,000
Total Assets	**$750,000**
Accounts Payable	$150,000
Bank Loan	350,000
Total Liabilities	$500,000
Stockholders' Equity	$250,000
Liabilities and Equity	**$750,000**

However, note a prominent element in that structure—that Energy Window presently has a $350,000 bank loan.

In fact, the loan provides the cash capability essential for the business to
generate its present $200,000 monthly volume, while paying suppliers for all pur-
chases within the prescribed thirty-day terms. Elimination of the loan would lead
to a severe drop in sales, or a serious violation of Energy Window's trade payment
policy. The presence of the bank loan also explains the need for the $50,000 min-
imum cash balance. Those funds meet the bank's compensating balance requirements for the loan.

Finally, the need for the bank loan also suggests the critical constraint that
imposes the natural limit on Energy Window's growth rate. That is, while observ-

ing the firm's operating requirements, the growth rate cannot outpace the financing available to support the increase in assets that naturally accompanies higher sales.

The problem is even more severe, since the need for financing typically expands more rapidly than the sales volume in a growing business. Thus, lenders set the brake on growth sooner than you might imagine.

To prove these assertions, let's review Elliot's analysis of Energy Window's circumstance. That analysis began with the constraints set above, and it proceeds in two logical steps.

First, Elliot identified the financing required to support the increase in Energy Window's assets associated with various growth rates. Second, he identified the upper limit on the available financing. Table 13–2 summarizes the first phase in that analysis. It projects the anticipated increase in assets and corresponding demands for financing that will come from growth rates ranging from 10% to 50%.

We again ignore the contribution earnings make toward balancing the firm's rising assets. While that contribution is real, it does not affect the principal point of this discussion: That is, the growth rate in a business is limited by the external financing available to support the accompanying increase in assets.

Now, let's concentrate on the critical points in Table 13–2.

TABLE 13–2 Growth-Financing Requirements

ENERGY WINDOW COMPANY

Growth Rate	10%	20%	30%	40%	50%
Total Asset Increase	$75,000	150,000	225,000	300,000	375,000
Less: Accounts Payable Increase	(15,000)	(30,000)	(45,000)	(60,000)	(75,000)
Additional Financing Required	**$60,000**	**120,000**	**180,000**	**240,000**	**300,000**
Increase in Necessary Financing in Proportion to Bank Loan	17%	34%	51%	68%	85%

Note that a modest 10% increase in sales leads to a $75,000 increase in assets. While an increase in supplier debt—that is, accounts payable—provides $15,000 in support, Energy Window needs an additional $60,000 in financing to carry the higher asset investment. (We assume here that accounts payable automatically expand at the same rate as sales.)

As we increase the projected growth rate, the need for additional financing rises rapidly. Indeed, a 50% expansion rate calls for a $300,000 increase in bank (or other) financing. Moreover, observe that the 50% increase in sales requires an

85% increase in new external financing. Proportionate debt requirements out-pace the expansion in assets.

Unfortunately, this analysis probably underestimates Energy Window's real growth-financing needs. In the actual business world, assets often expand more rapidly than sales. That is, a 20% growth rate may lead to a 30% increase in assets. Indeed, Elliot's projections are too optimistic.

Nevertheless, armed with those projections, Elliot then proceeded to the second step in his analysis: He identified the bank's lending limits applicable to Energy Window's circumstance.

By normal bank credit standards, the firm's financial structure does not jus-tify the additional $300,000 in credit consideration necessary to support a 50% growth rate. The financing required to fund a 30% or 40% expansion rate also is out of the question. Without that financial assistance, of course, Energy Window must hold its growth rate below those levels.

We can't specify the exact amount of financial aid available from Energy Window's bank. The final determination must follow more precise credit analysis, complemented by negotiations with upper management. Nevertheless, Elliot's analysis, coupled with the financing limits, prove the critical point emphasized in Cash Flow Concept 34. Exceeding those limits pushes a business into a cash flow problem.

Of course, Energy Window might pursue some alternative sources of fi-nancing to overcome the limits imposed by its bank. However, no alternative source of cash completely eliminates the practical restriction held in Cash Flow Concept 34. Only the limits vary, not the principle.

GROWTH CONTROL

Positive cash flow management recognizes the effect rapid growth has on the financial structure and cash needs in a business. It also recognizes the re-striction that limited external financing sets on the firm. Consequently, growth control, or holding a firm's expansion rate within the limits set by its financial structure and cash flow, should become a major management tenet.

Available financing isn't the only factor limiting growth in a business. Growth control as a management principle has a broader dimension. You can remember that dimension as Cash Flow Concept 35:

35: Growth control recognizes the natural limits set by a firm's plant, personnel, management, and financial circumstances.

At first glance, these considerations may appear to be beyond the concern of the cash flow manager. However, a growth rate that exceeds the boundary set by any element in a business usually leads to cash flow problems that have costly consequences. This means that the cash flow manager must recognize the complex considerations involved in practicing growth control throughout the business. First, he must accept the limitations on growth set by a firm's physical facilities. While that limitation may appear obvious, many businessmen overlook the expensive inefficiencies that become prevalent as sales volume approaches plant or warehouse capacity.

A manufacturer sees these problems in the form of a larger number of breakdowns or a loss in quality control. Even should these specific problems not become more common, unit production costs inevitably rise as a plant approaches capacity. A wholesaler might see analogous costs expressed more subtly. Thus, as his warehouse fills with the merchandise necessary to serve an expanding volume, inventory control problems increase. Delayed shipments increase and a backlog of unfilled orders begins to develop. Such problems translate into a drop in the quality of customer service, the major element in the success of most wholesalers. At best, the damage to customer relations will stymie further expansion.

Of course, expanding your plant or moving to a larger facility eliminates the physical restrictions on growth. But either option must be anticipated. Such foresight doesn't always accompany the pressure for an expanding sales volume.

Growth control also recognizes the limits on the collective operational abilities and physical capacities of a firm's employees. That merely suggests that, to handle any volume of business, your employees must have an adequate body of knowledge, and you must have an adequate number of bodies. Indeed, an insufficient number of employees, or poorly trained employees, raises a significant obstacle to growth.

That same consideration applies to the administrative quarter of your business. You need the proper accounting system, complemented by a staff sufficient to absorb the natural flow of paper from a larger sales volume. Failure to recognize these needs raises additional obstacles to expansion.

Finally, as the most difficult consideration for the entrepreneurial businessman, growth control also requires observance of the natural limits on his own managerial capacity.

Typically, a young business centers on the talent of the founder. His vision provides the foundation for the enterprise. His drive makes it go. Moreover, as the business grows from an idea into a reality, he makes all of the major (and most of the minor) decisions, whether operational, financial, or administrative. All problems come to him for solution.

However, as a business grows, the daily management problems grow more rapidly. The proliferation easily can tax the talent and stamina of the strongest businessman. Consequently, as a business expands, the founder must yield the reins of total control. He must delegate decisions to others, concentrating his efforts in those areas most complemented by his ability. Failure of the entrepreneur —or of any manager—to recognize the natural limits on his capacities can turn a success story into a disaster.

OFFSETTING THE FINANCIAL LIMITS ON GROWTH

No businessman wants to impose limits on the growth rate in his business. That holds true even though exceeding those limits leads to cash flow problems. Consequently, we will discuss some fundamental concepts that can help you overcome, at least partially, the limits on expansion enforced by external lenders. Managing your accounts receivable and inventory more efficiently generates cash that you can then devote to the demands of an increasing sales volume. Remember this as Cash Flow Concept 36:

36: Better component management facilitates growth in a business.

To help cement some important relationships, we will take another look at the Energy Window Company. Remember that Energy Window's sixty-day average collection period would remain constant as sales increased. Thus, the firm's investment in receivables would expand as rapidly as sales.

However, Herb Elliot, seeking to overcome the firm's financing limits, connected two important facts. First, he recognized that the market demand for Energy Window's product provided a major impetus in the firm's drive for expansion. In fact, the lack of adequate financing stands as the only obstacle to a 100% increase in sales. Second, that same demand, which Elliot surmised correctly, gave the firm the flexibility to impose shorter payment terms or a more stringent credit policy without hurting sales. Effecting either policy would lower the company's average collection period and improve its cash flow.

These facts encouraged Elliot to cast a new projection estimating the growth potential held in the cash that would flow from reducing Energy Window's average collection period from sixty to forty-five days. Again, the proposition required two steps.

As the first step, Elliot considered the potential benefits from enforcing the shorter collection period on the firm's present $200,000 monthly sales volume. He found that the new policy would lower Energy Window's investment in receivables from $400,000 to $300,000. That reduction provides the firm with $100,000 in cash for investment elsewhere and increases its cash capability by that amount. Certainly, that is a substantial benefit even if the company did not press for a higher volume.

But Energy Window does want to expand sales, so Elliot proceeded with the second step, projecting the financing requirements associated with a higher sales volume. However, Elliot altered three of his working assumptions. In this instance, he assumed that:

1. Energy Window would quickly develop and maintain a forty-five day average collection period
2. The first $100,000 increase in assets from the sales increase would absorb the cash initially generated by the lower collection period at 8/31/79

3. The initial asset base from the present sales volume becomes $650,000, after the reduction in accounts receivable

Table 13–3 reflects the results of Elliot's analysis. The $100,000 in cash that came from reducing Energy Window's receivables at 8/31/79, coupled with the spontaneous increase in accounts payable, provides the funds necessary for the company's first 20% increase in sales. The business can generate that increase without any other external financing.

TABLE 13–3 Effect of Lower Average Collection Period on Growth Financing Requirements

Growth Rate	10%	20%	30%	40%	50%
Total Asset Increase	$65,000	$130,000	$195,000	$260,000	$325,000
Less: Accounts Payable Increase	(15,000)	(30,000)	(45,000)	(60,000)	(75,000)
Less the amount presumably generated by reducing the collection period from 60 to 45 days	(100,000)	(100,000)	(100,000)	(100,000)	(100,000)
Financing Requirements	($50,000)	—	$50,000	$100,000	$150,000

At the same time, the lower initial asset base reduces the total asset growth that comes with any increase in sales (although the rate of growth remains the same). Consequently, a 50% increase in sales requires $150,000 in additional bank financing, only one-half of that called for in the previous projection. And, in the firm's new financial position, gained with the aid of a shorter collection period, Energy Window's bank is more likely to provide the smaller amount of funds now necessary to achieve the 50% rate of expansion.

Of course, the bulk of the contribution comes from better accounts-receivable management. The bank merely lends the funds necessary to complete that objective. Thus, better receivables management offsets a major portion of the limits set by the external source of financing.

14

Structural Management: Fixed Assets and Depreciation

To maintain our focus on the day-to-day cash flow cycle in a business excludes consideration of the impact an investment in fixed assets has on cash flow. This impact can be significant, and the significance increases as fixed assets become a larger element in a firm's financial structure. Thus, this chapter reviews the initial effect a new investment in fixed assets has on cash capability. Certainly, that effect may appear obvious: It matches the cost of the asset. However, it usually proceeds well beyond the purchase price of the asset. Failure to foresee that fact can make a cash flow problem one of the first products of a promising investment.

Next, we consider the specific source of the cash capability you might use to acquire fixed assets. Of course, you have the choice between using cash reserves or acquiring the assets with the aid of external financing. Either alternative may be appropriate. However, good business sense encourages financing the purchase of most fixed assets. That generally holds true even though you have the cash reserves necessary for that purchase.

Then, we look into the future to measure the effects an acquisition in fixed assets has on cash flow. That look no longer considers a fixed asset as a purchase. Instead, it involves the depreciation process, the natural deterioration in fixed assets as they are used in the normal course of business. Many businessmen have an erroneous view of how depreciation affects future cash flows. Our approach emphasizes the distinction between the cash capability used for the initial investment and the cash that flows from future depreciation.

We also include a review of the comparative effects of straight-line and accelerated depreciation on cash flow, and we will examine the cash benefits a business derives from any tax credit granted for making an investment in fixed assets.

Then, we recognize an important analogy between a firm's investment in fixed assets and the components in the cash flow cycle and show how either an overinvestment or underinvestment in fixed assets can be expensive. We identify some of those costs and then suggest a fundamental approach that helps to identify the proper fixed-asset investment level in a business.

Finally, we review the elements that enter into a specific fixed-asset investment decision, concentrating on the cash outlay required and the future cash flow promised from that investment.

THE INITIAL INVESTMENT

Measuring the relationship between fixed assets and the cash flow process requires a clear distinction that we can summarize as Cash Flow Concept 37:

37: Distinguish between the initial investment and the future depreciation associated with an investment in fixed assets.

A new investment in fixed assets permanently absorbs some of your cash capability, so you must commit cash reserves, perhaps coupled with external financing, sufficient to make up the total purchase price of the assets. Certainly, you easily can measure that direct requirement. However, the total cash capability required for a new fixed-asset investment usually exceeds the direct acquisition cost. Failure to anticipate these additional requirements can lead to a cash flow problem. Therefore, keep in mind Cash Flow Concept 38:

38: Anticipate the *total* cash capability necessary for an investment in fixed assets.

Consider a proposed $200,000 fixed-asset acquisition by the Growth Company. The assets will facilitate an increase in production and provide the potential for a $30,000 monthly increase in sales. As a direct requirement, of course, the Growth Company needs $200,000 in cash capability to complete the acquisition. However, that does not measure the total cash capability necessary to fund the new investment. Indeed, the Growth Company also should anticipate the cash capability required to support a larger investment in accounts receivable and inventory.

For example, assume that the Growth Company maintains:
1. An investment in inventory equal to two months' sales volume.
2. A forty-five-day average collection period.
If the company completes the fixed-asset acquisition and achieves the projected

increase in sales, the investment in the two major components in the cash flow cycle will rise as follows:

Inventory (2 times projected sales increase) = $ 60,000
Accounts Receivable (45 × $1,000 increase in daily sales) = $ 45,000
Total Increase in Component Investment $105,000

Thus, the total cash capability required to fund the Growth Company's proposed acquisition is $305,000, or the cost of the investment plus the natural increase in other assets. Should the firm's total cash capability fall below $305,000, the investment will lead to a cash flow problem.

Note that Cash Flow Concept 38 holds true even if a proposed investment does not relate to projected expansion. For example, upgrading your plant with modern equipment may require retraining your employees. You may suffer operating losses—a drain on your cash capability—during the training period. In another circumstance, merely replacing old equipment with new often requires a halt in production during installation. Again, you suffer temporary losses that increase the cost of the investment.

The cash capability required for an investment in fixed assets is seldom limited to the purchase price. Recognizing this fact can reduce the chances of an unhappy surprise—a cash flow problem.

CASH RESERVES VS. EXTERNAL FINANCING

External financing is often the preferable source of funds for an investment in fixed assets, even though a business has cash reserves adequate for the purchase.

We know that the total cash capability required for a particular investment often exceeds the direct acquisition costs. A practical businessman maintains his cash reserves to meet such needs. Indeed, a business can finance the purchase of a fixed asset more easily than the cost overruns that follow its installation.

The logical extension of such caution leads to the major justification for financing the purchase of most fixed assets: That is, maintaining your cash reserves reduces the risk inherent in operating a business. This fact recognizes that today's profitable business may become unprofitable tomorrow. Management error, severe recession, or natural catastrophe can set back the most successful operation.

The business with sufficient cash reserves can survive such setbacks without irreparable damage. Adequate cash enables a business to absorb a loss, and it also provides the wherewithal necessary for recovery. This potential benefit also recognizes an important fact of business life: The lender who provides fixed-asset financing when you are well may not come to your rescue when you are ailing. Thus, you have to ensure your own survival.

Using the external financing to purchase fixed assets provides some of that insurance, and it leaves your cash reserves as an important line of defense against financial trauma.

DEPRECIATION: THE BASIC CONCEPT

In several instances, we have referred to the acquisition of fixed assets as an investment. With qualifications, this is a realistic view. Fixed-asset acquisitions should promise the same return as any other investment.

However, an investment in fixed assets has an important distinguishing characteristic: With the usual exception of real estate, most productive fixed assets deteriorate. Indeed, most assets have a limited life, and ultimately they become worthless. This fact moves a fixed-asset acquisition from the realm of an investment into the category of a normal operating cost. Accountants and tax authorities define that cost as depreciation. A business recognizes the deterioration in any depreciable asset, then, as an expense pro-rated over its useful life.

Without losing ourselves in complex accounting considerations, we will review the effect depreciation has on the income statement in a business—in other words, its effect on the cash flow process. As an example, we will take the experience of the KBA Corporation, a small manufacturer of specialty steel products.

KBA began operations four years ago with an initial $100,000 cash investment in machinery and equipment. Original estimates indicated that those assets would have a five-year life. At the end of that term, the original investment would have no value at all.

Relying on those projections, KBA's accountant recognized the average annual deterioration in the equipment with a $20,000 depreciation expense. Thus, using the operating statement for the firm's fourth year in business as an example, that expense reduced the firm's $20,000 in operating profits as follows:

Earnings before depreciation	$20,000
Depreciation expense	(20,000)
Net earnings	—

After its fourth year in business, KBA found that it had break-even results. Thus, depreciation has the same effect on earnings as any other expense.

DEPRECIATION AS A NON-CASH EXPENSE

Depreciation prorates the cost of a fixed asset over its useful life. Thus, it stands apart from most other operating expenses in a business because it is a *non-cash expense*. We crystallize this fact in Cash Flow Concept 39:

39: Depreciation does not require a cash outlay.

Consequently, depreciation can be viewed as an *addition* to the annual cash flow in a business.

To prove that point, we will take the KBA Corporation and note the effect of the break-even operations on its cash account.

Table 14–1 compares the fiscal year-end balance sheets for KBA's third and fourth years in business. We will assume that the company's accounts receivable, inventory, and total liabilities remain constant from one year to the next.

TABLE 14–1 Effect of Depreciation on Annual Cash Flow

KBA CORPORATION

	Third Year	Fourth Year
Cash	$ 40,000	$ 60,000
Accounts Receivable	200,000	200,000
Inventory	200,000	200,000
Net Fixed Assets (of $60,000 accumulated depreciation in the third year and $80,000 in the fourth year)	40,000	20,000
Total Assets	**$480,000**	**$480,000**
Total Liabilities	$300,000	$300,000
Stockholders' Equity	$180,000	$180,000
Liabilities and Equity	**$480,000**	**$480,000**

Despite the break-even operating results in the fourth year, KBA's cash balance increases by $20,000. This cash represents the effect of depreciation on the company's income statement. Although recognized as an expense, no cash flowed out of the business in the fourth year to pay it.

However, note that depreciation does not represent the return of KBA's original investment in fixed assets. Instead, it merely recognizes the annual expenses incurred from the natural deterioration in those assets. The expenses were paid at the time of acquisition. Consequently, no cash flows out when the business recognizes them in the income statement.

Note also that financing the acquisition of fixed assets has no effect on the depreciation process, regardless of the source of funds used to purchase them. Of course, the cash flow from depreciation contributes to the periodic note payments that result from external financing. In fact, the lender measures that potential as an element in his decision to extend fixed-asset financing. At the same time, you relate those two elements—the cash flow from depreciation and your debt amortization requirements—in a cash flow budget, not in an operating statement.

Also, another implication for management suggested by the depreciation process is that you must foresee the eventual need to replace your depreciable assets. You may not reserve the cash flow from depreciation specifically for that purpose. But you must maintain access to the cash capability necessary to replace worn-out equipment.

Returning to the concept of earnings as annual cash flow, remember that earnings become a direct increase in cash reserves. We will apply that as Cash Flow Concept 40:

40: Earnings plus depreciation measure the total annual cash flow generated by the operations in a business.

This identifies the internal cash a business has to expand its reserves, invest in other assets, or reduce debt.

CASH BENEFITS FROM ACCELERATED DEPRECIATION

The KBA Corporation example demonstrated the benefits a business derives from *straight-line* depreciation: In a straightforward approach to the depreciation process, KBA recognized the presumed deterioration in its fixed assets in equal amounts each year.

However, many businesses use *accelerated depreciation* as an alternative to the straight-line process. This doesn't change the total cash benefits a business realizes from the depreciation process but the business gains those benefits more rapidly. Remember this as Cash Flow Concept 41:

41: Accelerated depreciation returns cash to the business sooner than the straight-line method.

We will look again at KBA's circumstance and compare the cash benefits that come from straight-line depreciation with those from two common approaches to accelerated depreciation. Table 14–2 shows that comparison over the full five-year useful life of the machinery and equipment.

TABLE 14–2 Comparative Cash Flows from Alternative Depreciation Methods ($100,000 Investment with a Five-Year Useful Life)

	Year				
	1	2	3	4	5
Straight Line	$20,000	$20,000	$20,000	$20,000	$20,000
Sum of the Years' Digits	33,333	26,666	20,000	13,333	6,666
Double-Declining Balance	40,000	24,000	14,400	10,800*	10,800*

* DDB allows switching to straight-line method for the latter years of an asset's useful life.

Of course, we already know that the straight-line process leads to $20,000 in depreciation in each of the five years. By comparison, the *sum-of-the-years'-digits* calculation increases the annual depreciation expense in the first two years. The calculation identifies the different rate of depreciation. The process begins by adding the digits that range from one to five, indicating the five-year anticipated life for the equipment. That sum—1 + 2 + 3 + 4 + 5—totals fifteen. Then, depreciation for the first year becomes 5/15 of $100,000, or $33,333. That is more than 65% above the depreciation charge allowed by the straight-line process. In the second year, the depreciation calculation becomes 4/15 of $100,-000, or $26,666. The process continues with the descending digits throughout the remaining life of the equipment.

The *double-declining-balance* method of depreciation increases the charge against income even more in the first year. This accelerated approach doubles the rate of depreciation that comes from applying the straight-line method. Since the straight-line method depreciates the equipment at a 20% annual rate, the DDB method applies 40% against each year's book value (that amount left after deducting previous depreciation charges).

Of course, you should consult your accountant before adopting any depreciation method. However, recognize that accelerated depreciation creates a larger charge against income in the early years of your fixed assets. That returns the cash flow from depreciation to you sooner than from the straight-line process.

Note that accelerated depreciation doesn't return more total dollars to your business: The ultimate cash benefit in any circumstance is the same. But accelerated depreciation enables you to regain those dollars more rapidly. You can reinvest that cash sooner than possible with straight-line depreciation. Properly reinvested, that cash can lead to higher earnings for your business.

THE INVESTMENT TAX CREDIT

A business that invests in fixed assets often obtains a cash benefit from a reduction in its federal income-tax obligation. That reduction, an investment tax credit, can total as much as 10% of the actual cost of each investment made during the year. We will illustrate the effect a tax credit has on the cash flow in a business. First, however, keep in mind Cash Flow Concept 42:

42: An investment tax credit provides a dollar-for-dollar reduction in a firm's federal income-tax obligation.

Table 14–3 compares the operating results of two firms with the same before-tax earnings. Thus, Company A and Company B generated $100,000 in earnings before taxes. Then, applying a 30% average tax rate, each company incurs a $30,000 income-tax obligation.

However, Company B has a $10,000 investment tax credit. We can assume that arose from a $100,000 investment in fixed assets. That tax credit becomes a direct offset against the company's income-tax obligation. Thus, the credit enables

TABLE 14-3 Effect of Investment Tax Credit on Federal Income-Tax Liability

	Company A	Company B
Earnings before Taxes	$100,000	$100,000
Tax Liability (30% average rate)	($30,000)	($30,000)
Investment Tax Credit	—	$ 10,000
Net Earnings	**$ 70,000**	**$ 80,000**

Company B to retain $10,000 in cash for use elsewhere. Or, from another perspective, you can view the benefit as a $10,000 reduction in the original cost of the new fixed-asset investment. Of course, from either perspective, the actual benefit is the same, and as you might expect, that benefit is designed to act as a spur to new business investment.

We should note one obvious limitation on the potential benefits promised by an investment tax credit. That is, those benefits don't apply to the business that fails to operate profitably because a loss operation has no income-tax obligation.

AN OVERINVESTMENT IN FIXED ASSETS

By now, we can anticipate the effect an overinvestment in fixed assets has on the cash capability in a business. Any excess investment absorbs cash that might be used profitably elsewhere. Indeed, from a conceptual viewpoint, an overinvestment in fixed assets is analogous to an overinvestment in accounts receivable and inventory. However, an overinvestment in fixed assets is more difficult to cure. After all, a tighter credit and collection policy can reduce a firm's investment in accounts receivable, and a temporary reduction in purchases will encourage a drop in inventory. The rapid disposal of excess fixed assets typically is a more difficult task.

In some circumstances, the excess assets may be part of a production process that has capacity well in excess of the demands set by the firm's sales volume. The business can't eliminate any of the assets without eliminating all of the assets. In that event, of course, the business must concentrate on expanding sales volume sufficiently to justify the higher productive capacity. In the interim, the business must absorb the cost of carrying the excess investment. In other circumstances, a businessman lacks the time or expertise necessary to market unnecessary fixed assets. He absorbs the overinvestment until he stumbles into the sale of the assets, often suffering a significant loss in the process.

An overinvestment in fixed assets also is more expensive than an overinvestment in accounts receivable or inventory. Of course, the financial or opportunity cost from carrying excess assets in any instance is the same. Using a 10% annual rate, a $100,000 excess investment in fixed assets leads to a $10,000 reduction in earnings.

This detrimental effect is increased by the insurance, storage, and maintenance costs associated with the excess assets. Analogous to inventory, it costs more to carry an investment in fixed assets than in accounts receivable. However, in a major distinction from accounts receivable and inventory, an overinvestment in fixed assets commits still further injury to the earnings in a business because of the higher depreciation expense that comes from that overinvestment. Thus, a $100,000 excess investment in fixed assets may lead to a $10,000 reduction in annual earnings. That reduction comes from the annual depreciation charge associated with that overinvestment, applying straight-line depreciation over a ten-year useful life. In any circumstance, higher depreciation charges lead to lower earnings.

From another perspective, the higher depreciation expense, which is a fixed cost, makes it more difficult for a business to reach a break-even level of operations. We demonstrate that fact in Chapter 15 as an additional consideration in determining the proper fixed-asset investment for a business.

AN UNDERINVESTMENT IN FIXED ASSETS

An underinvestment in fixed assets should impose no direct cash flow problem on a business. Fewer assets in one account leave cash capability available for use elsewhere. However, such an underinvestment often leads to direct and indirect costs. We emphasize this as Cash Flow Concept 43:

43: An underinvestment in fixed assets can hurt earnings.

The higher direct costs arise from operations that, because of underinvestment, remain less efficient than an operation possible with a larger investment in fixed assets. Higher labor costs and lower productivity associated with an inefficient manufacturing process inevitably shrink the profit margin in a business.

While the business may remain profitable, you can view the profits lost from the lower margin as an opportunity cost: The firm earns less than it should. Another opportunity cost may come from sales lost as a result of inefficient or insufficient productive capacity. Of course, these opportunity costs may be difficult to measure, but they are real nonetheless.

THE PROPER INVESTMENT IN FIXED ASSETS

Obviously, the proper investment in fixed assets relative to total assets will vary widely among businesses. A wholesaler may require no fixed assets except the shelves necessary to store his products and the trucks necessary to deliver them. Alternatively, a manufacturer may carry a larger investment in fixed assets than either accounts receivable or inventory.

Although the correct investment in any specific circumstance involves many complex variables, we can demonstrate one fundamental financial tool that can orient your analysis. That tool, the *sales-to-net-fixed-assets ratio,* enables you to relate your sales volume to your net investment in fixed assets, and allows you to measure your fixed-asset turnover rate. For example, a business with $1,000,-000 in annual sales, and a $100,000 net investment in fixed assets will relate the two totals as follows:

$$\text{Sales to Net Fixed Assets} = \frac{\text{Sales}}{\text{Net Fixed Assets}}$$

$$\text{Sales to Net Fixed Assets} = \frac{\$1,000,000}{\$\ \ 100,000}$$

$$\text{Sales to Net Fixed Assets} = 10$$

The firm's sales volume exceeds its investment in fixed assets ten times. Or, viewed from another perspective, the business turns its fixed assets ten times in the course of a year. Of course, the assets don't turn in the same way as your accounts receivable and inventory, but at the same time, your fixed-asset turnover rate becomes the primary criterion for measuring the efficient use of your fixed assets.

Perhaps the best use of that criterion again comes from a comparison with the fixed-asset turnover rates demonstrated by your competitors (using, for example, Dun and Bradstreet, or Robert Morris Associates *Statement Studies*). Thus, should your fixed-asset turnover rate fall below your competitors', you may have an overinvestment relative to your sales volume. Conversely, a turnover rate significantly above your competitors' may suggest an underinvestment.

In either circumstance, of course, the turnover rate is influenced significantly by the specific characteristics of a business. Moreover, since the calculation relies on depreciated equipment values, turnover rates may vary significantly, because the assets held in one business are several years older than the assets held in another.

Nevertheless, subject to the logical qualifications, the fixed-asset turnover calculation at least provides the starting point for identifying the appropriate investment level in a business. You must adapt that calculation to your own special circumstance.

THE FIXED-ASSET INVESTMENT DECISION

Although managing the fixed-asset investment in a business involves other complex considerations, here we can identify a sensible three-step approach for analyzing the financial promise from a proposed fixed-asset acquisition. That approach concentrates on several interrelationships:

1. The cash outlay required for the acquisition

2. The future incremental cash flow anticipated from the acquisition

3. The firm's financial or opportunity cost associated with the cash outlay

Professional analysts add esoteric elements to this approach, but a fundamental view will answer the practical requirements in most business circumstances. We emphasize that view in Cash Flow Concept 44:

44: The incremental cash flow from a fixed-asset acquisition must be sufficient to justify the investment.

We use the Proctor Printing Company to help illustrate that view. Proctor is contemplating the purchase of a new printing press. As an element in the decision process, Proctor used the three-step approach.

First, the company found the total cash outlay required for the proposed acquisition. The total cost for the purchase, delivery, and installation of the press amounted to $50,000. Proctor had no equipment suitable as a trade-in that would reduce that cash outlay.

However, the firm does anticipate a $5,000 investment tax credit from the acquisition. To simplify analysis, Proctor considers that credit a direct offset to the purchase price of the equipment. So, the net cash investment drops to $45,000.

Next, Proctor projected the anticipated incremental cash inflows from the proposed investment. Table 14–4 summarizes that projection.

TABLE 14–4 Projecting Increment Cash Flow from a Proposed Fixed-Asset Acquisition

PROCTOR PRINTING COMPANY

Incremental Earnings	$10,000
Less: Annual Depreciation	(6,250)
Incremental Earnings before Taxes	$ 3,750
Less: Taxes (at 50%)	(1,875)
Net Incremental Earnings	$ 1,875
Plus: Depreciation	6,250
Incremental Cash Flow	**$ 8,125**

Proctor anticipates a $10,000 increase in earnings before taxes and the depreciation expense associated with the new investment. Here, the gain comes from a $10,000 reduction in annual labor costs. In another circumstance, the increase in earnings might come from a higher sales volume.

Of course, the annual depreciation charge of $6,250 reduces that increase in earnings to $3,750, applying straight-line depreciation to the eight-year useful life of the new press. A 50% tax rate further reduces the incremental earnings to

$1,875. That measures the addition to the firm's annual cash flow from earnings directly attributable to the proposed acquisition.

Cash Flow Concept 40 reminds us that the annual cash flow in a business comes from adding depreciation to net earnings. As indicated in Table 14–4, that raises the annual incremental cash flow from the project to $8,125. The net $45,000 cash outlay for the new printing press will generate $8,125 in incremental cash inflow for eight years (the life of the new equipment), or a total of $65,000. This is $20,000 more than the net cost of the investment.

Next, Proctor considers the firm's financial or opportunity cost associated with the new investment by merely measuring the potential return available from investing the $50,000 at Proctor's present 10% cost of borrowing. Should Proctor have cash reserves sufficient for the investment, we can use that 10% rate to measure the firm's opportunity cost. A $50,000 investment would provide a $5,000 annual return for the firm, or a total of $40,000 over eight years. The 50% tax rate, of course, lowers that to a net $20,000.

Finally, Proctor compares the net cash flow from the proposed fixed-asset acquisition against that anticipated from investing the same cash outlay in an instrument providing a 10% annual return. In this instance, the proposed investment provides no benefit. The cost of the funds committed to the project—financial or opportunity—equals the projected return from the total incremental cash flow. Proctor would gain no real benefit from the new fixed asset.

In another circumstance, a business can justify a fixed-asset acquisition if the incremental cash flow from the project exceeds that theoretically available using opportunity cost as a criterion. Of course, the advantage should be significant enough to justify the risk and analytic error inherent in a look at any proposed fixed-asset investment.

Certainly, this example oversimplifies the analytic process. A project often promises incremental cash flows that change from year to year. Or a business might use accelerated rather than straight-line depreciation. In such instances, the time value of money complicates the process. Nevertheless, in most business circumstances, those complicating factors will have little effect on the outcome predicted by the basic analytic approach.

If the incremental cash flow doesn't provide a return that exceeds the firm's opportunity costs, a proposed acquisition will hurt your bottom line.

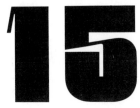

Structural Management: Two Break-Even Points

Most businessmen recognize the concept of break-even analysis. This kind of analysis identifies the sales volume where total revenue exactly matches expenses. At that point, the business neither makes nor loses any money. However, a business also has a *break-even cash flow* volume, a point where cash income exactly matches cash expenses. Proper cash flow management requires a clear distinction between the two break-even points. We demonstrate that distinction in this chapter.

We will review the fundamentals of standard break-even analysis and then illustrate cash flow break-even analysis. You will find that a business operating at a loss can have a break-even or a positive cash flow. Of course, that condition cannot continue indefinitely. But it can reduce the immediate impact of a financial reverse.

We will also interrelate break-even analysis and the proper investment in fixed assets in a business. Break-even analysis doesn't identify that investment level, but it raises some questions that should enter into the analysis.

BASIC BREAK-EVEN ANALYSIS

Traditional break-even analysis identifies the exact volume where a firm's total sales revenue equals its operating expenses. This can be restated in Cash Flow Concept 45:

45: A business breaks even when the contribution from sales exactly covers fixed costs.

We will identify the three elements that enter into the logical process of break-even analysis and then illustrate how those elements interrelate in the calculation itself. Break-even analysis begins with the proper division of a firm's operating expenses into two categories. Thus, every expense can be defined as either a fixed or a variable cost.

Fixed costs hold constant across a specific range of sales. For example, a business might increase sales from $1 million to $1.5 million without incurring any increase in rent, utility, or office salary expenses.

However, *variable costs* fluctuate proportionately with any change in sales. Thus, a 20% increase in sales naturally produces a 20% increase in variable costs. Product expenses, sales commissions, and delivery charges are the more obvious examples of the variable costs in a business. These costs are not incurred unless a business generates a sale, and then they are incurred proportionately to any sales volume.

Contribution margin is the critical third element that enters into break-even analysis. Specifically, it is the difference between the selling price and the variable cost-per-unit volume generated by a business. Thus, contribution margin represents the proportion of each sales dollar available to pay fixed costs and, ultimately, to provide any earnings the business might enjoy.

To establish a critical concept, we will concentrate on the relationship between contribution margin and operating results.

First, a business suffers a loss from operations so long as the total contribution margin that flows from sales remains insufficient to cover fixed costs. Remember, fixed costs hold constant regardless of the sales volume generated.

Second, a business breaks even at that volume where the total contribution from sales exactly equals its fixed costs. Identifying that point is the obvious objective of break-even analysis.

Third, as sales exceed the break-even point, the total contribution margin exceeds fixed costs. The excess margin over fixed costs represents earnings. Thus, a business operating above the break-even point generates a profit.

Figure 15–1 gives a conceptual view of the relationship between contribution margin and the break-even point.

The foundation for the illustration is (a). The quantity in the rectangle on the left represents the total selling price per unit for the product. That price is then separated into its two elements: contribution margin and variable costs. The square on the right represents the firm's fixed costs, segmented by the number of unit contribution margins necessary to cover those costs. In this case, there are six.

Now, observe the relationship as the business begins to generate sales.

First, in (b), five unit sales leave total fixed costs uncovered. The firm's loss at that unit volume is equivalent to the contribution margin from a single sale.

FIGURE 15–1 Break-Even Analysis: A Conceptual View

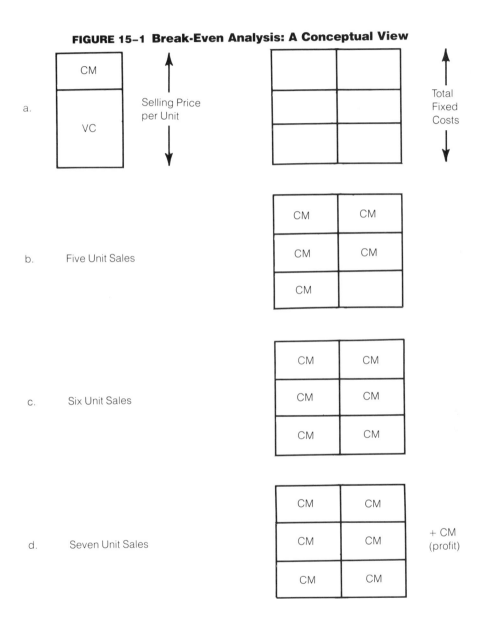

Then, increasing sales by one unit, the firm reaches the break-even point, illustrated in (c). Six unit sales provide the contribution margin that exactly covers fixed costs. At this point, total revenue equals total expenses: The business breaks even.

Finally, (d) visualizes the benefits that come from operating above the break-even point. Thus, the firm produces earnings equal to the contribution margin from each unit sold in excess of the break-even volume. After fixed costs are covered, the margin from each additional sale proceeds directly to the bottom line.

Let's translate this conceptual view into the calculation that actually identifies the break-even point in a business. We will use the simplified circumstances of the Strong Electric Motor Company (SEMCO) as an example. SEMCO carries only one product, a small motor that sells for $7. Since the firm incurs a $4 variable cost from each unit sold, we can calculate the contribution margin from each sale:

Contribution Margin = Selling Price − Variable Cost
Contribution Margin = $7 − $4
Contribution Margin = $3

Now, assuming SEMCO's fixed costs total $90,000 per year, we can use the contribution margin per unit to calculate the firm's break-even sales volume. From Figure 15–1, we know that the break-even volume occurs at that point where the total contribution margin from all units sold exactly equals fixed costs. Calculating the break-even point proceeds as follows:

$$\text{Break-Even Volume} = \frac{\text{Total Fixed Costs}}{\text{Contribution Margin per Unit}}$$

Entering the data from SEMCO's circumstance:

$$\text{Break-Even Volume} = \frac{\$90,000}{\$3} = 30,000 \text{ Units}$$

Thus, the sale of 30,000 units enables SEMCO to break even. The company's sales price per unit translates that into an annual volume of $210,000 (30,000 × $7).

Now, relate this example to two points asserted above. First, each sale in excess of 30,000 units per year contributes $3 to SEMCO's earnings. The margin in excess of fixed costs proceeds directly to the bottom line. Alternatively, should SEMCO sell fewer than 30,000 electric motors, the firm will suffer a loss. The total contribution margin will fall short of the amount necessary to cover fixed costs. The amount of the loss will be $3 for each unit SEMCO drops below the 30,000-unit sales level. For example, sales of only 28,000 units will leave SEMCO with a $6,000 loss.

Of course, few businesses restrict themselves to only one product. Most have a variety of items that carry different sales prices, different variable costs, and, hence, different contribution margins. That makes break-even analysis more complex, but it does not affect the essential concept.

AVERAGE CONTRIBUTION MARGIN

An alternative approach to break-even analysis recognizes the difference in contribution margins because of different sales prices and costs. It uses data extracted directly from your income statement, relying on the average contribution margin that comes from each sales dollar. The Able Company's experience illustrates this approach to break-even analysis.

As indicated in the summary of its income statement, the Able Company presently operates profitably:

Sales	$275,000
Variable Costs	(87,500)
Fixed Costs	(140,000)
Earnings	$ 47,500

However, John Able, the company's founder, anticipates a recession, and a consequent reduction in sales. Thus, he wants to identify the sales decrease the firm can absorb without falling below a break-even level of operations. Since Able's product costs and sales prices vary widely, there will be a wide variation in the contributing margin that comes from the sale of different products.

Conceptually, of course, the alternative seeks the same objective: It identifies the sales volume where the firm's cumulative contribution margin from all sales exactly equals total fixed costs. However, since the contribution margin varies among the firm's products, Able must use a three-step process to achieve that objective.

First, he must calculate the total contribution margin included in the income statement. The calculation proceeds as follows:

$$\text{Total Contribution Margin} = \text{Total Sales} - \text{Total Variable Costs}$$

$$\text{TCM} = \$275,000 - 87,500$$

$$\text{TCM} = \$187,500$$

The $187,500 total represents the contribution margin generated from all sales, so the next step involves calculating the *average* contribution margin per sales dollar. That average measures a straightforward proportional relationship:

$$\frac{\text{Average Contribution}}{\text{Margin per Unit}} = \frac{\text{Total Contribution Margin}}{\text{Total Sales}}$$

$$\text{ACM} = \frac{\$187,500}{\$275,000}$$

$$\text{ACM} = 68\% \text{ (or } 68¢ \text{ per dollar in sales)}$$

Thus, on the average, each dollar in sales provides 68¢ in margin to contribute to the coverage of fixed costs—and ultimately to any earnings realized by the firm.

Now, we can use that average contribution margin per unit to calculate Able's break-even point:

$$\text{Break-Even Sales Volume} = \frac{\text{Fixed Costs}}{\text{C/M as \% of Sales}}$$

$$\text{Break-Even Sales} = \frac{\$140,000}{.68}$$

$$\text{Break-Even Sales} = \$205,882$$

The Able Company can suffer a drop in sales of approximately $75,000 and still not suffer an operating loss. At the same time, note the general nature of the calculation process: It applies to any business. If you can identify your average contribution margin per sales dollar, you can calculate your break-even point.

One major qualifying assumption applies to this alternative approach: It presumes that as sales fluctuate the proportionate product mix that makes up any volume remains constant. A change in that mix naturally will change the average contribution margin received from each sales dollar.

Obviously, this assumption is not totally realistic. As sales fluctuate, product mix varies. Consequently, this approach to break-even analysis is less precise than the fundamental calculation. Nevertheless, the calculation provides a satisfactory estimate for most management purposes.

CASH FLOW BREAK-EVEN ANALYSIS

Standard break-even analysis identifies the particular sales volume in a business where revenues equal expenses. However, not all expenses incurred within a particular time period are cash expenses. Depreciation, as well as some less significant expenses, represents non-cash expenses. Thus, a business pays for machinery and equipment when purchased and then amortizes (discharges) the cost of the equipment over its useful life.

From our special perspective, it is significant that depreciation represents a major element in the total fixed cost in many businesses. Consequently, a business can have a cash flow break-even point—where the cumulative contribution margin from sales covers fixed cash expenses—that falls well below its financial break-even point.

Figure 15–2 illustrates this. First, (a) shows the contribution margin provided by each unit sale, together with the firm's total fixed costs. Again, it is apparent that it requires six unit sales to cover fixed costs fully. However, in this instance, the total fixed costs include depreciation that is equivalent to the contribution margin from two unit sales.

FIGURE 15–2 Cash Flow Break-Even Analysis: A Conceptual View

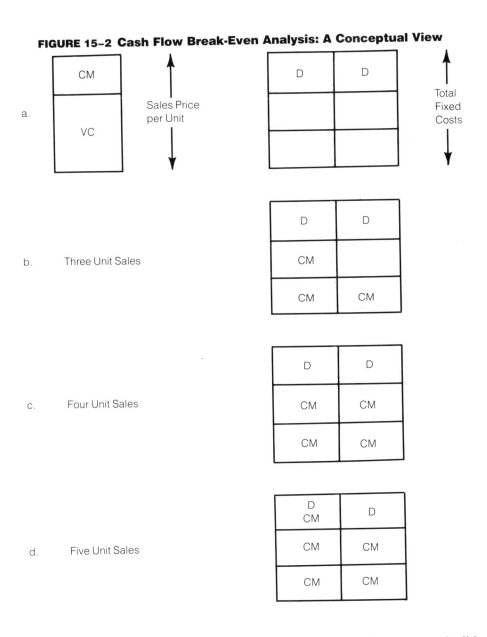

Note what happens as sales increase. A three-unit volume, shown in (b), leaves the business well below both the financial and cash flow break-even points. That volume creates a negative cash flow from operations: Cash expenses exceed cash income. In (c), we see that a four-unit volume provides a break-even cash flow. The total contribution margin from sales adequately covers actual cash expenses.

Finally, (d) demonstrates the effect of one unit sale above the cash flow break-even point. That sale provides a positive cash flow from operations, even though it leaves the business below the financial break-even point. One more unit sale returns the business to the proper break-even point. We can summarize the results in this illustration as Cash Flow Concept 46:

46: A business has a break-even cash flow when the contribution margin from sales exactly covers fixed cash costs.

The calculation process that identifies the cash flow break-even point in a business is identical to that illustrated above. However, instead of using a firm's total fixed costs, the calculation recognizes only fixed cash expenses. In most circumstances, that amount is merely the total fixed expenses less depreciation.

For example, looking at SEMCO again, assume that the firm's $90,000 annual fixed costs include $30,000 in depreciation. Then, its cash flow break-even point is found as follows:

$$\text{Cash Flow Break-Even Point} = \frac{\text{Fixed Cash Expenses}}{\text{Contribution Margin per Unit}}$$

$$= \frac{\$60,000}{\$3.00} = 20,000 \text{ units}$$

SEMCO has a break-even cash flow when sales reach $140,000 (20,000 × $7).

Again, if your business sells a variety of products, hence with different contribution margins, you must use the latter calculation to find the cumulative contribution margin necessary to cover fixed cash expenses.

Break-even cash flow analysis is a useful management tool, but it has limitations because it relies on accrual analysis. Thus, it does not reflect the actual timing of the cash flow into and out of business. Indeed, only an actual cash flow budget anticipates the physical collection and disbursement of cash.

Over a relevant period, cash flow break-even analysis can still be valuable because it identifies the sales volume that matches cash revenues to cash expenses. But keep it in perspective: You cannot equate accrual and cash flow accounting.

FIXED ASSETS AND THE BREAK-EVEN POINT

In Chapter 14, we introduced the fixed-asset turnover rate calculation, which identifies the proper fixed-asset investment level for a business. Break-even analysis contributes another important perspective: It recognizes depreciation as an element in the total fixed cost in a business. Thus, the relationship between a firm's investment in fixed assets and break-even analysis follows logically.

The annual depreciation charge as an element in the fixed cost increases as a business expands its investment in fixed assets. That increases the sales volume the business must generate to achieve break-even operating results. Alternatively, a lower investment in fixed assets leads to a lower break-even point.

Of course, the relationship is more complex. Indeed, a larger investment in fixed assets may lead to production efficiencies that reduce the variable product costs, increasing the contribution margin available from each sales dollar. At the same time, that doesn't negate the basic relationship between the size of the investment in fixed assets and break-even analysis. Nor does it eliminate the implications for the fixed-asset investment decision process.

Thus, before making a fixed-asset investment, you should measure how it will affect the break-even point in your business. If you can't be assured of the additional sales necessary to offset the higher fixed costs from the investment, you may wisely defer the acquisition.

Alternatively, if you can operate efficiently with a smaller fixed-asset investment, you lower the sales volume necessary to break even and reduce your operating risks. Of course, you also must measure the effect of your fixed-asset investment on the contribution margin you realize from each sale. This consideration falls naturally into the calculations that translate into break-even analysis.

Indeed, in any circumstance, a firm's investment in fixed assets influences its break-even sales volume. That suggests the value of using break-even analysis as an element in any fixed-asset investment decision.

THE BENEFITS OF BREAK-EVEN ANALYSIS

Prudent business management often calls for the use of break-even analysis. But the manager must recognize it as a tool, and know how to use it. It is more than a gauge of the effect that a firm's investment in fixed assets has on the break-even point.

From the pessimist's viewpoint, break-even analysis identifies the worst circumstances that can exist without suffering a loss from operations. If the business doesn't generate a profit, at least it *breaks even.*

However, the realistic manager recognizes break-even analysis as a step toward improving the firm's performance. Indeed, the analysis categorizes the critical relationships that determine whether or not a business operates profitably. Thus, should a business fall below the break-even point, the manager can use the analysis to consider the alternative solutions to his problem. Of course, the obvious corrective action in any instance will appear to be a higher sales volume. However, that often may not be the best approach, and it certainly isn't the only approach.

The best alternative in any event depends upon the operating constraints set by the external market and its internal operating requirements. Whatever the circumstance, however, break-even analysis isolates the major considerations for study and serves as a convenient tool for forecasting the results from any major change.

Almost every management decision in business—to hire or fire, to buy or sell, to lend or borrow—ultimately affects the cash flow process. Similarly, the economic environment in which the business operates also exerts a direct influence on cash flow management.

In Part Four, we will discuss two environmental considerations that have a particularly significant impact on the cash flow in a business.

First, in Chapter 16, we examine the relationship between the cash flow process and the administrative environment in a business. That relationship arises simply because of the quantity of paper work—invoices, delivery evidence, bank checks—that is involved in every business transaction. Thus, any problem that hampers the paper flow also disrupts the cash flow.

In Chapter 17, we turn our attention to the relationship between the inflationary economic environment and the cash flow process. Certainly, inflation always has had important implications for the cash flow manager. However, as the rate of rising prices

PART FOUR

Environmental Management

moves into double-digit levels, those implications become major management considerations.

Of course, the inflationary environment can't be altered to suit the administrative structure in your business, but you can isolate the impact inflation has on the cash flow process. Then, you can practice some defensive maneuvers to prevent that impact from producing a serious cash flow problem. As the rate of inflation accelerates, those maneuvers may become essential for survival.

Cash Flow Management in the Administrative Environment

A credit decision must precede an open-account sale. A customer seldom pays for a purchase until he receives an invoice. A past-due account pays more promptly when you politely remind the customer of his delinquency.

However obvious these facts appear to be, many businessmen overlook the direct relationship between the administrative environment and the cash flow process in a business. Inevitably, the two are interwoven. We illustrate that point in this chapter and review some principles that will help orient your management of that relationship. Our discussion proceeds in two steps.

First, in terms of its relationship to the cash flow process, we establish the primary objectives of administrative management. On occasion, these narrowly defined goals may conflict with other aims served by that management effort. However, from our perspective, no objective stands higher than the need for an efficient cash flow. Second, we review the major management principles that contribute to these objectives.

We also discuss the fundamentals of float management, *float* meaning the time lapse between the day you write a check and the day it reaches your bank for payment. Properly managed, float expands your cash capability, increases your earnings, and reduces the potential for cash flow problems in your business. In any circumstance, it should become a major consideration in positive cash flow management.

ACCELERATING CASH FLOW:
THE CASH CONVERSION PERIOD

An administrative environment should encourage efficient cash flow and contribute to two primary objectives:

1. Accelerating cash flow into the business
2. Deferring cash flow out of the business

Most businessmen recognize the first objective as a rational goal, but, at first glance, many find the second harder to accept, because prompt payment is critical to a firm's creditworthiness. However, if you can delay cash disbursements without violating that principle, you can enjoy an increase in your cash capability. Certainly, that remains the ultimate objective of cash flow management. In Part Two, we analyzed the rate of cash flow using the average collection period and turnover-rate calculations. A lower average collection period or a higher turnover rate indicated a more rapid conversion of accounts receivable into cash.

However, the collection period and turnover-rate calculations don't take into account all of the factors that affect how rapidly cash flows into a business. Both calculations measure cash flow from the date a business generates a sale to the date it receives payment. This limitation precludes the sequence of events before and after the sale that affect the efficiency of cash flow.

To measure the rate of cash flow properly, we need to adopt a broader perspective that we define here as the *cash conversion period*. This period measures the total time lapse between each customer's decision to purchase a product and the date the payment for that purchase becomes cash.

Figure 16–1 lists the factors that enter into the total cash conversion period. Between the purchase decision and the cash collection are most of the administrative tasks usually required to complete a sale. You accelerate the cash flow into your business as you complete each administrative task more efficiently. We summarize this fact as Cash Flow Concept 47:

47: Reducing your cash conversion period accelerates the cash flow into your business.

Below we discuss each step in the administrative process included in Figure 16–1. In terms of their influence on the cash flow process, we can identify the common problems that tend to stretch the cash conversion period. We also suggest some practical principles that can help compress that period.

The Purchase Decision and the Purchase Order

A customer's decision to purchase your product initiates the cash conversion period. However, we concentrate here on the time it takes to convert the purchase decision into cash in your bank account. Encouraging the most rapid communication of the customer's purchase decision into your business—that is, making it as quick and easy as possible for him to place an order—is the first step in compressing your cash conversion period. A purchase order serves as

FIGURE 16–1 Cash Conversion Period

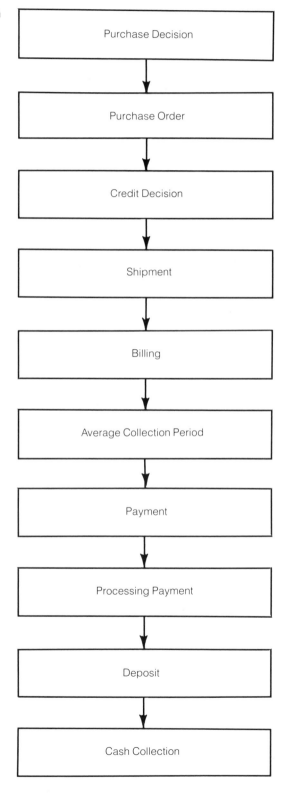

the medium of communication. Of course, the nature and complexity of the business dictate the format of the purchase order. But regardless of the format, your customer should be able to transmit his order to you as rapidly as possible.

The need for rapid communication usually eliminates the postal system, which even in the best circumstances extends your total cash conversion period from one to three days. Often, the delays in mail delivery reach seven days or more.

Of course, for items that don't affect your earnings, the postal service still provides the most efficient service because of its low cost, but remember that any delay in receiving your customer's purchase order affects your bottom line. Consequently, to overcome the deficiencies in mail service, you should provide an alternative method for your customers.

For significant purchase orders, you should use electronic communication, such as the telephone, a data-phone wire service, or xerographic transmission. Unfortunately, many businessmen concentrate on the personnel and equipment costs involved in these alternatives and overlook the one to seven-day reduction in their cash conversion periods that results from eliminating mail delays. Certainly, that benefit often is more difficult to measure.

Of course, electronic communication of purchase orders generally is suitable only when you have an ongoing relationship with a customer. Repeat customers usually make up the bulk of the sales, so using electronic communication at least for them helps you improve service and accelerate your cash flow.

After you receive a purchase order, you should complete the sale smoothly and with a minimum of paperwork. However, the flow of paperwork often is less of an obstacle to the completion of a sale than the credit decision that must precede it.

The Credit Decision

The credit decision, which authorizes a sale, is necessary to evaluate the probable fulfillment of the customer's promise to pay. As soon as a purchase order is received, the credit decision should be made. Each day that the decision is delayed, the cash conversion period is lengthened. Thus, it is important to approve in advance *lines of credit* for major customers. In other words, you should anticipate their needs *before* they exceed their credit limits.

You lose little if a customer does not use his full credit line. However, customers that do increase their purchases will find their orders delivered more promptly. Indeed, preapproved credit facilitates the completion of a sale and improves your service capability. A faster response inevitably offers a competitive advantage.

You can use the same procedure for prospective new customers: Check the creditworthiness of a new account in advance, before you receive a large order. Obtaining the information for a credit estimate—bank checks, supplier checks—can take several days and thus lengthens your cash conversion period. Moreover, if you delay too long, you risk losing the sale to a competitor with a more efficient credit-decision process.

Of course, don't sacrifice reliable credit analysis for speedy approval. Even a modest increase in bad-debt losses can offset the benefits from a lower cash-conversion period. At the same time, any element in the administrative environment that delays the completion of a sale hampers the smooth flow of cash into your business.

The Shipment

A delay in shipment lengthens the cash conversion period and hurts your cash flow. To avoid such delays, you should have a well-organized shipping department that meshes with your administrative environment.

Inefficient shipping procedures seldom become a major problem for most businesses. However, often a less obvious administrative problem interferes with prompt shipment: an inefficient inventory control system.

An inventory control system should answer two essential needs in a business: (1) it should maintain a current record of the amount of each inventory item held in stock; and (2) it should locate that stock. Neither element should be left to chance or memory.

Accountants refer to this system as a *perpetual* inventory. The system logs the sale and purchase of each item in inventory on a stock ledger card. Then, at any time, the ledger cards specify the total inventory of each item held in stock. The stock ledger card also should identify the exact location of the items. This prevents a shipment delay because someone does not have to search for the stock in the warehouse.

The perpetual inventory system offers another benefit for the business that seeks an efficient administrative environment. That is, when you apply EOQ analysis to the major items in your inventory, you can specify the reorder point for each item on the stock ledger cards. When the inventory falls to the reorder point, the "buy signal" tells you to restock, thus avoiding unnecessary stock-out costs.

The Billing

Issuing the invoice is the final step in the administrative process that completes a sale. The invoice identifies the merchandise sold, the shipment date (usually supported by a copy of the bill of lading or other evidence of shipment), and the amount due from the purchaser. For two reasons, the prompt completion and transmission of the invoice is an important element in the cash conversion process.

First, few purchasers will pay for merchandise prior to the receipt of the invoice. Indeed, the invoice typically serves as the trigger for the payment process in the accounting system in most businesses. Second, the invoice date usually initiates the payment period defined by a firm's selling terms.

To illustrate the significance of timely invoice preparation, we will assume that your designated selling terms call for payment within thirty days from the date of the invoice. However, if your administrative structure delays preparation of an invoice for seven days after shipment, you actually allow the customer thirty-seven days for payment. The invoice preparation period lengthens your cash conversion period by seven days.

Thus, your administrative environment should allow for the completion and transmission of every invoice as soon as possible after shipment, preferably on the same day. Each day's delay reduces the rate at which cash flows into your business.

Also, unless precluded by industry standards, you should require payment for purchases in accordance with your designated invoice terms. That means that you should not render a monthly statement of account to trigger customer payments.

Rendering statements is a costly, time-consuming, and self-defeating administrative process. Moreover, allowing customers to pay in response to monthly statements, rather than to purchase invoices, adds from one to thirty days to the cash conversion period. Customers will ignore the invoices and wait for the monthly statements. That can extend your cash conversion period significantly. Moreover, it can damage your earnings, even though you may have the cash capability to support the associated increase in accounts receivable.

Average Collection Period

The average collection period usually is the largest fraction of the cash conversion period. Because of this, you need a competent credit and collection effort. Uninformed credit decisions can increase bad-debt losses. Certainly, thorough research into a prospective customer's credit history will lengthen the cash conversion period, but that is preferable to an increase in bad-debt write-offs. You should seek a balance between the need for an efficient decision process and the need to exercise sound credit judgment.

Of course, you should complement your credit decision with a collection effort that encourages payment within your designated terms. You must select the average collection period that satisfies your earnings objectives within the constraints set by your cash flow. Then, you must design and use a collection policy that supports your cash flow needs.

Those policies and the collection period remain the most significant considerations in the relationship between the administrative environment and the cash flow process in your business.

The Payment

The prompt collection of your accounts receivable naturally is important, but a customer's *method* of payment also affects your cash conversion period. Usually the customer mails a check to your office on the date payment is due. Of course, any postal delay lengthens your cash conversion period.

As an alternative, you might use one of three payment methods to reduce your cash conversion period.

One is to use a post office box as your business address. This can reduce mail delivery time from one to three days. Although the rental fee is only an incidental expense, a major expense could arise because of the time it takes each day to collect the payments. The size of the expense should be compared to the benefits you obtain from the reduction in your cash conversion period. A significant difference in either direction determines your choice.

A second collection method is to use a *lockbox,* a post office box controlled by your bank. Your customers mail payments to the box address, and the bank, as a fee-paid service, deposits them directly into your account.

Of course, you still must rely on the postal system, so you don't save much more time than with a post office box. But you do automatically eliminate the administrative and accounting delays involved in processing the payments. With the lockbox, your accounting system processes a photocopy of the customer's check. Thus, accounting suffers the delays, not your cash conversion period.

The lockbox system is the most widely used system for accelerating collections. Of course, you must compare the bank's fee against the benefits that accrue from a shorter cash conversion period. In many circumstances, the profit potential held in a more rapid cash flow can make the cost of the lockbox service insignificant.

A third payment method eliminates all of the delays that can result from the most efficient mail service. The *wire transfer* process collects payments for large purchases through an electronic network within the banking system. This process transfers money from your customer's bank account into your bank account in a matter of hours.

Because wire transfers eliminate the delays that can arise from the postal system, the administrative structure in your business, or the check clearing process, it allows you to use the collected funds immediately.

Unfortunately, your cash-conscious customers will be reluctant to approve your request for payment by wire transfer: The system improves your cash flow, but it hurts theirs. Because the benefits are significant when large accounts are involved, you may want to make an effort to persuade them.

Processing the Payment

The lockbox and wire-transfer collection systems allow collections to be deposited before they are processed through a firm's accounting system. The business that receives payments directly should also deposit collections before processing the accompanying paperwork. After all, your cash capability remains unchanged when you hold customer checks in your office. Those checks begin to contribute to your cash capability only after they are deposited.

We are not disputing the need for bookkeeping to record customer payments. However, that recording process can proceed from remittance advice or photocopies, instead of from the check itself. Indeed, you should use any procedure that reduces your cash conversion period and accelerates your cash flow.

The Deposit

Depositing a customer's check in your bank account does not necessarily mark the end of the cash conversion period: The check does not increase your cash capability until it clears. Until the clearing is complete, which takes from two to ten days, the deposit falls into the category of uncollected funds. Thus, the bank registers the deposit in your account but doesn't recognize the deposit as cash. A bank adopts that view for two reasons.

First, the customer's check may be returned unpaid. Although it is seldom a major concern, some businesses do remit checks in excess of their bank balances. If your bank previously honored your checks, relying on the ledger balance of uncollected funds, your own account could be overdrawn if a large customer check is returned.

Second, when a bank honors checks drawn on the uncollected amount registered in a business checking account, it must pay the funds from its reserves to the drawing bank. This practice hurts the bank's bottom line: It pays out funds that otherwise could be invested profitably. Indeed, the business that persists in drawing on uncollected funds soon ruins its banking relationship.

The prompt deposit is the last element in the cash conversion period. Shortening that period as much as possible improves your cash flow and increases your cash capability.

DELAYING CASH DISBURSEMENTS

Most businessmen recognize the benefits of accelerating the cash flow into a business. And delaying cash disbursements as long as possible is merely the other side of the same coin.

You should try to achieve the maximum *cash disbursement period* in order to increase your cash capability and your tangible bottom-line benefits. We can summarize this as Cash Flow Concept 48:

48: Delaying disbursements increases the cash capability in a business.

The maximum cash disbursement period comes from two complementary management practices: (1) liability management and (2) float management. In either instance, however, the objective remains the same—the retention of all cash in your business as long as possible. The cash retained can be used profitably elsewhere, or it can enhance your cash reserves. In either circumstance, the additional capability benefits your business.

Liability Management
Pay no bill before its time: This is the guiding principle of liability management. Of course, you should never abuse a creditor's consideration, and neither should you exceed the requirements set by his standard payment terms. However, if you are experiencing a tight cash flow, you can delay cash disbursements beyond the credit terms.

In some industries, such as electronics and printing, this practice is common if not stretched too far. In other industries, such as steel and food commodities, failure to observe supplier terms can eliminate any future credit consideration. Certainly, you should know where you stand before deferring any payment beyond its due date.

Also, although the option exists to delay a payment beyond its due date, a business maintains goodwill from prompt payment habits. Don't pay any sooner than necessary, but try to observe your creditor's terms.

Float Management

Float measures the time lapse between the date you write a check and the date that check reaches your bank for payment. It becomes significant for the cash flow manager because a business does not *need* the cash to cover the check until it actually reaches the bank. Keep in mind Cash Flow Concept 49:

49: Float management helps to delay cash disbursements and increase your cash capability.

We will establish the fundamental concept of float management and discuss how it contributes to your cash capability.

Assume that on Monday you mail a $10,000 payment to a supplier in Kansas City, Missouri, a thousand miles away. Perhaps the supplier receives the check on Wednesday and immediately deposits it in his bank account. Your bank will not receive the check for payment until Friday, or perhaps the following Monday.

In this circumstance, your float totals four to seven days, depending upon the day the check actually reaches your bank for payment. You do not need the $10,000 in cash until the check actually reaches your bank.

Properly managed, float directly contributes to your cash capability. When you write a check to a supplier (or to any other creditor), you expand your cash capability by the amount of the check. Of course, you lose that additional capability, plus the actual cash, when the check clears.

As a practical concept, consider how that temporary expansion in cash capability benefits a business in the midst of a cash flow squeeze. Float provides the capability to pay suppliers within their original terms, even though the amount of the checks exceeds the funds on hand when written. The business that uses float should have realistic expectations of receiving the cash to cover those checks before the termination of the float period, either from anticipated collections or from external financing.

Of course, the cash flow manager recognizes that any business always has some checks floating through the system. Moreover, he knows that he can estimate fairly accurately the total float available to his business at any time. To make that estimate, he charts the date he writes the checks to pay his creditors and compares those dates to the time the checks actually reach his bank for payment. The latter date is stamped by the bank on the back of each check. Assuming that his monthly payment habits are regular, the manager can measure his float with enough precision to make it a profitable management tool.

Table 16–1, a simplified approach to float management, tracks the actual movement of cash into and out of a business and interrelates that movement with the cash capability that comes from float.

TABLE 16-1 Float Management

	(1) Beginning Checking Account Balance	(2) Checks Mailed	(3) Cash Deposits	(4) Ending Checking Account Balance	(5) Checks Cleared	(6) Actual Bank Balance	(7) Total Float	(8) Total Cash Capability (6) + (7)
8/1	$100,000	—	—	$100,000	—	$100,000	—	$100,000
8/2	100,000	$30,000		70,000	—	100,000	$ 30,000	130,000
8/3	70,000	—	$ 25,000	95,000	—	125,000	30,000	155,000
8/4	95,000	60,000		35,000	—	125,000	90,000	215,000
8/5	35,000	—		35,000	$30,000	95,000	60,000	155,000
8/6	35,000	75,000		(40,000)	—	95,000	135,000	230,000
8/7	(40,000)	25,000		(65,000)	—	95,000	160,000	255,000
8/8	(65,000)	—		(65,000)	60,000	35,000	100,000	135,000
8/9	(65,000)	—	150,000	85,000	—	185,000	100,000	285,000
8/10	85,000	—	50,000	135,000	75,000	110,000	25,000	135,000

Thus, on 8/1, the business begins with $100,000 in collected cash in its checking account. No unpaid checks are presently outstanding. On 8/2, the business writes and mails $30,000 in checks to pay suppliers. Although the checking account balance drops to $70,000, the actual cash held in the bank account remains unchanged: The checks are in the mail and are not affecting the firm's cash account.

While the checks are outstanding, the business could use the cash in its bank account. Consequently, the float in this instance raises its total cash capability to $130,000.

On 8/3, the business writes no more checks but receives $25,000 in cash collections on account. That raises the checking account balance to $95,000 and the actual bank balance to $125,000. (We assume here that the bank allows the customer immediate credit for all deposits, not an unrealistic expectation for the business that carries a reasonable collected balance throughout most of the month.)

Coupled with the float from the $30,000 in checks written on 8/2, the firm's total cash capability rises to $155,000. On 8/4, the business writes and mails another $60,000 in payments to suppliers. That raises the total float to $90,000 and the cash capability to $215,000.

Then, on 8/5, the $30,000 in checks written on 8/2 reach the bank for payment. We assume a conservative four-day average float period in this instance. That lowers the firm's bank balance to $95,000 and its cash capability to $155,000. The $60,000 reduction measures the total of the unpaid checks no longer outstanding, plus the actual reduction in cash required to pay the checks.

On 8/6, the firm writes another $75,000 in checks. This lowers the check book balance to a *negative* $40,000. The company has a book overdraft, although the actual bank balance remains a comfortable $95,000. Now, we can estimate the real significance of float management.

Perhaps the payments mailed on 8/6 enable the firm to take 2% discounts that would be missed if the firm delayed payment until it received the actual cash collections necessary to honor the checks. Or the firm may be observing payment within the supplier's terms in order to maintain its credit rating. In either circumstance, the firm gains benefits that would be lost without the use of float.

Continuing the example set in Table 16–1, on 8/7 the company writes another $25,000 in checks. This raises its book overdraft to $65,000. On the same day, the firm's actual bank balance drops to $35,000 as the $60,000 in checks reach the bank for payment. However, the firm's total cash capability remains at $135,000 on the same day.

Finally, on 8/9, the business receives $150,000 in collections, easily sufficient to cover all checks outstanding. The bulk of the firm's float evaporates on 8/10 as the $75,000 in checks written on 8/6 reach the bank for payment.

Obviously, you can't manage your float with the precision presumed in Table 16–1. Some checks clear in two days, some in ten. Absolute predictability is impossible. Nor can you be assured that your bank will provide instant credit for collections. However, this is the usual procedure so long as you don't continuously demand the use of the balances represented by your uncollected checks.

Proper float management also can increase your earnings. Indeed, you don't need to suffer from a cash flow squeeze to benefit from float. If your business has adequate cash for normal operations, you can improve your earnings by investing the cash equivalent to the float.

You should also recognize that two separate components make up the total float available to a business. One component, *postal float,* measures the length of time it takes for a payment to be delivered to a creditor. The other, *bank float,* registers the length of time it takes your creditor's deposit to reach your bank for payment.

Of course, you have no influence over bank float: You can estimate the time it takes your check to clear, but you can't extend it for your benefit. At the same time, the perceptive manager will anticipate the potential in lengthening the postal float. Indeed, he doesn't mail his payments to his supplier's post office box, but to his firm's address.

That increases the delivery time by a day or two, thus adding to your total float. So long as your payment is postmarked on the due date, most suppliers will consider your payment as prompt. What extends your cash conversion period when you look at your collections also extends your cash conversion period when you consider payments.

Again, never abuse a creditor's consideration, but use float to expand your cash capability and increase your earnings.

Cash Flow Management in the Inflationary Environment

Inflation, simply defined as persistently rising prices, is a pervasive problem in our modern economic environment and, hence, a major cash flow management consideration. This chapter reviews some concepts designed to help you successfully contend with inflation as an inevitable fact of business life.

First, we show how inflation affects earnings in a business, an effect that often misleads many businessmen. Unfortunately, in an inflationary environment, higher earnings cannot always be equated with financial growth.

Next, we will expand our illustration and demonstrate the impact inflation has on the cash flow process. That impact stands as an obstacle to the success —and to the survival—of many businesses.

Finally, we will discuss the principles of a good defensive strategy and illustrate the defensive maneuvers that can help you combat the detrimental effects of inflation.

HOW INFLATION AFFECTS EARNINGS

We can summarize one aspect of the impact of inflation in Cash Flow Concept 50:

50: Inflation generates deceptive profits and drains cash from a business.

A comparison of the operating results of two companies, referred to as the Fantasy Corporation and the Real Company, illustrates the tangible impact that deception has on the cash flow process. In most respects, the two companies are remarkably similar:
  1. Both operate as wholesalers distributing plumbing fixtures to home builders
  2. Both began a recent year with identical financial structures
  3. Both generate exactly the same unit-volume sales during the year
  4. Both begin and end the year with exactly the same unit volume in inventory
The only factor that distinguishes the two firms is the inflationary environment in which each operates.

The Fantasy Corporation functions in an economy that enjoys a zero inflation rate. Prices remain constant throughout the year. The Real Company is less fortunate: The firm has to contend with an economy encumbered with a 20% annual rate of inflation. Prices at the end of the year are 20% above those at the beginning of the year. Table 17–1 demonstrates how that fact affects the comparative operating results of the two firms.

TABLE 17–1 How Inflation Affects Earnings

	Fantasy Corporation (Zero Inflation Rate)	**Real Company** (20% Inflation Rate)
Sales	$2,000,000	$2,200,000
Cost of Goods Sold*	1,500,000	1,590,000
Operating Costs	300,000	330,000
Earnings before Taxes	$ 200,000	$ 280,000
Taxes at 50%	(100,000)	(140,000)
Earnings after Taxes	**$ 100,000**	**$ 140,000**
* Cost-of-Goods-Sold Calculation		
Beginning Inventory (10,000 units)	$ 300,000	$ 300,000
Purchases	1,500,000	1,650,000
Ending Inventory (10,000 units)	300,000	360,000
Cost of Goods Sold	**$1,500,000**	**$1,590,000**

First, note that the Real Company's sales and expenses are 10% above those posted by the Fantasy Corporation, although its inflationary environment registered a 20% annual increase in prices. This 10% difference measures the *average* effect of the annual rate of inflation. The firm's year-end inventory costs reflect the full impact of the inflationary environment: The costs are 20% above the beginning total. (Remember, both firms begin and end the year with exactly the same unit inventory in stock.)

Recognizing those facts, the comparison suggests that the Real Company actually benefits from the inflationary environment. By adjusting prices in line with inflation, the firm realizes after-tax earnings $40,000 above those generated by the Fantasy Corporation.

However, another look raises a question about the Real Company's apparent advantages. Observe the comparative costs associated with each firm's year-end inventory. Again, both businesses begin and end the year with exactly the same physical inventory on hand. However, the Real Company paid $360,000 for that stock, while the Fantasy Corporation's costs for the same inventory totaled only $300,000.

Thus, the Real Company's apparent earning advantage is more than offset by the higher prices paid for its final inventory. However, the detrimental influence of the inflationary environment is even worse than this comparison suggests. A review of the comparative cash flows for each firm proves that fact.

HOW INFLATION AFFECTS CASH FLOW

Deceptive profits are prevalent in an inflationary environment. Rising inventory replacement costs more than offset the apparent earnings advantage gained from higher prices. To see how that environment affects a firm's cash flow, we will compare the changes in the Fantasy Corporation's and the Real Company's financial structure effected by their comparative operating results. To isolate these changes, we will draw two new restrictive assumptions:

1. Each company's investment in accounts receivable averages 10% of its annual sales volume
2. Liabilities for each company hold constant from one year to the next

Observing these constraints, Table 17–2 demonstrates the full, detrimental impact the inflationary environment has on the Real Company's cash position.

Inflation translates the Real Company's apparent $40,000 earnings advan-

TABLE 17–2 How Inflation Affects Financial Structure

	Beginning Structure (Both Firms)	End of Year	
		Fantasy Corporation	Real Company
Cash	$ 50,000	$150,000	$110,000
Accounts Receivable	200,000	200,000	220,000
Inventory	300,000	300,000	360,000
Total Assets	**$550,000**	**$650,000**	**$690,000**
Total Liabilities	**$250,000**	**$250,000**	**$250,000**
Stockholders' Equity	$300,000	$400,000	$440,000
Equity and Liabilities	**$550,000**	**$650,000**	**$690,000**

tage into cash reserves that are $40,000 *less* than those accumulated by the Fantasy Corporation. Inflation absorbed the higher profits and imposed an additional cash penalty on the Real Company. Not only were the firm's profits deceptively higher, but inflation drained cash from the business. Measured by its cash reserves, the Real Company actually fell behind the Fantasy Corporation.

Another perspective of the same effect emphasizes the point of this illustration: Table 17–3 also traces the ultimate disposition of each firm's pre–tax earnings. The Real Company suffers every step of the way.

TABLE 17–3 How Inflation Affects Cash Flow

	Fantasy Corporation	Real Company
Pre-tax Cash Gain (total earnings from operations)	$200,000	$280,000
Less: Cash Paid Out		
1. Income Taxes	(100,000)	(140,000)
2. Replacement Inventory	(—)	(60,000)
3. Increased A/R Investment	(—)	(20,000)
Net Cash Gain	**$100,000**	**$ 60,000**

First, the Real Company has to pay a $40,000 cash penalty to fulfill the higher income-tax obligation associated with inflationary profits. The Real Company pays that penalty even though both businesses sold exactly the same unit volume.

Second, the Real Company has to pay a $60,000 penalty for its year-end inventory. Although both businesses end the year with the same physical inventory, inflation raises the Real Company's replacement costs by 20%.

Third, the Real Company must supply the cash capability to carry a $20,000 larger investment in accounts receivable. That investment inevitably rises along with the company's own price adjustments.

In total, Table 17–3 registers the transformation of the Real Company's $40,000 earnings advantage into a $40,000 cash flow disadvantage—an $80,000 turnaround!

Of course, the Real Company did produce a cash gain despite the inflationary environment. However, if the company continues in that environment, the increasing cost of replacement inventory, as well as operating costs, eventually will become an obstacle to any gain at all.

TIGHT MONEY IN AN INFLATIONARY ENVIRONMENT

Unfortunately, the effect of inflation on cash flow is often more detrimental than illustrated by the Real Company's experience. An inflationary environment also imposes strains on cash flow when a limited supply of funds forces financial institutions to restrict their lending activities. This is the *tight money* phenomenon, and it has several interrelated effects on the cash flow in a business. We crystallize this in Cash Flow Concept 51:

51: Tight money adds to the strains on the cash flow of the business operating in an inflationary environment.

First, as the demand for borrowed funds approaches the limits set by the short supply, interest rates inevitably rise. A business pays a higher price for the privilege of expanding its cash capability. At the same time, even the business willing to pay higher interest rates may find a limit set on its borrowing power. As demand for cash increases relative to supply, lenders begin to "ration" their loans. One form of rationing restricts loans to firms with high or above-average credit ratings, while less creditworthy borrowers receive little or no consideration at all.

Second, credit rationing restricts the size of the loans approved by lenders. Thus, the financially strong borrower may expand his cash capability, but often by a smaller amount than desired. Lenders approve the quality of the credit but ration the quantity.

Moreover, the rationing process sends a ripple throughout the economic environment. This affects a firm's cash flow even further. You feel that impact both in your role as a customer and in your role as a supplier.

In your role as a supplier, you extend credit to your customers. You allow a predetermined period of time for payout after the actual purchase. Presumably, you couple your designated selling terms with your credit policy to achieve an objective average collection period. That period satisfies the constraints set by your cash capability while also contributing to your earnings.

Unfortunately, attaining your collection period objective is more difficult in an inflationary environment. As the rationing process imposes borrowing limits on your customers, they begin to suffer strains on their own cash flows. Often, they pass part of that strain on to their suppliers: They pay less promptly.

That circumstance, in turn, increases the burden on your cash flow. You either absorb some of your customers' strains or risk losing them to financially stronger, more lenient competitors. Inevitably, their cash flow problems become *your* cash flow problems.

From the other perspective, you may also suffer an impact on your cash flow in your role as a customer. Thus, as you try to ease your cash squeeze by paying for purchases more slowly, you confront increasing supplier pressure for payment. A strong supplier may refuse future sales unless you honor his designated terms.

Many businessmen find themselves in a dilemma: They must balance their suppliers' demands for prompt payment against their customers' need for longer payment terms. That dilemma often presses the limits of a firm's cash capability. Whenever this happens to your business, the strains impose demands on your cash flow management effort. Inevitably, the constant battle against the detrimental effects of inflation becomes a business necessity. Contending with such an environment requires a well-developed defensive strategy that rests on two fundamental principles: *defensive accounting* and *defensive management.*

DEFENSIVE ACCOUNTING

One element in a good defensive strategy can be summed up in Cash Flow Concept 52:

52: Defensive accounting helps combat inflation.

We will reiterate the major policies that contribute to a good accounting defense: LIFO accounting and accelerated depreciation.

LIFO accounting operates on the assumption that a business sells its inventory in reverse of the order acquired: The last addition to stock presumably becomes the first sold.

Of course, LIFO accounting has no actual effect on the prices paid for replacement inventory. Nor does it influence the physical flow of goods through the business. However, a business derives a cash benefit because it increases the calculated cost-of-goods-sold total. That calculation lowers pre-tax earnings and ultimately reduces income-tax obligations.

To prove that benefit, we will again review the Real Company's circumstance. In the earlier illustration, the firm used FIFO accounting. Table 17-4 compares the original results with the outcome that would result from switching to LIFO accounting.

TABLE 17-4 LIFO Accounting vs. FIFO Accounting in an Inflationary Environment

THE REAL COMPANY

	FIFO Accounting	LIFO Accounting
Sales	$2,200,000	$2,200,000
Cost of Goods Sold*	(1,590,000)	(1,650,000)
Operating Costs	(330,000)	(330,000)
Earnings before Taxes	$ 280,000	$ 220,000
Income Taxes (at 50%)	(140,000)	(110,000)
Earnings after Taxes	**$ 140,000**	**$ 110,000**
* Cost-of-Goods-Sold Calculation		
Beginning Inventory	$ 300,000	$ 300,000
Purchases	1,650,000	1,650,000
Ending Inventory	360,000	300,000
Cost of Goods Sold	**$1,590,000**	**$1,650,000**

Thus, LIFO accounting generates $30,000 in additional cash for the Real Company. The higher calculated cost of goods sold lowers earnings sufficiently to reduce the firm's income-tax obligation by that amount. Although that doesn't offset the full effects of inflation, it certainly helps to blunt the attack.

Adopting accelerated depreciation for any fixed-asset investment also helps offset the cash sting a business feels from inflation. Of course, it has no effect on the total cash flow a business ultimately realizes from the process. However, it does affect the timing of the cash flow. Accelerated depreciation returns the same cash to the business, but it returns it sooner. This becomes critical in an inflationary environment.

To further emphasize that fact, we will look at the effect of an inflationary environment from a slightly different viewpoint and concentrate on the purchasing power cash loses in that environment. A simplified example demonstrates that loss.

The Wag Company operates in an inflationary environment that suffers a 10% rise in prices each year. An item that costs $1.00 today will cost $1.10 a year from now. Recognizing that, the Wag Company uses all excess cash to purchase inventory in anticipation of the rising prices. To see the benefits the firm derives from that policy, we will make two assumptions:

1. The Wag Company has the option of receiving $1,000 today or $1,000 a year from today, perhaps from an outside investor

2. The company's material costs today average $1.00 per unit

Recognizing that inflation will drive those costs to $1.10 over the next year, compare the number of units the Wag Company can buy with $1,000 today versus the total the same dollar will buy one year from now.

	Purchasing Today	**Purchasing One Year from Today**
Cash	$1,000	$1,000
Cost per Unit	$1.00	$1.10
Units Bought	1,000	909

Thus, if the company receives $1,000 today, it can anticipate the rise in prices and purchase 1,000 units for stock. Delaying receipt of the $1,000 for a year means that inflation will reduce the purchasing power of the same number of dollars to 909 units. Thus, the Wag Company realizes direct benefits—increased purchasing power—by having $1,000 now instead of a year from now.

The Wag Company's experience helps demonstrate the contribution accelerated depreciation makes to the defensive strategy against inflation. The policy returns the same cash to the business that comes from straight-line depreciation. But because it returns those dollars sooner, accelerated depreciation increases a firm's total purchasing power.

DEFENSIVE MANAGEMENT

Defensive management requires anticipation and action, rather than wait-ing and reaction. It calls for persistent exercise of three management actions:
1. Upward sales price adjustments
2. Anticipatory purchasing
3. Internal cost control
Implementing these defensive maneuvers will not defeat inflation, but it can help you offset its detrimental effects. Remember these actions as Cash Flow Concept 53:

53: Defensive management against inflation requires the proper price adjustments, anticipatory buying, and cost control.

Sales Price Adjustments

When not precluded by customer resistance or competitive pressure, you must maintain persistent upward pressure on your own price structure. Of course, every businessman recognizes that to maintain profitability he must increase his prices sufficiently to offset rising costs.

However, many overlook the fact that raising prices in an amount equal to the rise in costs is not sufficient to offset the effects of inflation. Indeed, as a busi-nessman raises prices to offset rising costs, he also must increase his profit mar-gin to maintain the purchasing power of the dollars he retains in his business.

To illustrate the need for a growing profit margin, we will look at the Sample Company, a hypothetical business with only one product. As the Sample Com-pany began its most recent year, it recognized the following facts:
1. The company's product sells for $4.60
2. With product costs that total $4.00 per unit, the company earns 60¢ from each sale (after covering all fixed costs)
3. Economists project a 12% inflation rate for the year.

The Sample Company, concerned with rising product costs, initially antici-pated increasing its prices by an amount sufficient to offset the 12% (or 48¢) in-crease in product costs. However, further analysis identified a flaw in that deci-sion.

Of course, a 48¢ increase in product costs will lead to a $5.08 selling cost per unit by the end of the year. That selling price will maintain the firm's 60¢ profit margin prevalent at the beginning of the year: $5.08 − $4.48 = 60¢. However, the purchasing power of that profit margin would have decreased as follows:

$$\frac{\$\ .60}{1.12} = \$.53$$

That means that each 60¢ in earnings at the end of the year would carry purchas-ing power equal to only 53¢ at the beginning of the year. Although profits per unit remained constant, the company actually would forfeit significant financial ground to inflation.

As an alternative to that undesirable outcome, the company then determined the price increase necessary to maintain the purchasing power contained in its profit margin. It found the selling price necessary to achieve that objective with the aid of the following calculation:

$$\text{Required Year-End Selling Price} = \frac{\left(\dfrac{\text{Beginning}}{\text{Product Cost}}\right)\left(\dfrac{1 + \text{Inflation}}{\text{Rate}}\right)}{\dfrac{\text{Beginning}}{\text{Product Cost}} \div \dfrac{\text{Beginning}}{\text{Sales Price}}}$$

Applying the data from the Sample Company, the calculation becomes:

$$\text{Required Year-End Sales Price} = \frac{(\$4.00) \quad (1.12)}{\$4.00 \div \$4.60}$$

$$\text{Required Sales Price} = \frac{\$4.48}{.87}$$

$$\text{Required Sales Price} = \$5.15$$

To have a unit profit margin at the end of the year equal in purchasing power to that held in the margin prevailing at the beginning of the year, the Sample Company's selling price must rise from $4.60 to $5.15. Thus, the calculation recognizes that product costs will rise at a pace equivalent to the annual rate of inflation—from $4.00 to $4.48 per unit, or a 12% increase.

At the same time, the analysis suggests a sales price that will increase the company's profit margin from 60¢ to 67¢ per unit. That increase will enable the company to maintain the same profit-margin purchasing power.

Of course, maintaining the purchasing power of your profit margin is a valuable management precept. However, recognizing the need for higher prices and forcing those prices onto your market are separate considerations. After all, your customers operate in the same inflationary environment. Should your rate of increases exceed your competitors', you risk losing your price-conscious customers.

At the same time, if you hold your price adjustments below competition, you may gain an increase in volume. But that volume will generate partially deceptive profits. How do you solve this dilemma?

Unfortunately, no simple answer exists. You want to increase your prices as rapidly as possible to maintain the purchasing power of your profit margin. At the same time, you must observe the natural restraints set by competition. Since they operate in the same inflationary environment, of course, neither you nor your competitors can lag too far behind one another.

Indeed, recognizing the need for appropriate price adjustments is an element of management science. Implementing those adjustments at the proper time and in the proper manner is a management art.

Anticipatory Purchasing

As you combat inflation, you should complement your upward price adjustments with purchasing practices that recognize the inevitable rise in your own product costs. That is, you should practice anticipatory purchasing.

First, you must accept inflation as an inevitable, pervasive fact of business life, and assume that prices will continue to rise. In other words, you must adopt an inflationary psychology. Certainly, you can't predict the precise time every supplier will increase his prices, but you can assume that a rise in prices is always pending. Thus, you must purchase as much inventory at present prices as your cash capability allows.

If you can assume realistically that suppliers will increase the prices of your major lines at least 10% over the next six months, then every item you purchase before the higher prices become reality will offset inflation to some extent and help your bottom line.

From one perspective, anticipatory purchasing will help you maintain lower costs for a period of time after any particular price increase becomes official. You don't eliminate the pain, but you do defer it.

From another perspective, you often can use the merchandise acquired by anticipatory purchasing to increase earnings. You derive that benefit when you increase your price structure simultaneously with your suppliers. In that event, you enjoy a higher profit margin until you exhaust your stock of the lower-cost merchandise.

We will use the Calculator Company as an example. The company sells its most popular hand-held calculator for $14.00. The firm pays the supplier $10.00 per unit, thus enjoying a $4.00 gross profit margin per unit. However, the company anticipates a $2.00 increase in the supplier's selling price—to $12.00 per unit—and purchases 1,000 calculators at the $10.00 price.

Subsequently, when the supplier announces the $2.00 price increase, the Calculator Company immediately increases its selling price to $16.00. The following summarizes the firm's benefit from anticipatory purchasing:

One Calculator Bought and Sold	Cost	Selling Price
Price at Time of Purchase	$10.00	$14.00
Price at Time of Sale	$12.00	$16.00
Actual Profit per Unit = $6.00		
Normal Profit per Unit = $4.00		
Anticipatory Purchasing Benefit	$2.00	

Thus, the Calculator Company realizes a $2.00 per unit benefit, or a $2,000 total, from an appropriately timed price increase.

Of course, you shouldn't strain the limits of your cash capability to achieve the benefits of anticipatory buying, but you should recognize that it at least provides one more tool to offset the effects of inflation on your business.

Internal Cost Control

Internal cost control also contributes to your fight against inflation. If you can hold some costs constant as prices increase, you will be under less pressure to raise your own prices point for point. In other words, you don't have to run as hard to stay even.

By comparison with the other two elements of defensive management, internal cost control actually helps to stem the prevailing inflationary trends. Thus, anticipatory purchasing and upward price adjustments respond only to inflation. They both seek to keep a business in pace with rising prices. Indeed, both may contribute to the inflationary spiral, however undesirable that may appear.

Internal cost control, in contrast, can contribute to a lower rate of inflation because it also helps you offset the effects of inflation on your business. As an illustration, we will introduce two alternative definitions for terms introduced in our discussion of break-even analysis: fixed costs and variable costs. From that discussion, we assumed that fixed costs remained constant over some reasonable range of sales volumes. Alternatively, variable costs changed in direct proportion to any fluctuation in sales.

Here we will view variable costs as those uncontrollable product costs that rise in line with the prevailing rate of inflation. A business must absorb these variable costs and pass them on to customers in the form of higher selling prices.

Fixed costs become those internal costs subject to some influence, if not complete control, by a business. Of course, some costs, such as rent, utilities, and maintenance, do remain fixed over reasonable periods of time. However, many others are semifixed, subject to inflation unless offset by internal cost control.

For example, as prices increase, a business feels pressure from rising production costs. Internal cost control encourages managerial resistance to those pressures. Perhaps the business can increase production with the same number of employees or maintain the same production with fewer employees. Either instance helps it maintain its fixed costs and reduces the need for upward price adjustments.

We will look again at the Sample Company to see how internal cost control can benefit a business and also contribute to a reduction in the prevailing rate of inflation.

Remember, the Sample Company opened its latest business year with a $4.60 selling price for its only product, the total cost of which was $4.00. Also, it anticipates a 12% rate of inflation for the year.

However, here we will recognize that the company's total product costs included two components: That is, $2.00 out of that total is a variable cost, directly responsive to any external price increases. Thus, the firm anticipates a 12% rise in variable costs over the year.

The other $2.00 in product costs are considered fixed. While these costs also increase over the year, we will assume that creative management enables the company to hold the increase to a 4% rate, well below the hike encouraged by inflation.

Before we see what effect the lower increase rate in fixed costs has on the company's required selling-price calculation, we must alter one element in the calculation to reflect the effects of internal cost control. Instead of using the 12% annual rate of inflation, we will use the "average" cost inflation absorbed by the company. That average allows proper consideration of the increase in both variable and fixed costs anticipated for the year.

We find the company's average product-cost increase for the year as follows:

	Annual Increase	Proportion of Total Product Costs	
Variable-Cost Increase	12%	× 50%	= 6%
Fixed-Cost Increase	4%	× 50%	= 2%
		Average Product-Cost Increase =	8%

Thus, the company's average product-cost increase totals 8%. We will use this 8% increase in the required sales-price calculation. Note that this approach can be used to calculate the average product-cost increase regardless of the distribution between fixed and average costs.

$$\text{Required Sales Price} = \frac{\left(\begin{array}{c}\text{Beginning} \\ \text{Product Cost}\end{array}\right)(1 + \text{Average Inflation Rate})}{\dfrac{\text{Beginning}}{\text{Product Cost}} \div \dfrac{\text{Beginning}}{\text{Sales Price}}}$$

$$\text{Required Sale} = \frac{(\$4.00) \quad (1.08)}{(\$4.00) \div (\$4.60)}$$

$$= \frac{\$4.32}{.87}$$

$$\text{Required Sales Price} = \$4.97$$

Exercising internal cost controls enables the Sample Company to reduce its price increase for the year from $5.15 to $4.97. This reduction allows the company to maintain its profit margin at the level necessary to keep up with the average cost increase for the year. At the same time, holding its price increase below the general rate of inflation ultimately can contribute to a reduction in the pace of price increases.

Of course, the Sample Company might practice internal cost control and still adjust its prices in line with the inflationary trends. That would enhance the individual benefits the company could derive from internal cost controls. Whichever path you select, don't overlook the contribution internal cost controls offer against inflation.

Practicing the tenets in this chapter won't beat inflation, of course, but it can make the terms of our coexistence with inflation more equitable.

Few businesses grow and prosper without using leverage, which simply means credit extended by an external lender. In some instances, leverage may solve a problem because it fills a temporary gap in cash flow. In other instances, it enables a business to take advantage of profitable opportunities, or to increase the return on the stockholders' investment. Whatever the purpose, leverage inevitably becomes a major consideration in cash flow management.

Chapter 18 introduces the fundamental concept of leverage. Obviously, leverage involves debt, so we will discuss the criteria for evaluating the potential contribution of leverage as well as its practical limits. Certainly, a business benefits when leverage helps increase earnings. At the same time, another criteria, return on investment, may justify the use of leverage even though the business has lower profits. Thus, you will see how

to measure the value of leverage from both viewpoints.

Chapter 19 discusses the mechanical processes of leverage. Because different loans have different structures and requirements, they do not all serve the same purpose. Thus, we will review the common lending mechanics as a natural prelude to discussing the specific uses of leverage as well as its sources.

We will also illustrate the methods lenders use to calculate direct interest charges. Those charges do not necessarily include the total cost of borrowing. In many circumstances, less obvious factors increase that direct cost. Nevertheless, the calculated interest remains the major portion of your borrowing cost. We also include a discussion of collateral considerations and borrowing power.

Chapter 20 examines the specific practical purposes that encourage the use of leverage in a business. Then, we illustrate the potential profits

PART FIVE

Leverage Management

that derive from its proper use in each circumstance. This translates the concepts that underlie the use of leverage into terms an earnings-oriented businessman can relate to directly.

In Chapter 21, we will discuss the alternative sources of borrowed funds. All creditors are not the same; some cost more than others, and some serve specific borrowing purposes better than others. All may be appropriate at different times in different circumstances.

Chapter 22 deals with the types of leverage available from the bank. We will illustrate the calculations that determine the true cost of borrowing, as well as the criteria banks use to evaluate a borrower's potential. Then, in Chapter 23, we discuss the same calculations and criteria from the viewpoint of commercial finance companies.

In both chapters, we touch on the fundamental guidelines that orient the credit decision

process for each lender. A better understanding of the lender's viewpoint will enhance the communication process. And better communication enhances the potential credit consideration.

As a natural complement to the discussion of leverage, we also consider two other external sources of funds for a business. Chapter 24 compares the potential benefits of leasing as an alternative to financing the purchase of fixed assets. Typically, you will find that the total cost of leasing exceeds the costs of financing. However, higher costs spread over several years often become less important to a businessman than near-term cash considerations. Indeed, in such circumstances, leasing may gain an advantage.

Then, Chapter 25 considers another source of external funds that is often ignored by the entrepreneurial businessman. That source—the external investor—stands ready to inject cash permanently into a business in the form of equity, rather than temporarily as leverage. Few small businesses become large businesses without the aid of external investors, so this consideration remains a valid alternative to the business that needs additional cash.

Chapter 26 facilitates the comparative analysis of the alternative sources of cash available to a business. This chapter should enhance your leverage management ability by taking the confusion out of the comparison process.

Leverage: A Conceptual View

Leverage measures the percentage of a firm's assets supported by debt. For example, a business with $1,000,000 in total assets and $600,000 in debt has a 60% *leverage factor.* Understanding the concept of leverage as a basic principle of financial management will enable you to use leverage to enhance your profit potential. And that is the point of this chapter.

In addition, we will examine the practical limits on the benefits a business can derive from leverage. One limit arises from the natural relationship between the cost of borrowing and the return on assets. Failure to observe that limit can turn a profitable operation into a losing one.

A second, less obvious limit comes from the element of risk involved in using leverage. Thus, as leverage enhances your profit potential, it also increases the chances for financial failure. That inevitable association means that risk should be given considerable weight in any decision to use borrowed funds. In many circumstances, the desire for survival may loom larger than the potential for higher profits.

MEASURING THE BENEFITS OF LEVERAGE

The benefits that accrue from the proper use of leverage can be measured in the form of higher earnings. However, in other circumstances, setting one earnings total against another can be misleading. The criterion for measuring the potential benefits comes from the calculation of a firm's *return on investment,* or ROI.

The ROI calculation measures the earnings a business generates as a proportion of stockholders' equity. For example, if a business with $200,000 in stockholders' equity earns $30,000 in a year, the calculation becomes:

$$\text{Return on Investment} = \frac{\text{Earnings}}{\text{Stockholders' Equity}}$$

$$\text{ROI} = \frac{\$\ 30,000}{\$200,000}$$

$$\text{ROI} = 15\%$$

On one level, the ROI calculation measures the increase in the value of the stockholders' investment from a firm's earnings. On another level, it becomes a tool for analyzing the comparative performance of different businesses: That is, a larger ROI suggests a better performance.

The earnings total used in the ROI calculation recognizes a firm's income-tax obligation. After all, the business—and its stockholders—ultimately benefits only from after–tax earnings. Also, the denominator in the calculation employs the stockholders' equity total as it stands at the beginning of the business year. While that may appear obvious, some financial philosophers believe the calculation requires an *average* equity total, since earnings accrue incrementally throughout the year.

That approach complicates a straightforward concept. Moreover, using the equity total as it stands at the beginning of a business year provides a criterion more suitable for comparative analysis.

LEVERAGE AND RETURN ON INVESTMENT

One of the direct benefits of leverage can be summarized in Cash Flow Concept 54:

54: Leverage increases the stockholders' return on investment.

For an existing business, that result also leads to higher earnings. However, as our first illustration of the relationship between leverage and ROI indicates, the two results are not necessarily synonymous.

Let's look at the experience of Brad Tallmann, an entrepreneurial investor who recently considered a major investment in a new plumbing supply operation. Tallmann centered his analysis on the following characteristics of the proposed investment:

1. The business required $1,000,000 in total assets to operate profitably

2. Given those assets, the business promised earnings of $150,000 in the first year, excluding any potential interest expenses

3. The cash was available to finance the $1,000,000 in required assets with an equal dollar equity investment

4. Alternatively, he could utilize as little as $200,000 in cash equity and borrow the funds necessary to finance the difference in required assets

5. Any borrowed funds will carry a 10% annual cost

Recognizing his options, Tallmann analyzed the proposed investment using four different financial structures. Table 18–1 measures the net earnings (after interest costs) and ROI that would result from each alternative. Let's examine Tallmann's potential return using both the earnings and ROI criteria.

TABLE 18–1 Leverage and ROI

| | Alternative Financial Structures | | | |
	1	2	3	4
Total Assets	$1,000,000	$1,000,000	$1,000,000	$1,000,000
Total Liabilities (10% annual cost)	—	200,000	500,000	800,000
Stockholders' Equity	1,000,000	800,000	500,000	200,000
Earnings before Interest Costs	150,000	150,000	150,000	150,000
Interest Cost	—	20,000	50,000	80,000
Earnings	$ 150,000	$ 130,000	$ 100,000	$ 70,000
Return on Investment	15%	16 1/4%	20%	35%

First, as he increases the use of debt instead of equity, Tallmann sees the projected earnings from the new venture drop. For example, using $1,000,000 in equity, with no debt, promises $150,000 in earnings. At the other extreme, coupling $800,000 in debt with $200,000 in equity, earnings from the venture drop to $70,000. The interest costs associated with the debt absorb the $80,000 difference.

Thus, using earnings as a criterion, leverage actually appears to be detrimental to a business. However, the ROI criterion contradicts that assessment and substantiates Cash Flow Concept 54. Tallmann increases the return on the dollars he invests in the new business by using less equity and more leverage. Indeed, an 80% leverage factor raises his ROI on the minimum $200,000 investment to 35%, compared to the 15% return he gains by avoiding any debt at all.

Obviously, if Tallmann seeks the maximum possible return on his investments, he will select the option that requires the fewest equity dollars. That allows him to use the remaining cash for profitable use elsewhere. Carried to the limit, an investor will never commit a single dollar more than necessary. However, he cannot make the investment decision without considering the element of risk inevitably associated with leverage, as discussed later in this chapter.

Let's look at the same concept from a more familiar perspective.

LEVERAGE AND EARNINGS

Leverage does *not* have to lower earnings to induce a higher return on investment. Indeed, the example of Brad Tallmann's analysis emphasized the critical relationship between leverage and return on the stockholders' investment.

Here, we will examine the benefits an existing business gains from the use of borrowed funds. Our illustration relies on an analysis performed by the Hopeful Company, a growing business seeking to expand. We will assume that the company will open the next business year with the financial structure illustrated in Table 18-2: that is, $1,000,000 in total assets, balanced by $500,000 each in liabilities and stockholders' equity.

Based on several assumptions, the company projected the results of financing the next year's anticipated growth with either debt or equity:
1. Earnings from operations (before deducting interest expenses) historically provide a 15% return on the firm's average investment in assets.
2. The projected expansion calls for a $500,000 increase in the firm's average investment in assets.
3. The firm can finance the increase in assets with either debt or new equity; the firm absorbs a 10% average expense from the use of debt.

Proceeding from the beginning financial structure, Table 18-2 summarizes

TABLE 18-2 Debt vs. Equity Financing for Expansion

THE HOPEFUL COMPANY

	Beginning	Equity Financing	Debt Financing
Total Assets	$1,000,000	$1,500,000	$1,500,000
Total Liabilities	500,000	500,000	1,000,000
Stockholders' Equity	$ 500,000	$1,000,000	$ 500,000
Earnings before Interest (15% of average investment in assets)	$ 150,000	$ 225,000	$ 225,000
Less: Interest Expense	(50,000)	(50,000)	(100,000)
Net Earnings	**$ 100,000**	**$ 175,000**	**$ 125,000**
Return on Investment	**20%**	**17.5%**	**25%**

the effect that both debt and equity will have on Hopeful's earnings, as well as the return on the stockholders' investment.

Thus, the Hopeful Company increases earnings in either instance. Certainly, proper financial management should use any external funds profitably, whether debt or equity. No other result justifies or attracts cash from either source.

However, as might be anticipated, using debt to finance Hopeful's expansion provides a larger return on investment for the firm's stockholders. Net worth, as a proportion of the firm's beginning equity, increases more with the proper use of leverage. This reinforces Cash Concept 54.

Of course, leverage is not automatically beneficial. Indeed, to use borrowed funds properly, you must work within some natural constraints.

ONE LIMIT ON LEVERAGE

One of the limits on leverage can be summarized in Cash Flow Concept 55:

55: To benefit from leverage, a firm's return on assets must exceed the cost of debt.

Before illustrating this natural limit, we should establish a common view of the term *return on assets,* or ROA.

ROA measures a firm's earnings as a percentage of its total asset investment. For example, if a business has $100,000 in earnings and $1,000,000 in total assets, the ROA calculation becomes:

$$\text{Return on Assets} = \frac{\text{Net Earnings}}{\text{Total Assets}}$$

$$\text{ROA} = \frac{\$100,000}{\$1,000,000} = 10\%$$

In this instance, the total assets figure may represent the firm's investment at the beginning of the year, the end of the year, or the average that prevails throughout the year. The latter alternative, perhaps using monthly balance-sheet totals to compute average assets, offers the more logical approach. At the same time, any of the three alternatives should be satisfactory so long as you maintain consistency from one year to the next.

We will return to the analysis done by the Hopeful Company to illustrate the relationship between ROA and leverage costs. The firm still projects a $500,000 increase in assets. Also, we still assume that using leverage to finance those assets will impose a 10% annual interest expense. However, we will alter one point in the analysis and assume that the firm is unsure of the return it can anticipate from the *incremental* assets associated with the expansion. Consequently,

TABLE 18–3 How ROA Limits Leverage

THE HOPEFUL COMPANY

ROA ($500,000 in incremental assets financed with borrowed funds)	5%	10%	15%
Leverage Cost	10%	10%	10%
Incremental Earnings before Interest	$25,000	$50,000	$75,000
Interest Expense (10%)	(50,000)	(50,000)	(50,000)
Net Change in Earnings	**($25,000)**	**—**	**$25,000**

the analysis considers the ultimate change in earnings across the three most likely outcomes—a 5%, 10%, and 15% ROA.

Table 18–3 reflects that analysis and affirms Cash Flow Concept 55. Thus, should the Hopeful Company realize less than a 10% return on the proposed incremental assets, the expansion will actually reduce earnings. Achieving a 10% return on the new assets leaves earnings unchanged.

However, should the return on assets exceed the cost of the debt (as in Column 3), the use of leverage leads to higher earnings. In that event, borrowing benefits the bottom line.

ASSET TURNOVER AND RETURN ON INVESTMENT

Part Two demonstrated the benefits a business derives from a reduction in the average size of its investment in accounts receivable and inventory. A reduction in either instance reduces the total cash capability necessary to support those investments, contributes to a better cash flow, and leads to higher earnings.

Now, we can use the ROI calculation to measure those benefits from another perspective and find that a lower average asset investment for any constant sales volume increases the stockholders' return on investment.

Table 18–4 helps prove that point as it compares the ROI generated by two closely comparable businesses: Company A and Company B.

Both firms enjoyed $100,000 in earnings from a $2,000,000 annual sales volume. Moreover, each business employs a 50% leverage factor: One-half of each firm's assets is financed with debt.

However, Company A carries a $1,000,000 investment in total assets, while Company B generates the same sales volume with only $800,000 in assets. By dividing annual sales by each firm's total investment in assets, we see that Company B turns its total asset base two and a half times a year, while Company A manages to turn its assets only twice.

Ultimately, the faster turnover rate reduces the stockholders' investment required to achieve any sales volume. As indicated in Table 18–4, then, Company B's stockholders enjoyed a 25% return on investment, while Company A's investors earned 5% less.

TABLE 18–4 Asset Turnover and ROI

	Company A	Company B
Total Assets	$1,000,000	$ 800,000
Total Liabilities	$ 500,000	$ 400,000
Stockholders' Equity	500,000	400,000
Liabilities and Equity	$1,000,000	$ 800,000
Sales	$2,000,000	$2,000,000
Profit Margin	5%	5%
Earnings	$ 100,000	$ 100,000
Asset Turnover	2	2.5
ROI	**20%**	**25%**

To match that return, Company A must increase its sales to $2,500,000 while holding its asset investment at $1,000,000. (We ignore the lower cost of debt that also comes from a faster asset turnover. As you turn your assets more rapidly and reduce the size of your average investment, you also reduce the need for leverage.)

That potential provides another boost for earnings and improves the firm's ROI even more. This should encourage you once again to exercise the tenets of competent component management. Turning your assets more rapidly—meaning that you are using them more efficiently—increases your return on investment.

LEVERAGE AND RISK

The relationship between the cost of leverage and the return on a firm's assets implicates the other major limit on the use of leverage: That is, while leverage can increase earnings and ROI, the opposite outcome is always a possibility. Remember this fact as Cash Flow Concept 56:

56: Risk is a natural companion of leverage.

Indeed, using leverage *inevitably* imposes an element of risk on the firm. On one level, the risk may lead to lower rather than higher earnings. On another, leverage may temporarily turn a profitable business into a losing operation. Carried to the worst extreme, the improper use of leverage can destroy a business.

Financial analysts employ complex models to measure the element of risk associated with various degrees of leverage in a firm's financial structure. However, complex models are not necessary to illustrate the fundamental relationship. Instead, we will examine a simpler view.

The Uncertainty in Futurity

A business seldom increases its leverage—debt as a percentage of total assets—merely to finance its current level of operations. Of course, a business might use debt to replace obsolete or worn-out equipment. But in most instances, leverage usually precedes—indeed, anticipates—a projected increase in sales volume.

The process follows a logical course. First, a business projects a larger sales volume. Perhaps it intends to expand into new areas, introduce a new product, or merely press for a larger share of its existing market.

Then, as a necessary precedent to achieving any such projection, the business must increase its investment in inventory. That, in turn, may also be preceded by an expansion in fixed assets. Using borrowed funds to finance the necessary increase in assets increases the leverage factor in the business.

Should a business achieve the projected sales increase, then leverage again offers benefits. At the same time, should the higher volume fail to follow the projected course, the increased leverage costs may lead to lower earnings.

The potential for more than one outcome defines the element of risk associated with leverage: Uncertainty is a constant companion of futurity. A business's projected volume is subject to all of the vagaries of an uncertain economic environment.

Thus, a business may find resistance to projected expansion from a general economic decline or from increased competition. Technological innovation or a change in consumer tastes may alter customer purchasing habits. A supplier strike may stymie any projection in the best circumstances. Whatever the source of the problem, the presence of such potential makes the use of leverage a risky proposition.

Of course, even the business that uses no leverage at all confronts risk as a natural element of the economic environment. However, when leverage enters a financial structure, the element of risk acquires greater importance. Thus, as leverage increases the return for the business that achieves its goals, it also increases the penalty inflicted on the business that falls below its projections. Now, let's examine the alternative outcome.

LEVERAGE, RISK, AND RETURN

Our discussion serves two functions.

First, it demonstrates the interrelationships between risk, return, and the use of leverage. Although leverage can benefit a business that achieves its goals, when volume falls below projected levels, the business using leverage suffers a larger setback.

Second, as a logical extension of the basic concept, it shows how the risks associated with any operation increase as leverage increases. Low levels of leverage involve little risk; high levels of leverage involve high levels of risk. You must find the level for your business that provides the best return for the risk you are willing to accept.

These two points can be crystallized in Cash Flow Concept 57:

57: Leverage imposes risk on a business in exchange for the promise of a higher return.

We will go back to part of Brad Tallmann's analysis of his proposed investment in a new plumbing supply operation to illustrate the fundamental relationships. Tallmann's initial analysis compared the earnings and return on investment that came from four alternative financial structures. However, the analysis proceeded on the assumption that the new business would earn $150,000 before deducting any interest expense. Recognizing the uncertainty inevitably associated with that expected outcome, Tallmann expanded his analysis.

Thus, he estimated the risk associated with the alternative financial structures based on the following assumptions:

1. At any level of sales, the new business would incur $200,000 in fixed costs.
2. Variable costs will average 50% of any sales actually generated.
3. In the worst circumstance, the new company will generate no sales at all; the most optimistic projection anticipates a $2,000,000 sales volume.

Tallmann's analysis proceeded in two steps.

First, he calculated the expected earnings the business would realize from four alternative sales volumes, ranging from the worst to the best possible outcomes. (The calculations measure Earnings Before Interest and Taxes, or EBIT.) Table 18–5 shows the calculations associated with each outcome.

TABLE 18–5 Four Potential EBIT Operating Results

	(1)	(2)	(3)	(4)
Sales	—	$500,000	$1,000,000	$2,000,000
Fixed Costs	($200,000)	(200,000)	(200,000)	(200,000)
Variable Costs (60% of sales)	—	(300,000)	(600,000)	(1,200,000)
EBIT	**($200,000)**	**—**	**$ 200,000**	**$ 600,000**

We note that $500,000 stands as the operational break-even point. Sales in excess of $500,000 will generate profits; sales below that level will leave the firm with a loss. Of course, the break-even point presumes the firm uses no leverage at all.

Then, as the second step in his analysis, Tallmann completed the earnings and ROI calculations, using each of the four alternative leverage factors illustrated in Table 18–1: 0%, 20%, 50%, and 80%. Table 18–6 also includes those calculations in order. (Again, we ignore any potential income-tax obligation as a complicating element. Nevertheless, it would not change the point of the illustration.)

TABLE 18-6 Leverage, Risk, and Return

	Financial Structure 1 (Table 18-1, Zero Leverage)			
EBIT	($200,000)	—	$200,000	$600,000
Interest Expense	—	—	—	—
Net Earnings	($200,000)	—	$200,000	$600,000
ROI	**(20%)**	**—**	**20%**	**60%**
	Financial Structure 2 (Table 18-1, 20% Leverage)			
EBIT	($200,000)	—	$200,000	$600,000
Interest Expense	(20,000)	($20,000)	(20,000)	(20,000)
Net Earnings	($220,000)	($20,000)	$180,000	$580,000
ROI	**(27.5%)**	**(2.5%)**	**22.5%**	**72.5%**
	Financial Structure 3 (Table 18-1, 50% Leverage)			
EBIT	($200,000)	—	$200,000	$600,000
Interest Expense	(50,000)	($50,000)	($50,000)	($50,000)
Net Earnings	($250,000)	($50,000)	$150,000	$550.000
ROI	**(50%)**	**(10%)**	**30%**	**110%**
	Financial Structure 4 (Table 18-1, 80% Leverage)			
EBIT	($200,000)	—	$200,000	$600,000
Interest Expense	(80,000)	($80,000)	($80,000)	($80,000)
Net Earnings	($280,000)	($80,000)	$120,000	$520,000
ROI	**(140%)**	**(40%)**	**60%**	**260%**

Tallmann's analysis emphasizes the critical interrelationships among leverage, risk, and return.

First, in any circumstance, a higher sales volume increases earnings and return on investment. That obvious fact holds true regardless of the financial structure. At the same time, as the firm achieves a higher sales volume, ROI increases dramatically because the financial structure includes greater leverage factors. Thus, if the firm achieves a $2,000,000 sales volume with a financial structure that contains an 80% leverage factor, the stockholders' return on investment reaches a remarkable 260%. Naturally, that result reaffirms Cash Flow Concept 54: Leverage increases ROI.

However, that is the best possible outcome among a set of projections looking into an uncertain future. We will look at the other side of the picture and measure the risk associated with the leverage factors used in the prospective investment.

As leverage enhances the return from a successful venture, it also increases the loss should the firm achieve a minimal volume.

Referring again to Table 18–6, examine the alternative outcomes should the new business achieve only a $500,000 sales volume. If the firm has no leverage, that volume produces a break-even operation. However, using leverage converts the break-even results into a loss, and more leverage leads to a larger loss. Indeed, the 80% leverage factor leads to an $80,000 loss and a 40% *reduction* in stockholders' equity.

As leverage increases the potential return in a business, it also exaggerates the effect of a loss. Table 18–7 summarizes the return on investment that Tallmann should anticipate from each sales volume, beginning with each financial structure distinguished by its leverage factor.

TABLE 18–7 Risk, Return, and Leverage: The Range of Potential Outcome

Range of Potential Sales Volumes	Leverage Factor			
	0%	**20%**	**50%**	**80%**
0	(20%)	(27.5%)	(50%)	(140%)
$ 500,000	—	(2.5%)	(10%)	(40%)
$1,000,000	20%	22.5%	30%	60%
$2,000,000	60%	72.5%	110%	260%

ROI at Each Leverage Factor and Sales Volume

Range of Expected ROIs: Low to High

80%	100%	160%	400%

At the bottom of Table 18–7 is the *range of expected outcomes* associated with each leverage. That range is most relevant to the risk associated with leverage. Thus, when Tallmann projects the results from using absolutely no leverage, the range between the best and worst possible outcomes is 80%. In the worst circumstance (no sales at all), he stands to lose 20% of his original investment. Should the new business achieve a $2,000,000 sales volume, however, using no leverage yields a 60% ROI.

Compare those outcomes to the range that results from the 80% leverage factor. In the worst circumstance, Tallmann could lose, theoretically, 140% of his original investment. When the firm uses leverage, interest expense continues regardless of sales volume.

At the same time, should the business generate $2,000,000 in sales, Tallmann's ROI will reach 260%. In one year, he will realize a return that is more than two and a half times his original investment.

Thus, with an 80% leverage factor, using ROI as a criterion, we find a 400%

range in the anticipated results from the alternative possible sales volumes. That range is five times more than that using no leverage.

The range differentials demonstrate the critical interrelationships among leverage, risk, and return. Thus, a successful outcome returns larger benefits to the business that uses leverage. And an unsuccessful outcome leads to a larger loss.

Leverage: A Mechanical View

This chapter, which offers a view of leverage more familiar to most businessmen, outlines the distinguishing characteristics associated with the alternative forms of leverage available to a business. We separate these alternatives into three major categories and differentiate the mechanics involved with the extension and repayment of the borrowed funds. Adopting a mechanical view of the major borrowing alternatives is designed to help you better fit each lending method to the circumstance that raises the need for leverage. Indeed, one alternative form of leverage serves some purposes better than others.

More important from our perspective, however, is that using the improper alternative for a particular circumstance can lead ultimately to a cash flow problem. That threat exists even though the other elements in the firm's financial structure appear balanced.

We also include illustrations of the two primary methods lenders use to calculate interest charges, and later we extend the discussion to review the collateral requirements often associated with a business loan. Those requirements can affect the amount of leverage available to a business as well as to the source. Indeed, except for the few businesses that qualify for unsecured credit consideration, the question of collateral often is a major element in the potential use of any leverage at all. That consideration affects both the borrower's decision to request a loan and the lender's decision to grant it.

Certainly, not all lenders are the same. Different credit criteria, lending methods, and external constraints make one more suitable for some circumstances than others. As those differences become apparent, you can better relate your own needs to the appropriate lender and facilitate the use of leverage profitably.

Most business loans fall into one of three categories: (1) single payment, (2) revolving, and (3) installment. Of course, any specific business loan may contain elements associated with more than one category. We will discuss each separately.

THE SINGLE-PAYMENT LOAN

A single-payment loan requires repayment in full, including the interest charge, on a predetermined date. Typically, repayment follows the granting of the loan by ninety days or six months. Less frequently, a single-payment loan may extend for only a few days or even for as long as a year.

One characteristic of such a loan is noted in Cash Flow Concept 58:

58: A single-payment loan answers a specific business purpose that provides a well-defined source of repayment.

The lender specifies the required repayment date in the loan document. Before he extends the loan, a well-informed lender also knows the probable source of funds necessary to meet the payment schedule. That source isn't specified in the note, but it should be well understood in advance.

Another characteristic is that most single-payment loans are extended for only a short term, usually for less than a year. The exact maturity of the single-payment loan should coincide with the purpose of the loan, coupled with a realistic projection of the date the funds will be available for repayment. Indeed, both the maturity and the repayment date should be directly related to the purpose of the loan.

The more common single-payment loan answers the seasonal needs of a business. For example, a business may borrow to build inventory in anticipation of its major selling season. The collection of the accounts receivable from the sales provides the cash to repay the loan on schedule.

Of course, the farmer remains the classic example of the seasonal borrower. He borrows to finance his spring planting and then raises (rather than buys) his inventory during the summer. In late summer or early fall, when he harvests his crops, the farmer repays the lender from the proceeds of his sales. The terms and source of repayment are recognized clearly by both the borrower and lender on the day the loan is granted.

Many manufacturers and wholesalers also use seasonal loans. For example, the lawnmower and fertilizer manufacturers and bathing suit and ski distributors need seasonal financing. Indeed, the single-payment loan smooths the cash flow across many business cycles.

Single-payment loans also answer specific, short-term purposes apart from the seasonal requirements that arise in a business. In one instance, a business might borrow to fill a temporary gap in its cash flow. Perhaps the inventory requirements for an unusually large sale drain a firm's cash reserves. Collection of the receivables that result from the sale provides the cash to retire the loan. Or, a business might want to take advantage of a unique and profitable opportunity. The loan may facilitate the purchase of some bargain merchandise or enable the business to obtain quantity or trade discounts.

Calculating the Single-Payment Interest Charge

Elements associated with calculating the borrowing cost of a single-payment loan can increase that cost significantly. The lender extending the loan charges a stated annual interest rate, pro rated for the fraction of the year that usually makes up the term of the loan.

For example, assume a business borrows $100,000 from a lender who charges a 12% annual interest rate. If the loan extends for a full year, the interest charge totals $12,000. However, should the term of the loan be only six months, the interest calculation becomes:

1. $100,000 × 12% = $12,000
2. $12,000 × .5 (six months) = $6,000

This is a straightforward *simple interest-rate* calculation.

Unfortunately, the simple interest rate is often not so straightforward. Measuring the true cost is actually more complicated because of two traditional lender practices.

First, lenders seldom calculate interest charges based on the calendar year or specific fractions of that year. Instead, they measure the term by 90, 180, or 365 days.

Second, lenders do not use an annual interest rate applied to the pro rata portion of the year of the loan. Instead, they charge a daily rate derived from the annual stated rate. While that may imply a proper pro rata application, the result differs because of the calculation process that determines the daily interest charge.

That calculation operates on the presumption that a year has only 360 days. Thus, using the 12% annual charge, the average daily charge is found as:

$$\frac{12\%}{360} = .000\overline{33}\% \text{ per day}$$

The lender applies that rate to each dollar you use each day. Unfortunately for the business borrower, that daily rate exceeds the rate that would come from the same calculation using a 365-day year.

To illustrate the effect that difference has on the actual annual cost of borrowing, let's compare the actual dollar cost a business incurs from the above daily rate versus a true 12% annual cost:

1. $100,000 × .000$\overline{3}$3% per day × 365 = $12,165
2. $100,000 × 12%   =   12,000

Incremental Cost $ 165

In this instance, using the 360-day year increases the cost of borrowing by $165.

Of course, that difference isn't significant to any business in a position to use substantial funds profitably. At the same time, as a matter of business principle, recognize that the practice increases the lender's earnings at your expense.

We should also note a significant advantage you gain from a lender who charges you a daily rate: You usually incur no prepayment penalty for retiring a loan prior to the original maturity date.

For example, assume you obtained the above $100,000 loan for a six-month, or 180-day, period. However, 45 days after obtaining the loan, you find that you can repay the lender. The lender will therefore charge you only for the 45 days you actually used his funds, rather than for the 180 days. That is a logical, equitable approach for both the borrower and the lender.

THE REVOLVING LOAN

A revolving loan serves as a natural complement to the cash flow cycle in a business. Remember the potential benefit as Cash Flow Concept 59:

59: A revolving loan provides a source of flexible leverage that answers a number of cash needs.

A revolving loan begins with the lender's approval of a specified *line of credit,* which authorizes the advance of any loan amount up to the limit specified in the line. However, the revolving loan agreement involves more than a single advance followed by a scheduled repayment. Instead, the loan fluctuates in direct response to the peaks and valleys in the borrower's cash flow cycle.

Thus, whenever the borrower foresees a demand that will exhaust his cash reserves, the lender advances funds sufficient to maintain a positive cash position. Conversely, as the natural cycle generates funds in excess of those needed for normal reserves, the business repays all or part of the funds advanced by the lender.

The process repeats itself as often as these peaks and valleys occur in the firm's cash flow. Figure 19–1 provides a simplified picture of that relationship.

The figure includes the normal cash flow cycle. However, as suggested by the overlapping circles, the normal collection of accounts receivable is insufficient to pay for inventory purchases in a timely manner.

Foreseeing that gap, the business obtains an advance from its revolving loan to ensure a prompt payment record. The eventual collection of the receivables repays the advance. In most circumstances, however, while the size of the cash flow gap expands and contracts in response to the fluctuating needs of the business, it seldom disappears completely.

You should recognize the revolving loan as a source of flexible leverage that can answer a number of business needs not served by a single-payment or installment loan.

One measure of flexibility comes from the elimination of any predetermined

FIGURE 19–1 The Revolving Loan and the Cash Flow Cycle

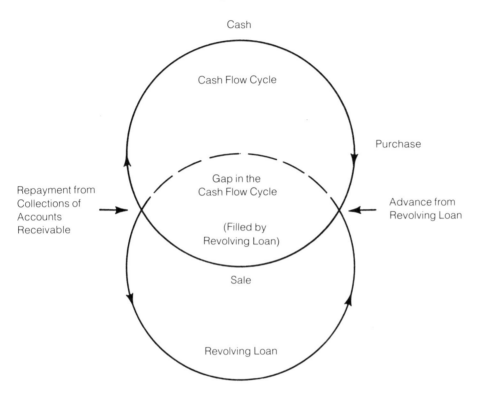

payment schedule. Of course, a revolving loan is not a perpetual, open-ended arrangement. Usually, the loan agreement matures one year after initiation. However, so long as the lender is satisfied with the relationship, he usually allows annual extensions or renewals.

The revolving loan also provides flexibility and a source of growth money for the business that is projecting expansion. At the same time, if the anticipated growth does not result, the firm suffers no unnecessary interest expense. Indeed, the revolving loan imposes no expenses, while it provides assurance that the cash needs that come from expansion will not go unfilled.

The flexibility to borrow or not to borrow suggests another advantage that comes with the revolving loan: The borrower pays a simple daily interest rate for the funds used. This provides reasonable incentive to borrow as little as possible and to repay as soon as possible, which benefits both the borrower and the lender. The borrower can hold the cost of his credit consideration to a minimum; at the same time, the lender is assured that the loan will revolve as agreed. That fluctuation adds some measure of insurance to the lender.

A revolving loan does not provide permanent credit consideration. The loan has a specified maturity date when all unpaid advances fall due. While that usually results in an extension of the original agreement for another year, the borrower usually must meet certain continuing financial requirements.

And recognize that the lack of positive action to ensure renewal makes the total amount of any unpaid advances a single-payment note on the expiration date of the revolving loan agreement.

THE INSTALLMENT LOAN

An installment loan requires repayment of a fraction of the original loan at regular intervals. The fraction repaid usually comes on a monthly basis proportionate to the terms of the loan measured in months. For example, each payment in a $12,000 installment loan repayable in one year will include $1,000 in principal repayment, plus a portion of the interest due to the lender. One year usually is the shortest term installment loan available to a business. While shorter terms exist, they are usually better served by single-payment loans.

At the other end of the continuum, it is not uncommon to see an installment loan extend for three, five, or ten years, depending upon the purpose and circumstance of the loan. Indeed, a business may repay a mortgage loan over a twenty- or thirty-year period with equal monthly installment payments.

The repayment schedule that distinguishes the installment loan should reflect the purpose of the loan. The main purpose is summarized in Cash Flow Concept 60:

60: Installment loans finance the purchase of productive assets that should contribute a positive cash flow.

Most businesses use installment loans to purchase fixed assets, and typically, those assets have a useful life that exceeds the term of the loan. Thus, a business might employ an installment loan repayable over three years to finance the acquisition of equipment with a five-year productive life.

Of course, the productivity of the equipment purchased, measured by the cash flow from a rise in revenues or a reduction in costs, should be sufficient to meet the required loan payments and provide some bottom-line benefits for the business.

When you analyze a prospective fixed-asset acquisition, don't forget the cash that flows from the depreciation process, a significant element in that analysis. Certainly, measuring the potential return from proposed fixed-asset acquisitions is natural for most businessmen. However, calculating the cost and repayment schedule associated with an installment loan is a less familiar task.

Calculating the Installment-Loan Interest Charge

Lenders use an *add-on* interest rate to calculate the total interest charge for an installment loan. However, the *true annual interest rate* is approximately twice the add-on rate, and that apparent discrepancy confuses many borrowers.

To eliminate that confusion, we will review the calculation process that determines the total interest charge and monthly payment for a standard installment loan. Then, we will bridge the gap between the add-on and true annual interest rate.

Our illustration begins with the Major Company's request to borrow $10,000 to finance the purchase of new machinery for its main production line. The company has the capacity to repay the loan in monthly installments over three years, or 36 months.

The Major Company's lender approves the request, noting that he will charge the firm a 7% add-on interest rate for the loan. The calculation of the total interest charge and required monthly payment then proceeds as follows:

1. The lender multiplies the principal balance of the loan ($10,000) by the add-on interest rate.
2. Then, the lender multiplies the product of that calculation ($700) by the term of the loan measure in *years*. The calculation provides the total $2,100 interest charge for the $10,000 loan.
3. To find the monthly payment necessary to repay the loan, the lender adds the total interest charge ($2,100) to the principal balance ($10,000); then he divides that total ($12,000) by the term of the loan measured in *months*.

In sequence, the calculation process becomes:

1. $10,000 × 7% × 3 = $2,100 = Total Interest Charge
2. $10,000 + $2,100 = $12,100 = Total Amount Payable to Lender
3. $12,100 ÷ 36 = $336.11 = Monthly Payment

Each monthly payment includes $277.78 in principal and $58.33 in interest each month, or 1/36 of each total.

Repeating the calculation process with any principal balance, add-on interest rate, and repayment period will provide the total dollar interest cost and monthly payment for an installment loan.

The Interest Rate Gap

The true annual interest rate a borrower pays for an installment loan is approximately *twice* the add-on rate used to calculate the actual dollar charge. For example, the Major Company's 7% add-on rate translates into a true annual interest rate of approximately 14%. That apparent discrepancy arises from two interrelated facts.

First, as shown in the calculation, the lender applies the add-on rate to the full amount of the original loan to calculate the total interest charge. However, a borrower initiates repayment of an installment loan one month after receiving the funds. Thus, the average size of the loan measured across the full term of repayment is one-half of the amount originally funded. That, in turn, approximately doubles the interest cost expressed originally as an add-on rate.

We can use the Major Company's installment loan to illustrate the translation of an add-on into a true annual interest rate. The company pays a total of $2,100, or $700 per year, for a $10,000 loan repayable in equal installments over three years. However, since the Major Company begins repayment one month after obtaining the loan, the average loan outstanding may be found as follows:

$$\text{Average Loan} = \frac{\text{Initial Loan} + \text{Principal Amount of Last Payment}}{2}$$

$$\text{Average Loan} = \frac{\$10,000 + 278}{2} = \$5,139$$

Now, to identify the true annual interest rate applicable to the borrowed funds, we relate the annual interest cost to the average loan outstanding for the term of the note:

$$\text{True Annual Interest Rate} = \frac{700}{\$5,139} = 13.6\%$$

Of course, the actual dollar cost of the loan remains the same. But using this calculation process, you can identify the true cost of borrowing. Or, you can avoid the calculation process altogether. Instead, use Table 19–1, which translates the common add-on rates into the true annual interest rate based on the term of the installment note.

The Declining-Balance Interest Charge

An installment loan with equal monthly payments may use a more straightforward interest charge calculation than the add-on method. That alternative applies the appropriate interest rate to the principal balance left outstanding after each installment payment. Consequently, although each installment payment is equal, the proportion devoted to interest decreases as the principal balance drops. A simple illustration demonstrates the concept.

Assume a business borrows $100,000, repayable in five equal annual installments over five years. If the lender charges the firm a 10% annual interest rate, the annual payments become:

Year	Annual Payment	Interest	Debt Retirement	Remaining Balance
1	$26,378	10,000	$16,378	83,622
2	26,378	8,362	18,016	65,606
3	26,378	6,561	19,817	47,789
4	26,378	4,579	21,799	23,990
5	26,389	2,399	23,990	—

Thus, the first annual installment payment includes $10,000 in interest. That is the appropriate charge, since the firm has the use of the funds for a full year. The remaining $16,378 in the payment reduces the principal balance of the loan.

In the second year, the 10% interest rate applies only to the $83,622 outstanding after the first principal reduction. The second annual payment includes $8,362 in interest, plus an $18,016 reduction in principal. The process then repeats itself until the borrower fully repays the principal balance. The last payment is slightly higher to complete the payoff.

TABLE 19-1 Converting Add-On to True Annual Interest Rates

Term of Loan (year)	Add-On Rates					
	5%	6%	7%	8%	9%	10%
1	9.10	10.90	12.68	14.45	16.22	17.97
2	9.32	11.13	12.91	14.68	16.43	18.16
3	9.31	11.08	12.83	14.55	16.24	17.92
4	9.24	10.97	12.68	14.35	15.99	17.60
5	9.15	10.85	12.50	14.13	15.71	17.27

True Annual Percentage Rates

The same concept applies to monthly installment loans established on the declining balance method of repayment. Of course, in that instance, the lender employs a daily interest rate to determine the interest due each month.

In any circumstance, you should recognize the true annual interest rate charged by a lender, the calculation method used to apply that rate, and the actual dollar cost of the loan. That is the only way to compare the costs of alternative sources of borrowed funds properly.

Hybrid Loans

Hybrid loans often combine one or more elements of the three categories of loans. For example, one hybrid loan might call for installment payments of $2,000 per month for twenty-three months, with a single "balloon" payment due in the twenty-fourth month. Alternatively, a revolving line of credit might reduce a firm's maximum credit line by $10,000 per month, allowing the business to fluctuate its loan within that maximum.

Most often, a lender designs a hybrid loan repayment schedule to correspond with some unique pattern in the borrower's cash flow. Thus, the installment loan with the balloon payment might reflect the borrower's limited cash flow in the early life of a fixed-asset investment. Presumably, the eventual productivity of the asset will generate the cash necessary for repayment. Similarly, the reducing line of credit may coincide with the expectation that cash from projected earnings will reduce the need for borrowed funds.

In any circumstance, don't restrict your financial vision to the three basic types of loans. A creative lender adapts his credit consideration to your special needs.

COLLATERAL CONSIDERATIONS

Few businesses borrow without pledging collateral to the lender to secure the loan. That pledge, which may include accounts receivable, inventory, or fixed assets, may be little more than a formality that adds confidence to the lender's credit decision. Or it may directly affect the firm's borrowing power.

A collateral pledge to secure a loan seldom justifies credit consideration. Instead, it provides the final margin of safety that protects a lender. The role collateral plays in the credit decision becomes apparent as we review the rank it holds as the anticipated source of repayment for a loan.

Of course, the primary source of repayment of any credit consideration should come from the normal operations of the firm. Thus, the source of repayment for a single-payment loan comes from the cyclical or seasonal liquidation of assets held in the cash flow cycle. Repayment for an installment or revolving loan should proceed from the projected earnings of the business.

In the latter instance, the lender looks for a historical earnings trend that promises the future profitability necessary to retire any credit consideration. Those potential earnings also provide a secondary source of repayment for a single-payment loan if the firm's cyclical asset liquidation does not proceed as planned.

Of course, earnings projections extend into an uncertain future. Consequently, the lender looks for a potential source of repayment in addition to projected earnings. The strength held in the borrower's financial structure usually serves as that source. The lender also measures the ability of a business to absorb a financial setback without losing the ability to honor its credit consideration.

Finally, the lender seeks collateral as the final hedge against an error in judgment. If a business loses instead of earns, thus eroding its financial strength too far, the lender can liquidate the collateral as the final source of repayment. Thus, collateral doesn't justify credit consideration: It merely adds support for the lender's positive view of a borrower's creditworthiness. Indeed, collateral makes a good loan better.

COLLATERAL AND BORROWING POWER

Although collateral does not directly justify the extension of credit, it often influences the amount of the credit. Thus, an approved loan might become some proportionate amount of the full value of the pledged asset.

Of course, numerous considerations interact to determine the advance rate, the funds a lender will grant against any collateral. However, the creditworthy borrower can expect the following general relationships to hold true:

Collateral	Advance Rate	Probable Loan Limits (per each $10,000 in collateral value)
Accounts Receivable	60–80%	$6,000–8,000
Inventory	20–50%	$2,000–5,000
Machinery and Equipment	70–90%	$7,000–9,000

Certainly, the specific applicable advance rate varies widely with the circumstance. For example, a financially strong borrower qualifies for a higher advance rate than a business confronting a major cash flow problem. And, of course, the more certain the value held in the collateral, the more the lender is likely to advance.

The advance rate also will vary among lenders. Commercial finance companies feel comfortable advancing funds at rates that approach the high end of the ranges listed above. Alternatively, banks will be more likely to adopt the lower limits. Moreover, lenders within the same category often adopt different views.

Of course, the lender still relies primarily on the profitability and financial strength of the borrower. Collateral doesn't justify a loan; it merely increases the probability of repayment.

Leverage: A Practical View

Few businessmen have the time or inclination to measure the risks associated with the use of leverage, or to calculate the relationship between the cost and the return on assets financed with any debt. Instead, most businessmen adopt a practical, functional approach to borrowing. They use leverage to solve a problem or to serve a specific, profitable purpose.

Recognizing these facts, we will identify the practical purposes that encourage businesses to borrow. Then, we illustrate the benefits that can come from that decision.

THE NEED TO BORROW

No business should incur any debt haphazardly. Any debt employed by a business should serve a specific, well-defined purpose. Borrowed funds may solve a problem, facilitate growth, or merely provide the cash capability to support a larger, more profitable investment in inventory. Whatever the circumstance, a clear purpose should precede the assumption of any obligation. Also, the form of leverage should be matched to the purpose.

Thus, it is illogical and financially dangerous to purchase a major fixed asset with funds obtained from a single-payment loan due in ninety days. The obligation will come due long before the asset generates the cash necessary to honor it. Indeed, the business may be forced to drain its cash reserves, or to seek some alternative credit consideration sufficient to retire the short-term loan.

A business also should not exploit a long-term installment debt to finance a seasonal increase in inventory. This exhausts credit lines that are better suited to finance the purchase of fixed assets.

Of course, when you borrow, you accept the risk that the funds will not return an amount sufficient to pay the cost of borrowing. That risk will hurt your earnings. You also accept the risk that your business might lack the capacity to honor its debt obligation in a timely manner. This is the risk of default. Should the lender allow extension or renewal, you suffer no more than a measure of financial embarrassment. Of course, chances are that the potential default will limit future credit consideration, and this could hurt your business as well as your reputation.

Finally, in the most unfortunate circumstance, you also accept the risk that the ultimate inability to satisfactorily honor your credit obligations will lead to financial failure. This is the risk of bankruptcy.

A business may borrow to satisfy any number of objectives. However, most circumstances fall into several categories:

1. Solve a cash flow problem
2. Facilitate growth
3. Generate supplier profits
4. Enhance financial flexibility

This list includes most business purposes for borrowing that fall within cash flow management. Reminding ourselves of that perspective, let's examine the most important justification for the use of leverage in a business.

USING LEVERAGE TO SOLVE A CASH FLOW PROBLEM

In the broadest sense, any use of leverage solves a cash flow problem. After all, the business with sufficient internal cash capability achieves its business objectives without external financing. However, this purpose for borrowing seldom threatens a company's financial integrity. It might earn less because it grows more slowly or misses supplier discounts, but the lack of external financing doesn't cause financial embarrassment.

Indeed, we concentrate here on the cash flow problems that can impair the performance or threaten the survival of a business. Thus, we will consider the potential benefits a business derives from using leverage to:

1. Fill a gap in the cash flow cycle
2. Gain the cash capability necessary to achieve a profitable level of operations

Of course, more than one potential solution exists for many of these problems. However, we will assume that the businessman, recognizing the fundamental precepts of component and structural management, finds the use of leverage the logical solution to his problem.

Filling a Gap in the Cash Flow Cycle

A business has a gap in its cash flow cycle anytime it lacks the capacity to meet all of its obligations in a timely manner. The problem appears when accounts payable remain unpaid beyond the seller's original terms; or when scheduled note payments fall past due; or, in the worst circumstance, when the business fails to pay its employees promptly. Certainly, most businessmen recognize these potential problems, but keep in mind Cash Flow Concept 61:

61: Leverage can fill a gap in your cash flow.

We will use a simple example to demonstrate a natural business circumstance that generates a gap in the cash flow cycle. Leverage erects the natural bridge across that gap. The example also reestablishes a fundamental concept that remains critical to positive cash flow management.

The example comes from the experience of the Tyson Company, an architectural design firm. As a financially conservative operation, Tyson traditionally has functioned on a cash basis. The firm used no debt. However, a recent management decision created a cash flow problem that necessitated a change in that policy. The problem came with the acceptance of a design contract that led to a $100,000 increase in the firm's monthly revenue. The terms of the contract, coupled with the special nature of Tyson's business, created an inevitable gap in the cash flow cycle.

One element of the problem was that Tyson's employees expected to be paid twice a month, on the fifteenth and the thirtieth. The other element came from the terms of the new contract, which restricted Tyson to a monthly billing schedule for work performed by the employees. Moreover, the contract allowed Tyson's customer an additional thirty days for payment after the billing date.

Table 20–1, a simple cash budget, identifies the gap in Tyson's cash flow that develops naturally from these circumstances.

The firm must meet payroll and cash overhead requirements for three pay periods prior to receipt of payment for the first month's billing. The budget projects a maximum $135,000 gap in the middle of the second month.

The gap then drops to $80,000 after Tyson collects payment for the revenue billed at the end of the first month, then it builds again to $125,000. Lacking adequate cash reserves, Tyson must use leverage to fill the gap or risk defaulting on the contract.

Of course, in many circumstances, a gap in cash flow is more subtle than in

TABLE 20–1 A Gap in the Cash Flow Cycle

TYSON ENGINEERING

	Cash Out	Cash In	Cash Gap
9/15	$45,000	—	$ 45,000
9/30	45,000	—	90,000
10/15	45,000	—	135,000
10/30	45,000	$100,000	80,000
11/15	45,000	—	125,000
11/30	$45,000	$100,000	$ 70,000

the case of Tyson Engineering. A business watches a prompt payment record deteriorate as a shrinking bank account forces a deferral of payments to suppliers. Or a business finds itself short of the cash required to retire a single-payment note originally extended for ninety days.

In fact, a business may have a large gap in its cash flow that is not directly apparent. We will illustrate that possibility and emphasize again the importance of matching the form of the leverage to the circumstance.

Filling Another Gap in the Cash Flow Cycle

A business with sufficient cash capability, measured by the requirements set by its investment in operating funds, accounts receivable, and inventory, can still suffer from a gap in its cash flow. This problem arises whenever the business improperly matches the structure of its debt to its needs. We summarize this problem in Cash Flow Concept 62:

62: A potential gap in cash flow is not always obvious.

Table 20–2 summarizes the circumstance of Darnell, Inc., a modestly successful automobile-parts distributor. The firm's cash flow cycle, partially represented by its investment in receivables and inventory, reflects several characteristics:

1. Darnell presently generates $90,000 a month in sales, which produces $3,500 a month in earnings
2. A 45-day average collection period (not subject to reduction) translates into a $135,000 investment in accounts receivable
3. The $189,000 in inventory, sufficient for three months' sales, represents the minimum practical investment for the present sales volume

TABLE 20–2 Leverage Management: Matching Form to Circumstance

DARNELL, INC.

	Before Restructuring	After Restructuring
Cash	$ 11,000	$ 23,000
Accounts Receivable	135,000	135,000
Inventory	189,000	189,000
	$335,000	$347,000
Accounts Payable	$126,000	$ 63,000
Single-Payment Loan	74,000	—
Installment Loan	—	150,000
Total Liabilities	**$200,000**	**$213,000**
Stockholders' Equity	135,000	135,000
Liabilities and Equity	**$335,000**	**$347,000**

Despite the firm's success, the balance sheet summary in Column 1 reflects haphazard leverage management that could lead to a serious cash flow problem. That problem could come from two sources.

First, supplier trade terms prevalent in the industry typically require payment thirty days after purchase. However, Darnell's accounts payable represent two months' purchases. Thus, $63,000 out of that total is one to thirty days past due.

Also, Darnell's balance sheet includes a $74,000 single-payment note. Whether that note is due in one day or ninety days is less important than the fact that Darnell lacks sufficient cash to honor it. The firm's investment in receivables and inventory is not subject to reduction; nor is a significant increase in cash reserves from earnings likely.

Indeed, Darnell presently has a $137,000 gap in its cash flow. This amount is necessary to honor the existing credit consideration as agreed. Of course, the indulgence presently displayed by the firm's creditors does provide the cash capability necessary for a $90,000 monthly volume. But maintaining that volume is subject to the whim of suppliers, who may cease shipments to a slow-paying customer, or a lender who may not renew or extend a single-payment note.

Now, consider the potential benefit Darnell can derive from rational leverage management. Assume the company negotiates a $150,000 installment loan repayable monthly over seven years, perhaps guaranteed or funded by the Small Business Administration. (We discuss such loans in Chapter 22.) The company uses the proceeds from the loan to retire the single-payment loan and pay all past-due accounts payable. Also, Darnell enjoys a $12,000 contribution to its cash reserve.

Of course, Darnell maintains sufficient cash capability for its sales volume. One form of leverage merely replaces another. However, the alternative form of leverage eliminates the gap in the firm's cash flow. No accounts payable remain past due. Darnell has no risk of defaulting on a single-payment note. The firm's earnings are more than sufficient to amortize the monthly payment required to repay the installment loan. Darnell no longer operates at the mercy of its creditors.

Darnell's experience directly demonstrates the relationship between debt service requirements and the cash flow in a business. The relationship between cash flow and debt service requirements often becomes an important element in a lender's decision to extend credit consideration. That relationship also should influence your decision to accept that consideration.

ACHIEVING A PROFITABLE LEVEL OF OPERATIONS

Leverage can help a business achieve a profitable level of operations, but only when the lone obstacle to profitability is insufficient cash capability. So, keep in mind Cash Flow Concept 63:

63: Leverage may provide the cash capability necessary to achieve a profitable sales volume.

Of course, leverage cannot help a business turn around a loss operation that stems from marketing, management, or production problems.

The case of the Bayline Bolt Corporation in Chapter 11 illustrated this potential use of leverage. In that circumstance, the $100,000 used to start the business provided cash capability sufficient for only a break-even sales volume. The firm's natural cash flow cycle at that volume absorbed the full $100,000 in cash.

Then, Bayline's founder negotiated $30,000 in trade credit consideration. This leverage provided the cash capability necessary for a profitable sales volume. Remember, however, that this potential realistically exists only when limited cash capability stands as the only obstacle to a profitable sales volume. Cash Flow Concept 63 is most beneficial for a business operating within reasonable proximity of its break-even sales volume, as in Bayline Bolt's circumstance. In that event, a relatively small increase in sales can have a dramatic effect on earnings.

At the same time, the further a business is from that break-even point, the more questionable the potential benefits from external financing. And, if the distance becomes too great, the business will be unlikely to find a lender to extend such financing.

Using Leverage to Facilitate Growth

Leverage is an essential requirement for any business that seeks rapid growth: That is, any expansion rate that exceeds the cash capability provided by stockholders' equity and retained earnings. We summarize this in Cash Flow Concept 64:

64: Leverage can facilitate growth in a business.

In Chapter 13, we used the Energy Window Company as an example to illustrate that an increasing sales volume inevitably leads to an expansion in asset investment, part of which must be financed with external financing.

Of course, we emphasized the limits on the growth rate imposed by the requirement for external financing. We also should refer to the experience of the Hopeful Company in Chapter 18. The Hopeful Company used leverage to finance growth that increased both earnings and the stockholders' return on investment.

Using Leverage to Generate Supplier Profits

Many businesses use leverage to facilitate profitable purchase and payment practices that help increase earnings. In general terms, we define these benefits as supplier profits. Cash Flow Concept 65 crystallizes these sources of supplier profits:

65: Leverage can lead to supplier profits from trade discounts, quantity discounts, and anticipatory purchases.

Of course, the business with sufficient cash capability doesn't have to use leverage to benefit from supplier profits. Cash capability—not borrowing—provides the benefits. At the same time, it is important to emphasize that a business often can justify the use of leverage and the associated cost to gain the cash capability to take advantage of substantial supplier profits.

Using Leverage to Take Trade Discounts

You will often find that you can profit from using leverage to gain the cash capability necessary to take supplier discounts. To demonstrate that fact, let's examine a case that identifies the actual dollar benefits held in that potential.

The Bonner Company purchases $200,000 in merchandise each month to maintain its investment in inventory at a level appropriate for its projected sales volume. Half of the firm's suppliers offer a 2% discount for payment within ten days, requiring payment in full in thirty days.

Bonner is losing those discounts, although it has the cash capability necessary to pay in thirty days. Presently, the discounts lost reduce Bonner's earnings as follows:

$$\$1,200,000 \times 2\% = \$24,000$$

Recognizing the substantial profit penalty imposed by insufficient cash capability, management decides to borrow the funds necessary to take the 2% discounts.

Since half of the total monthly purchases include the potential discounts, Bonner needs two-thirds of that amount to pay for all such purchases in ten days, leaving ten days' discount purchases constantly outstanding. Bonner needs $66,666 to achieve their objective.

Assuming the firm incurs a 12% annual borrowing cost, we can calculate the potential bottom-line benefits as follows:

Total Annual Discounts Taken	$24,000
Annual Borrowing Cost ($66,666 × 12%)	(8,000)
Net Bottom-Line Benefits	$16,000

Thus, leverage leads to substantial bottom-line benefits when it provides the cash capability necessary to take supplier discounts.

Note that Bonner would increase earnings even if the necessary leverage cost 24%, or even 30% per year. So, don't let the presumed high cost of borrowing make you miss out on an increase in earnings. Indeed, always measure the cost against the potential benefits.

Using Leverage to Take Quantity Discounts

Quantity discounts are a less obvious form of supplier profits that can justify the use of leverage. However, the potential benefits usually fall well below those from trade discounts. This follows logically when we remember that as you increase the size of your inventory purchases, you also increase the size of your average investment in inventory. That, in turn, increases the carrying costs associated with that component of the cash flow cycle. Adding leverage costs to carrying costs can diminish significantly the potential held in quantity discounts. Nevertheless, the potential does exist, and in the proper circumstances it can be substantial.

The Assembly Company manufactures standard desk lamps. The company doesn't produce any of the component parts of the lamps; instead, it purchases each component from various suppliers.

Projections for the upcoming year suggest the realistic potential for the sale of 20,000 desk lamps. Beginning with that projection, the firm measures the potential increase in earnings available from suppliers' quantity discounts.

The analysis began with a look at the quantity discounts offered by the lamp-base supplier. Table 20–3 includes the supplier's price structure. Thus, the unit price drops from $4.00 to $3.10 when a business increases its order size from 1,999 to 10,000 units.

Beginning with that schedule, the Assembly Company proceeded with the analysis on the following assumptions:

1. The company could make twelve monthly purchases of 1,666 units each or two semi-annual purchases of 10,000 units each

TABLE 20–3 Using Leverage to Obtain Quantity Discounts

THE ASSEMBLY COMPANY

Lot Size	Unit Price
0 – 1,999	$4.00
2,000 – 4,999	$3.70
5,000 – 9,999	$3.40
10,000 +	$3.10

	Annual Cost Based on Twelve Monthly Purchase Orders (1,666 each)	Annual Cost Based on Two Semiannual Purchase Orders (10,000 each)
Total Units	20,000	20,000
Unit Cost	$4.00	$3.10
Annual Purchase Cost	$80,000	$62,000
Plus: Leverage Cost	—	$ 2,400
Total Cost	**$80,000**	**$59,600**

2. The total acquisition and inventory carrying costs incurred at the two alternatives are exactly equal
3. To purchase the lamp bases in 10,000-unit lots, the company will have to borrow an average of $20,000 for the year, incurring $2,400 in interest costs

The Assembly Company reaps substantial benefits from the quantity discounts associated with the larger lot purchases, even after proper consideration of the leverage cost.

Using Leverage to Finance Anticipatory Purchases

In Chapter 17, we reviewed the potential benefits from anticipatory purchasing as a weapon against inflation. Thus, when a businessman anticipates a significant increase in supplier prices, he should purchase as much inventory as his warehouse capacity and cash capability will allow.

You can also use leverage to increase the benefits you gain from anticipatory purchasing. We will extend the circumstance of the Calculator Company in Chapter 17. In that example, the Calculator Company anticipates a $2.00 supplier increase in the price of the firm's most popular item. The cost per unit will increase from $10.00 to $12.00. Thus, the company purchased 1,000 units at the old $10.00 price. Possibly that purchase level was set by the limits on the firm's cash capability.

Let's assume here that, instead of buying 1,000 units, the Calculator Company purchases 10,000 units (inventory sufficient for a full year's sales) at the $10.00 price. However, a purchase of that magnitude required the use of leverage. In fact, we will assume that the company borrowed the full $100,000 necessary to make the purchase. Table 20–4 illustrates the benefits that flow from that purchase.

Again, we assume that after the anticipatory purchase the Calculator Company increases its own selling prices by $2.00 on the same day the supplier announces his increase. That increases the company's margin on those units from $4.00 to $6.00. What are the benefits?

**TABLE 20–4 Using Leverage to Finance
Anticipatory Purchases**

THE CALCULATOR COMPANY

Sales Revenue from Anticipatory Purchase ($16.00 average per unit)	$160,000
Less: Purchase Cost	(100,000)
Less: Interest Cost for Funds Used to Finance Purchase (12% per annum)	(6,000)
Less: $4.00 per Unit Normal Margin	(40,000)
Net Anticipatory Purchasing Profit	**$ 14,000**

Assuming it sells the inventory over the year, the company realizes $160,-000 in total revenue from the 10,000 units. After deducting the $100,000 purchase cost, the company has a $60,000 gross profit from those sales.

Of course, the company had to borrow the funds to finance the anticipatory purchase. Originally, that loan totaled $100,000, with the lender charging a 12% per annum rate. However, we assume that the company repays the loan as it sells the units acquired in the anticipatory purchase. This is not illogical, since the purchase did represent inventory sufficient for a full year's sales; the cash was not necessary for replacement purchases.

Operating on that premise, the Calculator Company incurs $6,000 interest cost for a loan that averaged $50,000 for the year. Now, after deducting those costs, we also must deduct the $4.00 per unit profit margin the company normally realizes on each calculator. Remember, to receive these benefits, the firm must buy at the supplier's old price and sell at his own new price.

After recognizing all of the appropriate costs, the Calculator Company realizes a $14,000 bottom-line benefit from the anticipatory purchase. Moreover, the firm enjoyed that benefit even after recognizing the interest costs associated with the leverage necessary to finance the purchase. That's another measure of the benefits leverage can provide to a business that uses it to take advantage of supplier profits.

Of course, in different circumstances, the actual benefits will vary. Few firms have the product, will, or capacity to purchase a full year's inventory. Also, we have not considered the carrying costs, which would lower the total benefit.

Don't forget the risks that accompany the use of leverage to chase supplier profits. But don't overlook the potential benefits either.

Using Leverage to Gain Financial Flexibility

The flexibility leverage provides enables a business to effect profitable decisions that otherwise might be precluded by a limited cash capability.

Some of those decisions may involve special, one-time opportunities for profit. For example, a business might use its financial flexibility to take advantage of a special supplier discount in exchange for cash payment. Or the firm may pursue a large prospective customer, certain that it has the cash capability necessary to service the customer's needs.

However, here we will emphasize the on-going bottom-line benefits available to the business that properly exercises its financial flexibility. This can be summarized as Cash Flow Concept 66:

66: Leverage can provide financial flexibility that leads to bottom-line benefits.

Thus, a business might use that flexibility to eliminate discounts from its selling terms. Of course, you must have the cash capability—the financial flexibility—to carry the larger investment in receivables that results from that policy.

Should your profit margin warrant, your financial flexibility might allow you to carry that policy another step and extend longer selling terms to induce a higher sales volume.Obviously, you must carefully weigh the cost against the benefits. But should the potential profits and your financial flexibility prove sufficient, the longer selling terms may make good business sense.

In other circumstances, you might use that financial flexibility to carry a larger investment in inventory, to move into other product lines, or to expand your geographical market.

Even the conservative businessman benefits from the financial flexibility provided by leverage. He knows that he has the cash capability necessary to absorb a financial setback.

Using Leverage to Serve Special Objectives

A business might profitably use borrowed funds to increase sales, take discounts, or fill a gap in its cash flow cycle. In each instance, however, those benefits ensue because leverage serves as a natural complement to the firm's existing cash capability.

However, a business can also use leverage in cases that are not directly related to its normal operations and that don't contribute directly to an increase in the firm's cash capability. Of course, any leverage inevitably affects the cash flow process: After all, the business that borrows also must repay.

A business might borrow to buy out some of its stockholders or to facilitate the acquisition of another operation. In another circumstance, debt may provide the cash to pay dividends. Although these objectives may benefit the business, directly or indirectly, they are beyond the scope of cash flow management.

21

Leverage from the Trade

A supplier contributes leverage to your business any time he extends open account credit consideration. This trade credit allows you to defer cash payment for a purchase in accordance with the supplier's standard selling terms.

Conceptually, trade credit provides the same benefits to a business as any other form of leverage. It increases your cash capability and enables you to satisfy objectives that might remain out of reach in the absence of external financing. However, it is more closely intertwined with the cash flow cycle than any other form of leverage. We illustrate that fact in this chapter.

First, we review the link between trade credit and cash capability from a new perspective. Next, we introduce an approach to the comparative analysis of the benefits a business can derive from alternative supplier selling terms. Of course, in some instances, longer payment terms are desirable. In others, a business benefits more from terms that allow discounts for early payment. We will show how to compare the alternatives.

Then, we illustrate the direct relationship between trade credit and the cash flow process with the aid of the average payment period calculation. Identifying that period contributes an important element to positive cash flow management.

Of course, that effort also requires a measure of consideration for the factors that influence a supplier's credit decision. Thus, we review the basic criterion of credit history that stands as the indispensable element in the supplier's credit decision process. Other elements also enter into that process, but payment history remains the crucial determinant. The businessman who recognizes that fact has

197

the key that opens the door to the maximum potential benefits available from that leverage.

Finally, we discuss the management practices that encourage good relations between a business and its suppliers. The consideration that flows from good supplier relations often provides the extra capability that solves a cash flow problem.

THE MECHANICS OF SUPPLIER LENDING

Properly managed, trade credit becomes another hybrid form of the three principal lending methods discussed in Chapter 19. Trade credit provides a permanent revolving loan in the form of an infinite series of single-payment loans.

Of course, the borrower doesn't execute a formal note each time he makes a purchase. Instead, the credit consideration becomes part of the firm's accounts payable, the inventory of amounts due to all suppliers. Each account represents a promise to pay for a purchase within the allotted time set by the supplier's payment terms.

However, trade credit can provide a constant contribution to the cash capability in a business. Accounts payable, a current liability, become permanent leverage.

A brief look at the experience of the Boone Company with a single supplier demonstrates that potential.

The Boone Company, a regional manufacturer of trailer axles, recently placed a $10,000 order for wheel bearings with a new supplier. The supplier approved open-account credit consideration for the purchase in line with the industry's standard thirty-day terms. Thus, payment for the September 1 purchase falls due on October 1.

However, concomitant with the payment scheduled on October 1, Boone repeats the $10,000 purchase on the same thirty-day terms. The simultaneous transactions lead to a $10,000 continuous contribution to Boone's cash capability. The following transaction record illustrates that contribution:

Date	Purchase	Payment	Creditor's Contribution to Cash Capabilities
9/1	$10,000	—	$10,000
10/1	$10,000	$10,000	$10,000

Assuming Boone continues the same purchase/payment cycle, the rollover effect translates into a $10,000 revolving line of credit that becomes a permanent addition to the firm's cash capability. Similar consideration from a number of suppliers provides Boone with the support necessary to carry a profitable investment in inventory.

Before we take a closer look at the Boone Company, let's review an approach to analyzing the benefits held in alternative supplier selling terms.

COMPARING THE ALTERNATIVES

Two interrelated factors ultimately determine the size of the contribution to cash capability that comes from a supplier's credit consideration.

The primary influence comes from the supplier's estimate of his customer's creditworthiness. The higher the estimate, the larger the line of credit extended. That line sets the maximum credit consideration available to the customer at any point. Viewed from our special perspective, the line of credit sets the maximum contribution a supplier will commit to the cash capability in a business.

Of course, a business often qualifies for credit lines that exceed its purchase requirements. In such instances, the supplier's selling terms specify the cash capability the business draws from that credit consideration. Obviously, the longer a supplier allows for payment, the larger the contribution he makes to your cash capability.

In both cases, you should remember the tenet held in Cash Flow Concept 67:

67: Use the supplier credit terms that answer the needs of your business.

We will illustrate the analytic approach that helps identify the appropriate supplier when cash capability is the primary consideration. However, this is not always the ruling factor that selects one supplier instead of another.

Indeed, many businesses favor supplier discounts for early payment over the additional cash capability that comes from larger lines of credit or longer terms for payment. Our illustration also includes that alternative view as an element in the comparative analysis of supplier selling terms.

Table 21–1 summarizes an analysis performed by Any Company, a diversified conglomerate. The analysis begins with the following facts:

1. As a logical necessity for good employee relations, Any Company purchases $10,000 in toilet tissue each month for internal use
2. Six potential suppliers (tagged by alphabetical designation in Table 21–1) can provide a competitive product
3. The list purchase price from any of the six suppliers is the same
4. Each supplier approves an unlimited line of credit for Any Company

Despite its size and financial strength, Any Company follows a regular pattern of analysis when no price differential exists among prospective suppliers of the same product. That analysis examines the competitors' selling terms from two perspectives. Each perspective usually favors different suppliers. One perspec-

**TABLE 21–1 Cash Capability and Profit Potential
Available from Alternative Credit Terms
(assumes $10,000 in monthly purchases)**

Supplier	Selling Terms	Maximum Potential Contribution to Cash Capability	Maximum Potential Contribution to Annual Earnings
A	Net 10 ROG (receipt of goods)	$ 3,333	—
B	1% 10, Net 30	$10,000	$1,200
C	2% 10, Net 30	$10,000	$2,400
D	Net 30	$10,000	—
E	Net 45	$15,000	—
F	Net 60	$20,000	—

tive considers the bottom-line benefits Any Company can gain from discounts allowed for early payment.

Note in Table 21–1 that Supplier C's 2% discount for payment in ten days rather than thirty gives that firm the advantage. Buying toilet tissue from Supplier C each month for a year yields a $2,400 benefit for Any Company.

The other perspective in Any Company's analysis contributes information to a contingency plan for operating in a tight money period. The plan calls for conservation of the company's cash as a singular corporate objective during such periods. Thus, if effected, Any Company will switch its preference from suppliers who offer discounts to those who provide the largest contribution to the firm's cash capability.

Note that Supplier F's sixty-day credit terms will gain the firm Any Company's business in a tight money period. These terms provide the maximum potential contribution of $20,000 to Any Company's cash capability. That will contribute to the contingency plan's primary objective—retention of as much cash in the business as possible, without eliminating toilet tissue as an employee benefit.

Even though Any Company's circumstances are hypothetical, the considerations involved in the alternative decision criteria remain valid. Thus, the firm with adequate cash capability will favor the profit potential held in supplier discounts. As illustrated in Chapter 20, that profit potential can prove substantial, even though a business uses other credit consideration to realize those benefits. Certainly, the cost of institutional credit seldom equals the cost of lost discounts.

Alternatively, the business suffering from a tight cash flow abandons trade discounts in favor of longer terms for payment. Longer terms contribute capability that can ease the strain imposed by a cash flow problem.

Typically, the analysis of alternative supplier credit terms is less complicated than implied in Table 21–1. Suppliers in any industry usually have similar designated selling terms. Of course, you certainly should compare any alternatives that do exist.

From another perspective, the analytic tasks increase in complexity when you look at implied terms rather than designated terms. Of course, prompt payment habits open the door to the maximum benefits available from supplier credit considerations. However, in the midst of a cash flow crunch, you might find welcome relief from a supplier who designates thirty days for payment but continues shipments to customers who fall thirty days or more past due.

Unfortunately, because implied terms are nebulous, they are less subject to objective analysis. Nevertheless, the careful manager can expand the cash capability in his business with the aid of lenient collectors. Don't abuse the privilege, but don't overlook the potential.

AVERAGE PAYABLE PERIOD

Average payable period measures the average length of time you use each dollar of trade credit consideration. In other words, Cash Flow Concept 68:

68: Average payable period defines the relationship between trade credit and the cash flow process.

To calculate that period and find how it contributes to positive cash flow management, let's assume that the Control Company has $170,000 in total accounts payable at the end of the first quarter of operations for the year. During that same quarter, Control received trade credit consideration for $240,000 in total purchases. In a ninety-day quarter, that translates into $2,666 in average daily purchases. Then, to calculate the average payment period for the accounts payable that remain unpaid at the end of the quarter, we can use the calculation:

$$\text{Average Payment Period} = \frac{\text{Accounts Payable}}{\text{Average Daily Purchases on Account}}$$

Using the Control Company's circumstance, we find:

$$\text{Average Payment Period} = \frac{\$170,000}{\$2,666}$$

Average Payment Period = 64 Days

Thus, each dollar of trade credit consideration contributed to the Control Company remains in the business for 64 days before being returned to the supplier in the form of a cash payment.

THE COMPLETE CASH FLOW CYCLE

Our conceptual view of the cash flow cycle includes cash, accounts receivable, and inventory. However, this view is incomplete for most established businesses, and indeed, it should include accounts payable as a natural component.

As the Boone Company's experience indicated, the business that manages a prompt payment record gains a permanent contribution to its cash capability. Thus, accounts payable (supplier credit consideration) substitute for the cash purchase of inventory. Sales convert that inventory into accounts receivable. Proceeds from the collection of the receivables provide the cash to retire the original account payable. Then, the cycle begins again.

Of course, a supplier's selling terms seldom coincide with the cash conversion period in a business—the length of time it takes to convert a customer's order into a collected account. So, accounts payable cannot substitute entirely for cash. Instead, they supplement the original cash invested in a business.

This leads us to a view of the complete cash flow cycle in Figure 21–1. The cash investment coupled with accounts payable provides the total capability necessary for the purchase of inventory. The cycle then proceeds normally.

However, part of the cash collection retires the original supplier debt, with the remainder—the gross profit margin—returning to the firm's cash account. That cash pays expenses, while any excess buys more inventory. So long as the cycle operates satisfactorily, then, accounts payable remain a natural part of the complete cash flow cycle.

Now, let's further refine our view of the role trade credit plays in a properly managed cash flow cycle and interrelate the payable period with the requirements set by a firm's cash conversion period.

FIGURE 21–1 The Complete Cash Flow Cycle

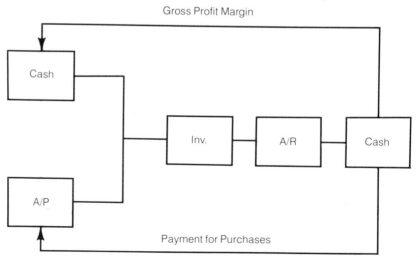

A closer look at the Boone Company and its present operating characteristics helps demonstrate the interrelationships:

1. Sales presently average $2,000 per day, or $60,000 per month.
2. A 60-day average collection period leaves the firm with a $120,000 investment in accounts receivable.
3. Product costs average 75% of each sales dollar.
4. The company maintains inventory on hand sufficient for two months' sales; the 60-day average investment period translates into $90,000 in inventory.
5. Experience indicates that a 40-day average payable period satisfies supplier implied terms for payment.
6. Boone maintains a minimum $10,000 cash operating balance.
   Figure 21–2 provides a view of Boone's complete cash flow cycle.

Thus, we find that the Boone Company has $220,000 in total assets revolving in the cash flow cycle. Accounts payable, with a 40-day average payment period, provide the cash capability for $60,000 of that amount. Purchases average $1,500 per day.

FIGURE 21–2 Trade Creditors' Contribution to Cash Capability

The Boone Company

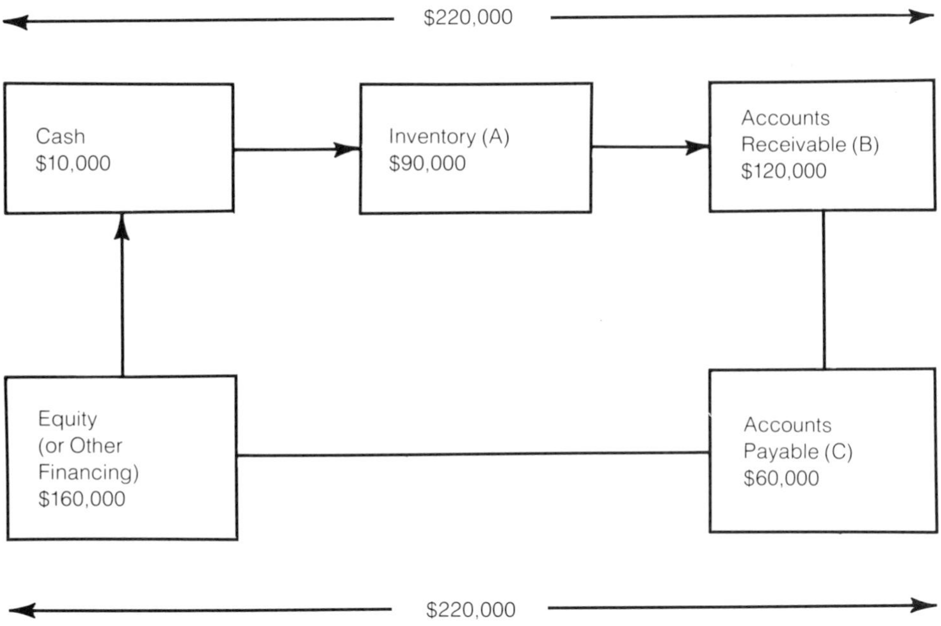

(A) 60-Day Average Investment Period
(B) 60-Day Average Collection Period
(C) 40-Day Average Payable Period

That leaves $160,000 in cash capability that comes from the Boone Company's original cash investment and retained earnings. Of course, part of that capability also might come from external financing available from other lenders.

Now, let's see how a change in the Boone Company's operation affects those interrelationships.

First, holding the above operating characteristics constant, how does an increase in sales affect the structure illustrated in Figure 21–2? Imagine that the Boone Company manages an instant 50% increase in sales.

We can anticipate the effect the sales increase has on the Boone Company's assets. Indeed, the firm's investment in cash, accounts receivable, and inventory increases by 50% or a total of $110,000.

Of course, to maintain the necessary balance, other changes in the firm's financial structure must provide the cash capability to carry higher asset investment. The support that comes from trade creditors emphasizes the natural place accounts payable hold in the complete cash flow cycle.

As sales increase, the cash capability contributed by trade creditors also rises in line with the higher volume. We note this fact in Cash Flow Concept 69:

69: Trade credit provides a spontaneous increase in cash capability for a growing business.

Of course, that increase occurs only so long as a business satisfies its supplier requirements.

Thus, the business must maintain an average payable period consistent with supplier expectations. In the Boone Company's circumstance, that means paying for all purchases in no more than forty days.

At the same time, the business must continue to satisfy the credit standards set by its suppliers. The firm must qualify for higher lines of credit. However, presuming the business satisfies these constraints, trade credit usually expands in direct proportion to sales volume. Figure 21–3 demonstrates how that contribution affects Boone's cash flow cycle.

Thus, the spontaneous increase in trade credit consideration provides $30,000 out of the $110,000 in cash capability necessary to support the firm's higher investment in assets. Boone's financial strength and ability to maintain a forty-day average payable period encourages its suppliers to grow with the business.

Of course, to support the sales increase, the Boone Company has to obtain $80,000 in cash capability from other sources. Nevertheless, we can still view the spontaneous increase in trade credit as a significant element in financing expansion.

TRADE CREDIT CRITERIA

As we have noted, the benefits you derive from trade credit partially depend on the line of credit each supplier approves for your business. Of course,

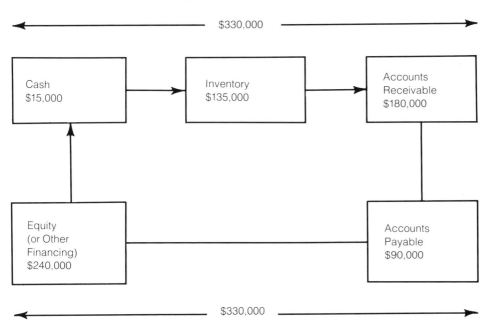

FIGURE 21–3 The Spontaneous Increase in Trade Credit

that line comes from the supplier's estimate of your creditworthiness. Before extending any credit, he assesses your capacity to pay.

The complexity of his assessment depends upon the circumstances of the sale. Indeed, a large sale to an existing customer or any sale to a new customer might call for extensive financial analysis similar to that performed by institutional lenders.

However, most trade credit decisions center on one pivotal consideration—payment history. What payment patterns does the purchaser follow? How long has he followed that pattern? Then, presuming that past history predicts future performance, the supplier estimates the probable payment pattern for future purchases.

Of course, a long, prompt payment history makes trade credit consideration easily accessible for a business. Alternatively, a record for slow payment may restrict a firm to little or no consideration. However, in many circumstances, a business achieves favorable results from a payment history that is consistent, although it exceeds the supplier's designated terms. Table 21–2 helps demonstrate that fact with a review of the payment histories of three businesses that buy from the Large Company.

All three customers have purchased the same amount from the company in the last six months. All three also have recently entered new orders for $10,000 purchases. Of course, the company's credit manager approves immediate shipment to the Established Company. The firm's recent history indicates prompt payment in accordance with the Large Company's designated thirty-day terms.

The credit manager also approves immediate shipment to Controlled

TABLE 21-2 The Supplier's Credit Decision

THE ESTABLISHED COMPANY

Month	Purchases	Outstanding at Month's End	Current	1-30 Past Due	31-60 Past Due	60-90 Past Due
January	$10,000	$10,000	$10,000			
February	12,000	12,000	12,000			
March	15,000	15,000	15,000			
April	10,000	10,000	10,000			
May	20,000	20,000	20,000			
June	10,000	10,000	10,000			

CONTROLLED GROWTH, INC.

Month	Purchases	Outstanding at Month's End	Current	1-30 Past Due	31-60 Past Due	60-90 Past Due
January	$10,000	$20,000	$10,000	$10,000		
February	12,000	22,000	12,000	10,000		
March	15,000	27,000	15,000	12,000		
April	10,000	25,000	10,000	15,000		
May	20,000	30,000	20,000	10,000		
June	10,000	20,000	10,000	10,000		

THE PROBLEM COMPANY

Month	Purchases	Outstanding at Month's End	Current	1-30 Past Due	31-60 Past Due	60-90 Past Due
January	$10,000	$10,000	$10,000			
February	12,000	12,000	12,000			
March	15,000	20,000	15,000	$ 5,000		
April	10,000	25,000	10,000	15,000		
May	20,000	40,000	20,000	10,000	$10,000	
June	10,000	45,000	10,000	20,000	10,000	$5,000

Growth, Inc. Although Controlled Growth does not pay within the designated terms, it does follow a consistent payment pattern: Controlled Growth doesn't let any payment fall more than thirty days past due.

This illustrates a critical point: Many trade credit decisions rely as much on consistent payment as on prompt payment. This often holds true even though the consistent pattern exceeds the boundaries set by the creditor's designated terms. Such consistency usually improves a firm's potential for credit consideration.

A look at Large Company's third customer, the Problem Company, suggests the rationale behind that presumption. The firm's prompt payment record has deteriorated over the recent six-month history. Indeed, it is ninety days past due for some purchases. That changing pattern probably disqualifies the Problem Company from any new credit consideration. Indeed, the slower payment record suggests a cash flow problem approaching serious proportions.

Of course, payment history isn't the only element in a supplier's credit decision. Consistent payment habits—in accordance with designated terms, or at least within a reasonable period—help reassure a supplier. Practicing consistent payment habits can increase the cash capability for trade credit.

SUPPLIER RELATIONS

A discussion of the elements that contribute to a sound relationship between a business and its suppliers may seem out of place in a book that concentrates on cash flow management. But the working relationship you have with your suppliers has a direct influence on your cash capability. That relationship affects both the amount and the terms of the credit consideration your business receives.

Of course, making a major purchase from any supplier involves considerations that proceed beyond any potential credit consideration. Price structures, product lines, delivery schedules, and service capabilities certainly remain most relevant.

However, most businesses eventually establish ongoing relationships with their major suppliers. From our perspective, once a business establishes such relationships, it should seek to develop and maintain the maximum potential cash capability from each supplier's credit consideration.

Two management practices contribute to good supplier relations.

First, practice consistent payment patterns. Erratic payment upsets even the most patient suppliers. So long as they know when to expect payment for purchases, even if persistently late, they can feel comfortable with the relationship.

Second, keep the lines of communication open. The more a supplier knows about your business, the more he can respond to your needs. After all, your purchases presumably are profitable sales for his business. The better he responds to your needs, the more bottom-line benefits you both realize.

From a positive perspective, inform major suppliers of your purchasing plans. Tell them if your projected requirements for credit considerations exceed presently approved lines. In this way, you can lay the groundwork for approval by giving your suppliers the information that will facilitate the credit decision process.

From another perspective, open lines of communication can help you slip unscathed through a cash flow problem. Thus, don't let a supplier learn about that problem from the break in your payment pattern. Instead, inform him in advance that you cannot pay according to your usual pattern. Explain your circumstance and your problem. Then, offer your best estimate of your revised payment schedule. Most trade creditors can live with a past-due account, and proper communication can prevent the loss of future credit consideration. Of course, the best supplier relations will not lead to unlimited credit consideration or to a cure for every cash flow problem. However, they often can lead to more credit consideration and less pressure for prompt payment. The cash capability gained from these effects make the effort worthwhile.

Leverage from the Bank

When a businessman seeks leverage in excess of the amount available from trade creditors, or leverage for a special circumstance, he first looks to his banker. In fact, bank loans are the second largest form of external financing used by businesses.

In this Chapter, we discuss bank credit consideration as a significant element in cash flow management. We begin with a review of the common bank lending methods, which provide the basis to illustrate the impact each method has on cash capability.

Of course, the initial contribution to that capability is the same as that obtained from any other form of leverage. However, the repayment schedule that accompanies a bank loan ultimately withdraws that contribution. Failure to anticipate that fact can lead your business into a cash flow problem.

Then, we consider the cost of bank credit and discuss the elements that make up the differential between the apparent cost, or the predetermined interest rate, and true cost.

Of course, the major element in that differential comes from the standard requirement for a compensating balance, which can increase the cost of the funds you actually use or make you borrow more than you need. From either perspective it increases the true cost of borrowing from a bank. Moreover, calculating that cost is essential for comparative analysis of the alternative forms of leverage.

Next, we review the basic criteria that justify the banker's lending decisions so that you will be able to anticipate the potential response to your loan requests.

Finally, we look at the substantive elements that contribute to a sound relationship between a businessman and his banker. More so than with any other source of leverage, that relationship directly influences the amount and terms of the credit consideration a business receives. Indeed, good bank relations become an important element of positive cash flow management.

CASH CAPABILITY AND THE SINGLE-PAYMENT LOAN

The single-payment loan serves a specific purpose and has a predetermined source of repayment. Of course, the purpose may not be fulfilled as predicted, nor does repayment always follow promptly. Nevertheless, the promise that justifies a single-payment loan identifies each.

We use the experience of Fawn Chemicals, Inc., to demonstrate the contribution a single-payment loan makes to a business and emphasize the proper relationship between the purpose of the loan and the ultimate source of repayment.

Fawn Chemicals manufactures fertilizer for sale to large agricultural producers. The operating characteristics of the business require a seasonal, single-payment loan. Thus, Fawn purchases the chemicals necessary for the fertilizer manufacturing process in January of each year. Chemical suppliers allow Fawn thirty-day terms, so all accounts payable must be retired by the end of February.

Fawn's customers purchase the fertilizer during the planting season in March and April. However, the producers command terms that allow six months for payment. This means that they defer payment until after they sell their harvests in September or October.

Table 22–1 summarizes the natural chain of events that justifies the use of a single-payment loan. The successive financial structures reflect the following additional characteristics of Fawn Chemicals:

1. Fawn ends each year with no investment in accounts receivable or inventory, and it has no debt. At 12/31/78, that left the firm with $400,000 in cash, $100,000 in fixed assets, and a $500,000 net worth.
2. Projections indicate that Fawn will earn $140,000 from a $1,000,000 sales volume in the upcoming year.
3. That sales volume will require the purchases of $560,000 in agricultural chemicals.
4. The firm's operating expenses, including interest costs, average $20,000 per month.
5. The firm incurs $100,000 in manufacturing expenses, all paid in February.

Now, let's trace the chain of events that justifies the need for the single-payment loan and also provides a natural, predictable source of repayment.

First, in January, Fawn purchases the $560,000 in chemicals necessary for the projected sales volume. The company pays $100,000 in cash for part of the inventory, while suppliers allow the balance to be paid in February. As indicated in Column 2, that leaves the firm with $460,000 in accounts payable due by Feb-

TABLE 22-1 The Mechanics of a Single-Payment Note

FAWN CHEMICAL COMPANY

			(Fiscal Year End)		
	12/31/78	1/31/79	2/28/79	4/30/79	10/31/79
Cash	$400,000	$280,000	$160,000	$ 120,000	$540,000
Accounts Receivable	—	—	—	1,000,000	—
Inventory	—	560,000	560,000	—	—
Fixed Assets	100,000	100,000	100,000	100,000	100,000
Total Assets	**$500,000**	**$940,000**	**$820,000**	**$1,220,000**	**$640,000**
Accounts Payable	—	$460,000	—	—	—
Bank Loan	—	—	$460,000	$460,000	—
Total Liabilities	**—**	**$460,000**	**$460,000**	**$ 460,000**	**—**
Stockholders' Equity	$500,000	$480,000	$360,000	$ 760,000	$640,000
Equity and Liabilities	**$500,000**	**$940,000**	**$820,000**	**$1,220,000**	**$640,000**

ruary 28. Even the firm's healthy $280,000 cash balance is insufficient to satisfy the obligation.

(Observe the $20,000 cash drain imposed by operating expenses for the month of January. The lack of any revenue during that period translates that into the $20,000 reduction registered in the stockholders' equity account.)

In February (Column 3), Fawn obtains a $460,000 bank loan to retire the entire amount due to suppliers. The bank extends the single-payment loan with repayment required on or before October 31, 1979.

Of course, Fawn incurs $20,000 in operating expenses again in February; also the firm must absorb $100,000 in fertilizer manufacturing expenses. The 2/28/79 financial statement registers the effects those expenses have on both the cash and equity accounts.

As predicted, Fawn sells its entire inventory by 4/30/79. The firm registers those sales in the form of $1 million in accounts receivable. All of the accounts are due no later than October 31.

Column 4 reflects the impact the sales have on Fawn's financial structure. Note, in particular, two elements in that structure. First, the accrued profits on the sales raise Fawn's equity account to $760,000. At the same time, the monthly operating expenses for March and April drain another $40,000 from the firm's cash reserves. This monthly cash drain continues until September, when the producers begin paying for their purchases as agreed. Indeed, by 10/31/79 Fawn collects all of its accounts receivable, retires its bank loan, and has a respectable $540,000 cash balance. The $20,000 in monthly operating expenses will reduce that balance to $500,000 by year's end, when the cycle begins again.

Fawn's experience clearly demonstrates the proper use of a single-payment loan. The loan answered a specific need, providing the cash capability necessary to pay for inventory purchases. As sales converted the inventory into accounts receivable, the loan then helped support the investment in receivables. The ultimate collection of those accounts served as the necessary source of repayment.

Of course, you don't need a seasonal business to benefit from a single-payment loan. Indeed, the loan can enable a business to take advantage of a special inventory purchase or generate an unusually large sale. At the same time, both you and the lender must relate the loan directly to the purpose and ultimately to the source of repayment.

CASH CAPABILITY AND THE INSTALLMENT LOAN

In Chapter 14, we suggested that a business should use external financing as the source of the cash capability required to purchase fixed assets. Then, in Chapter 19, we narrowed that perspective, indicating that the source of external financing could be an installment loan. An installment loan allows a business to repay on a schedule that coincides with the cash flow generated by the investment. Now, we relate the cash that flows from a new investment in fixed assets to the amortization requirements associated with an installment loan.

From the lender's perspective, to justify installment-loan credit consideration, the annual cash flow in the borrower's business must equal or exceed the principal amortization requirements set by any installment loan. Moreover, the lender relates that practical requirement to the firm's total installment debt service, existing as well as proposed.

Let's clarify this requirement with a look at the Collins Company, a small tubing manufacturer that presently operates at a break-even level. The company is contemplating the purchase of a $400,000 automated assembly line that promises a return to profitable operations. Indeed, the reduction in production costs from the new line should translate into $80,000 a year in earnings.

In conjunction with the proposed acquisition, Collins has requested a $400,-000 bank loan to finance the purchase and installation of the new line. Despite its break-even operation, the company satisfies the bank's basic credit criteria. However, final approval of the credit consideration hinges on the relationship between Collins's annual cash flow and the amortization requirements for the proposed loan. That phase of the analysis proceeds on several assumptions:

1. Estimates indicate that the new machinery and equipment will have a ten-year useful life
2. The application of straight-line depreciation to the new assets will contribute $40,000 per year to Collins's cash flow

3. The existing fixed assets are fully depreciated and have no effect on annual cash flow measurements

4. Collins presently has no other fixed-debt requirements

5. The bank's credit policy precludes extending any installment loan that will not be repaid in five years or less

Collins's banker analyzed these facts in two simple steps. First, he found the annual cash flow necessary to amortize the $400,000 loan over a five-year term. That amount came from the basic calculation:

$$\frac{\text{Annual Cash Flow}}{\text{Requirements}} = \frac{\text{Loan Amount}}{\text{Term (in year)}} = \frac{\$400,000}{5} = \$80,000$$

Consequently, Collins will need to produce an annual cash flow of at least $80,000 to meet the debt-service requirements on the proposed loan. We ignore interest expense in this instance, since it would fall into the category of normal operating expenses included in the projected earnings calculations.

Second, the banker measures the annual cash flow anticipated from the company's operations. However, recognizing the uncertainty inevitably associated with the proposed transformation of the business from a break-even to a profitable operation, the banker considered three alternative outcomes: pessimistic, optimistic, and an average view.

The pessimist's view presumes that the new investment will have no effect on Collins's operating results: The firm will remain a break-even operation. The annual cash flow will be equal to the annual depreciation.

The optimist's view accepts the company's projections. It presumes that the firm will produce $80,000 a year in earnings and a $120,000 annual cash flow — the earnings plus $40,000 in depreciation.

Logically, the average expectation splits the difference between the optimist and the pessimist. This view anticipates future earnings of $40,000 per year, which, when coupled with the depreciation, produce an $80,000 annual cash flow.

Below, we compare the annual cash flow anticipated from the three alternative projections with the annual debt amortization requirements. We also include the probable decision that will follow the particular view the banker adopts:

	Cash Flow from Earnings	Cash Flow from Depreciation	Total Annual Cash Flow	Amortization Requirement	Loan Decision
Pessimist	—	$40,000	$ 40,000	$80,000	Decline
Optimist	$80,000	$40,000	$120,000	$80,000	Approve
Average	$40,000	$40,000	$ 80,000	$80,000	?

Of course, the optimistic view encourages approval of the credit consideration. The prospective cash flow from that perspective is 150% of the amount required for debt amortization. The bank adopting that view will extend the loan.

The pessimist will decline the loan. Since half of the cash flow necessary to retire the debt comes from projected earnings, he foresees a $40,000 annual shortfall.

Finally, the lender who holds the average view is left without any clear decision criteria. Indeed, this view projects an annual cash flow exactly equal to Collins's debt-service requirements.

However, a slight drop in earnings below the $40,000 projected reduces the firm's annual cash flow below the required $80,000. Indeed, the average view must rely on other factors to justify the final credit decision.

Perhaps surprisingly, the ultimate credit decision in the Collins Company's circumstance actually may depend upon the banker's individual perspective: whether he is a pessimist, an optimist, or something in between. Whatever his attitude, however, when he analyzes a prospective installment loan, he will look closely at the relationship between the firm's annual cash flow and fixed-debt amortization requirements.

The logic of this attitude recognizes that the principal repayment of a loan is not a business expense: Indeed, it does not appear in the income statement. Instead, the repayment merely returns the cash capability borrowed. The cash for repayment must come from the liquidation of assets, from funds borrowed from another lender, or from the annual cash flow from operations.

However, lenders who approve an installment loan automatically tie themselves to the borrower for the term of the note, usually several years. In addition, they recognize that a business might be unwilling or unable to liquidate other assets to meet its fixed-debt requirements. And the lender cannot depend on some other creditor to provide the cash necessary for installment debt service.

The business with a tight cash flow is not the most welcome prospect for a loan. Consequently, the bank (or other lender) looks for an annual cash flow from operations sufficient to meet the debt-service requirements. The business that fails to satisfy that requirement usually has trouble obtaining installment-loan credit consideration.

CASH CAPABILITY AND THE REVOLVING LOAN

A revolving loan provides flexible leverage for a business. The business gains the discretionary use of the lender's funds up to the limit set by its line of credit. Table 22–2 provides a simplified look at the operation of a bank revolving loan.

The table presumes that a bank approves a $500,000 line of credit for a business, extending from the beginning to the end of the calendar year. The business uses the line during that term as a complement to its natural cash flow cycle. Thus, the borrower obtains $300,000 on January 15 and another $200,000 on March 7. Then, reflecting a cyclical operation, the firm generates the cash to repay $400,000 on April 7. The firm obtains another $300,000 on July 26 and then retires the full amount of the loan in three payments during the last quarter of the year.

TABLE 22–2 A Revolving Line of Credit
($500,000 maximum)

Date	Borrowed	Repaid	Loan Balance	Available Cash Capability
January 15	$300,000	—	$300,000	$200,000
March 7	200,000	—	500,000	—
April 7	—	$400,000	100,000	400,000
July 26	300,000	—	400,000	100,000
October 1	—	100,000	300,000	200,000
November 9	—	200,000	100,000	400,000
December 7	—	100,000	—	500,000

The flexibility available from a revolving loan is apparent. Unfortunately, only the stronger, more creditworthy borrowers qualify. Indeed, such firms most often have resources that preclude the need for such consideration altogether, so the revolving loan becomes a convenience rather than a necessity.

THE TRUE COST OF BANK BORROWING

Without properly measuring the costs, a borrower can't determine how profitable leverage is for his business, nor can he properly compare the costs among alternative forms of leverage. We can summarize these facts as Cash Flow Concept 70:

70: A businessman should measure all of the costs associated with bank credit consideration.

The interest charge sets the basic, or apparent, cost of a bank loan. However, to measure the true cost, you must recognize the expenses that arise from
1. Compensating balances
2. Commitment fees
3. Restrictive covenants
4. Legal fees
5. Negotiating renewals
6. Annual cleanups
Of course, the borrower does not absorb all of these costs, but when incurred, they can add substantially to the apparent cost of bank borrowing represented by the stated interest rate.

The Compensating Balance Requirement
A deposit relationship is usually necessary before any bank loan is approved. Thus, a business that borrows from a bank must have, or agree to estab-

lish, an operating account with the lender. This requirement serves two objectives.

First, a prospective borrower's cash management practices enter into the credit criteria that guide the lending decision. Thus, the business that maintains a comfortable cash balance has the first line of defense against the threat of a financial reverse. This adds an element of confidence to a lender's decision to extend credit.

In contrast, the business that holds little cash relative to its sales volume constantly confronts the risk of a financial setback. A supplier pressing for payment of past-due accounts, or a major customer who defers payment for large purchases, can translate that risk into reality. Consequently, the business has less chance of receiving bank credit.

In either circumstance, the bank's requirement for the borrower's operating account allows the bank to monitor the firm's cash management practices. Moreover, it enables the bank to update that estimate regularly. Indeed, it becomes an important element in a continuing lending relationship.

However, the second objective probably stands higher in the banker's mind: That is, it enables him to obtain a compensating balance, which increases the bank's earnings.

The cash a business holds for normal transactions often satisfies a bank's compensating balance requirements. However, if the average deposits are too low, the bank will require the borrower to carry additional, idle cash sufficient to make the compensating balance equal to 20 to 30% of the credit consideration. The compensating balance provides the bank with additional funds for profitable lending purposes.

Of course, as the compensating balance requirement increases the bank's earnings, it also increases your cost of borrowing and thus hurts your earnings. That follows naturally, since the necessity for a compensating balance forces you to borrow more than you actually need.

For example, a business that needs $400,000 in additional cash capability might have to borrow $500,000 to satisfy the bank's requirement for a 20% compensating balance. The firm pays for $100,000 in credit consideration, which lies idle in its checking account.

You measure the cost of a compensating balance by relating the actual dollar cost of bank credit to the net funds you actually employ. Assume that a bank approves a $100,000 single-payment loan for a business, repayable at the end of one year. The bank charges a 10% annual interest rate for that consideration but requires a 20% compensating balance for the term of the loan.

The compensating balance requirement raises the firm's apparent cost of borrowing as follows:

1. Annual Cost of Borrowing at 10% = $10,000

2. Interest Rate Based on Funds Actually Used $= \dfrac{\$10,000}{\$80,000} = 12\ 1/2\%$

Thus, the inability to use 20% of the total bank credit consideration raises the borrower's apparent cost of borrowing by 2 1/2%.

TABLE 22–3 Effect of Compensating Balances on the Apparent Cost of Bank Credit Consideration

Compensating Balance Requirements

Stated Rate	10%	20%	30%	40%	50%
6%	6.6	7.5	8.5	10	12
6 1/2%	7.2	8.1	9.3	10.8	13
7%	7.8	8.8	10	11.7	14
7 1/2%	8.3	9.3	10.7	12.5	15
8%	8.8	10	11.4	13.3	16
8 1/2%	9.4	10.6	12.1	14.2	17
9%	10	11.25	12.8	15	18
9 1/2%	10.6	11.9	13.6	15.8	19
10%	11.1	12.5	14.3	16.7	20
10 1/2%	11.7	13.1	15	17.5	21
11%	12.2	13.8	15.7	18.3	22
11 1/2%	12.8	14.4	16.4	19.2	23
12%	13.3	15	17.1	20	24

True Rate

Table 22–3 charts the effect of various compensating balance requirements on a firm's apparent cost of borrowing across a range of interest rates.

The Commitment Fee

A business may request a line of credit from a bank merely to provide a cushion of cash capability to contend with any unforseen problems. While it is true that obtaining a preapproved line of credit often makes good business sense, the businessman should recognize that he incurs a cost of borrowing, even if he never uses the committed funds.

Most banks charge a commitment fee for establishing a line of credit. The fee typically totals 1/4% to 1/2% of the *unused* portion of the approved line. Consequently, a business that uses only $100,000 of a $200,000 line of credit will pay an interest charge for the borrowed funds, plus a $250 to $500 fee for the funds committed but not employed.

A commitment fee may be a small cost to pay for a cushion of cash capability, but recognize that it increases the apparent cost of bank borrowing.

Restrictive Covenants

A bank often includes restrictive covenants as conditional elements associated with a term or revolving loan agreement. Violation of a covenant by a borrower allows the bank to make immediate demand for repayment of any credit consideration outstanding.

For example, without prior bank approval, common restrictive covenants may preclude a borrower from incurring additional debt, paying dividends, increasing the investment in fixed assets, or even increasing officers' salaries. The bank also might require the business to satisfy certain financial constraints: for example, to maintain current assets (cash, accounts receivable, inventory) that total at least twice the firm's current liabilities. Similarly, the firm's total debt in any circumstance might be restricted to an amount equal to the total stockholders' equity.

From the banker's perspective, restrictive covenants encourage a borrower to avoid any action that could prevent him from eventually repaying the credit consideration.

However, the borrower often finds that restrictive covenants are another addition to the apparent cost of bank credit. The business incurs that cost when the covenant delays or precludes management actions that can benefit the business.

Certainly, a bank can waive any covenant that hampers a borrower. However, while waiting for that waiver, the business might lose a profitable business opportunity to a competitor with the capacity for prompt action.

Moreover, no matter how much promise an opportunity may hold, the bank may ultimately refuse to bend the restrictive covenants. The business may find its potential limited or stymied altogether.

The cost of restrictive covenants may be difficult to measure, but it can become a substantial, if indirect, opportunity cost. Remember that fact before you accept such binding credit.

Legal Fees

The larger and more complex the lending arrangement, the more likely you will incur legal fees in addition to the apparent cost of bank financing.

In some instances, those fees arise when a cautious businessman employs his attorney to review a loan agreement before execution. In other instances, the bank passes the cost of preparing loan documents on to the borrower.

In either case, the legal fees often translate into a substantial increase in the true cost of bank credit consideration.

Negotiating Renewals

Often a business is unable to retire a single-payment loan as originally agreed. Perhaps the purpose that justified the loan remains unfulfilled, or a changing business environment necessitates a decision that absorbs the cash earmarked for the repayment.

The failure to meet the repayment obligation is seldom a cause for serious concern, so long as the borrower maintains the appropriate creditworthiness. However, negotiating an extension or renewal of the loan becomes another element in the cost of bank financing. You measure that cost in terms of the management time devoted to the negotiating process. It is another opportunity cost.

If negotiating a renewal requires no more than a phone call or a brief visit to the bank, the cost is small. You may consider it to be a part of your normal operating expenses. However, as the management time devoted to obtaining renewals (or new loans) increases, the cost of negotiating rises rapidly. After all, a businessman can't employ his management talents while he is locked into loan negotiations. Thus, too much time negotiating for credit consideration can damage the bottom line of a business. The more valuable your time, the larger the cost of negotiating renewals.

Annual Cleanups

Many banks expect its borrowers to repay all loans—that is, to operate free of any bank credit consideration—for thirty to ninety days each year. This requirement for an annual cleanup period can become another element in the true cost of bank credit consideration.

Of course, the requirement doesn't pose a problem for the seasonal business: The natural business cycle generates the cash necessary to satisfy the cleanup requirement. However, the business with a level or expanding sales volume may find the requirement a burden. Indeed, to satisfy the call for a cleanup, the business either must obtain comparable credit consideration elsewhere, usually from trade creditors, or temporarily scale down its operations.

If the burden falls on the trade creditors, the business may lose trade discounts that it previously took with the aid of the bank financing. In the extreme circumstance, the business may suffer injury to its credit rating, and this can restrict future operations even further. Alternatively, should the business scale down its operations for the cleanup period, it will suffer another opportunity cost—the potential profits on lost sales. In either circumstance, the cleanup period can prove costly.

BANK CREDIT CRITERIA

A banker's credit decision evolves out of a number of interrelated factors. First, the banker estimates the management ability of the business and its prospects within its industry and within the larger economic environment.

Ultimately, however, the credit decision focuses on the financial characteristics of the business, which we can summarize as Cash Flow Concept 71:

71: A banker's credit analysis centers on a firm's earning power, cash flow, and debt/equity ratio.

The banker estimates not only the firm's ability to repay the potential credit consideration, but its ability to absorb an unforeseen financial setback.

Earning Power

The banker begins his credit analysis with a look at the prospective borrower's historical earnings performance. Then, he measures the probability of whether the performance will hold constant or improve in the future. Of course, the term *satisfactory earnings* may seem to be a nebulous credit criterion. However, the lender expects earnings to remain realistic relative to sales volume, perhaps compared to other firms in the borrower's industry. Moreover, the earnings must be substantial enough to offer the reasonable promise that the credit considera- tion can be repaid over a realistic period.

On occasion, a bank may extend credit to a business with a recent history of losses rather than earnings. However, special circumstances must justify that consideration. Indeed, the banker seldom proceeds further in his analysis if the business lacks the prospective earning power sufficient to justify loan approval.

Cash Flow

A profitable operation does not necessarily generate a positive cash flow. Consequently, while a business must demonstrate satisfactory earnings, it must also have a cash flow satisfactory to meet all obligations in a timely manner. This means that the borrower should have cash capability to pay all trade creditors promptly, service any debt requirements, and maintain cash reserves sufficient to absorb disruptions in its cash flow cycle.

From a broader perspective, the bank also estimates the prospective bor- rower's *liquidity*. Thus, he measures the firm's total investment in cash, accounts receivable, and inventory against the obligations due to creditors in the near-term future.

This comparison of current assets against current liabilities—the current ratio—helps the banker estimate the probability that the firm will be able to meet its obligations satisfactorily, even in the event of some business reverse.

For example, a business with $500,000 in current assets and $250,000 in current liabilities (a two to one current ratio) has little risk of defaulting on its im- mediate obligations. Alternatively, a business with $500,000 in current assets and $500,000 in current liabilities has little margin of error. This doesn't necessar- ily imply any immediate financial distress, but it does raise the potential for prob- lems. In any event, the larger the potential for problems, the less likely it is that credit will be extended.

The Debt/Equity Ratio

As the third major element in his credit analysis, the banker examines the borrower's debt to equity ratio: He compares the borrower's total debt to the total stockholders' equity. For example, a business with $200,000 in total liabilities and $100,000 in equity has a debt/equity ratio of two to one. As debt increases relative to equity, the ratio rises.

A banker will usually be reluctant to lend to a business with a debt/equity ratio that exceeds two to one. Naturally, his reluctance increases as the debt/equity ratio rises. Conversely, a lower ratio lends more reassurance to any positive credit decision.

The debt/equity criterion adds two elements to the banker's credit analysis: one psychological, one financial.

From the psychological perspective, as a firm's debt/equity ratio rises above two to one, stockholders have less than one dollar invested in the business, compared to every two dollars (or more) supplied by creditors. Thus, stockholders have much less to lose than creditors.

Moreover, the more liabilities increase relative to equity, the more likely a business is to take higher risks. The psychological implications of gambling with someone else's cash—that is, the creditor's—tends to reduce the fear of failure.

From the financial perspective, a debt/equity ratio of two to one generally allows the business to absorb a short-term setback. A drop in sales or a rise in costs that leads to a temporary loss from operations does not push the borrower to the brink of financial disaster.

Of course, one negative element in the analysis will not necessarily disqualify a business from credit consideration. Indeed, unusual strength in one area can overcome a weakness in others.

For example, the prospects for a strong earnings performance can offset the detrimental influence that comes from a tight cash flow and a high debt/equity ratio. Collateral considerations also often add strength to the decision to extend credit consideration.

Of course, a banker often wants to extend credit to a business even though it fails the standard credit criteria. This often occurs when the potential promise in a young business exceeds the bounds set by its financial circumstance. When the credit consideration can help the business achieve its potential, the banker might justify the loan with the aid of a guarantee from the Small Business Administration.

LOANS FROM THE SMALL BUSINESS ADMINISTRATION

Insufficient cash capability often stands as the primary obstacle to profitability. That obstacle grows larger if a weak financial structure precludes standard bank credit consideration. However, many businessmen fail to take advantage of loans that are funded or guaranteed by the Small Business Administration.

SBA loans fall into two categories: (1) the direct SBA loan, and (2) the indirect SBA guaranteed loan.

The direct SBA loan means that the SBA accepts the application, approves the request, and extends the credit consideration. No intermediary is involved. Unfortunately, we can dispense with this category as a potential source of cash capability with two brief comments.

First, a business qualifies for a direct-funded SBA loan only when all other reputable avenues to credit consideration are closed. Such loans may provide start-up cash for the new, untested business or disaster financing for the business on the brink of failure. However, relatively few firms qualify.

Second, few direct-funded SBA loans are available relative to the number of applicants. In fact, this typically precludes practical consideration of this alternative source of funds.

In contrast, the indirect SBA guaranteed loan is readily available from many banks. Such loans are extended directly by the bank. However, the borrower's promise for repayment is supported by a guarantee provided directly by the Small Business Administration. That guarantee usually ensures repayment of at least 90% of the credit consideration.

Two unfortunate myths are often associated with this category of SBA loans.

First, the 90% guarantee for repayment means that banks do not consider these loans frivolously. Indeed, the lender still expects the borrower to demonstrate a fundamentally sound financial status.

However, that circumstance may still not satisfy the requirements set by the bank's credit criteria. Perhaps the firm's debt/equity ratio is somewhat higher than usual for normal bank credit consideration. Or the firm may be losing money, held back by insufficient cash capability. Or the prospective borrower's promise exceeds its past performance.

In such circumstances, the SBA's guarantee enables the bank to meet the needs of a worthy customer who fails to qualify for normal credit consideration. An SBA guarantee does not make a bad loan good; instead, it makes a good loan better.

Second, many businessmen still shy away from SBA loans because they fear that there are mountains of paperwork or government interference. In reality, neither obstacle exists.

After the initial application process, which is no more tedious than most other loan applications, the only paperwork is the monthly repayment (most SBA guaranteed loans come in the form of five- to seven-year installment loans). The imaginary mountain of paperwork becomes lost in the normal administrative process.

Because you obtain the loan from your bank and work with your banker, your contact with the SBA is minimal.

Bank-funded SBA guaranteed loans should not be overlooked as potential sources of credit consideration. In many circumstances, such loans are the logical answer to external financing.

BANK RELATIONS

A sound banking relationship is essential for the long-term success of a business. Indeed, that relationship can ensure that the business has a source of external financing to fill a gap in its cash flow cycle. Moreover, an experienced banker can provide valuable counsel.

Of course, you don't establish a sound banking relationship in your first meeting with a banker. Nor does that relationship automatically follow the extension of bank credit consideration. Instead, a business *builds* a bank relationship over a long period and in a manner that is mutually beneficial for both the business and the bank.

As with any other lender, the cornerstones of a sound banking relationship are (1) open lines of communication, (2) timely financial information, and (3) adequate lender compensation.

The communication process operates most effectively, if not most efficiently, when it relies on personal contact. The better your personal relationship, the better your bank relationship. To enhance the personal relationship, you should provide the bank with timely financial information about your business. You should give the bank your most recent balance sheets and income statements as soon as they are prepared. Indeed, the more the banker knows about your financial circumstance, the more he can contribute to your business.

Significantly, you should communicate any actual or potential financial setback to your banker immediately. He cannot feel comfortable with a relationship that reveals financial difficulties thirty, or sixty, or ninety days after the fact. So long as you maintain open lines of communication, whether the news is good or bad, your bank will be able to help solve your problems.

Finally, a bank deserves reasonable compensation for its services. While you should know the true cost of borrowing, you should not try to reduce that cost unnecessarily and make your account unprofitable for the bank. When the bank finds your account profitable, your line of communication open, and your financial information timely, you have set the structure for a sound, mutually profitable bank relationship.

23

Leverage from the Commercial Finance Company

Many businessmen view the commercial finance company as the lender of last resort, a source of leverage to be used only when other lenders refuse credit consideration. Unfortunately, this attitude most often arises from ignorance, and thus it becomes an obstacle to the success or to the full potential of many businesses.

This chapter will review the two major forms of credit consideration provided by commercial finance companies: factoring and accounts receivable financing. We will establish two fundamental concepts that provide the logical foundation for both financing methods.

One concept, collateral-based borrowing power, draws a direct line between the collateral pledged to a lender and the cash capability available to the borrower. Often, this provides more leverage than a business can obtain from any other source. The second concept, the collateral-based revolving loan, revolves the collateral-based loan according to a firm's fluctuating sales and collections. Together, these two concepts provide continuous cash flow financing that can lead to substantial bottom-line benefits.

After defining the collateral-based revolving loan, we distinguish between the two alternative approaches to utilizing it in a business—i.e. factoring and the accounts receivable revolving loan (A/R/R/L). Then, we will examine the special benefits that can proceed from cash flow financing. The unique attributes of cash flow financing often furnish a larger, more permanent contribution that can enhance growth and increase earnings.

Finally, we will review the basic credit criteria that guide the decision process in a commercial finance company.

THE COLLATERAL-BASED LOAN

Before extending any loan, a prudent lender assesses the borrower's credit-worthiness. A commercial finance company uses basically the same credit criteria. However, it does not approve a specific loan. Instead, it agrees to advance funds, subject to a realistic upper limit, in direct proportion to the amount of collateral pledged to secure the credit consideration.

For example, a commercial finance company might approve an 80% *advance rate,* secured by a borrower's investment in accounts receivable. Thus, the borrower gains access to cash capability in any amount up to the limit set by the proportional relationship. In this circumstance, a $100,000 investment in receivables warrants $80,000 in credit consideration. Should the borrower's receivables increase to $150,000, the potential loan rises to $120,000 (80% × $150,-000). Alternatively, a reduction in that investment to $50,000 reduces the firm's borrowing power to $40,000 (80% × $50,000).

In any instance, the total credit consideration extended by the finance company will not exceed the collateral value set by the specific advance rate.

Collateral-based loans secured by accounts receivable comprise the major portion of the credit consideration extended by the commercial finance industry.

With some modification, lenders employ the same concepts to provide leverage secured by inventory, and, less frequently, by equipment. The lender extends credit secured by assets that revolve through the business.

Revolving the Collateral-Based Loan

Unless financing the purchase of fixed assets, many borrowers pledge collateral only to secure single-payment loans. Thus, a business pledges $100,000 in accounts receivable to secure an $80,000 bank loan. Collections from the pledged accounts ultimately repay the loan. Should its cash requirements continue, the business obtains another loan secured by a new set of accounts receivable. Continuous requirements call for a series of repetitive, single-payment loans.

However, factoring and accounts-receivable financing both proceed beyond the limits set by a series of successive single-payment notes. Instead, each translates collateral-based lending into a fluid, revolving relationship of cash flow financing. This relationship can be summarized as Cash Flow Concept 72:

72: The collateral-based revolving loan fluctuates in direct response to the sales, collections, and cash requirements in a business.

Figure 23–1 illustrates this relationship. View (a) shows another perspective of the normal cash flow cycle in a business. Thus, after sales convert inventory into accounts receivable, the business must wait for the term of its average collection period to obtain the cash to pay expenses or reinvest in inventory.

FIGURE 23–1

a. Normal Cash Flow Cycle

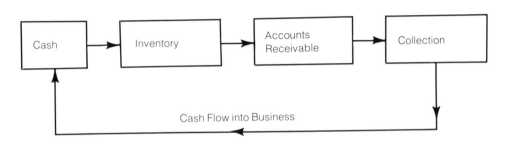

b. Cash Flow Financing

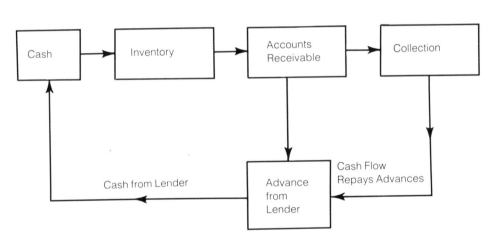

    The collateral-based revolving loan, as shown in (b), eliminates the waiting period and enables a business to obtain the bulk of its cash from sales immediately. That is, on a continuous basis, as it generates sales, a business can obtain cash secured by receivables up to the limit set by its advance rate. A business with an 80% advance rate generates $8,000 in borrowing power from $10,000 in new sales. That much cash is available immediately for profitable reinvestment.

    At the same time, the on-going collection of the borrower's receivables completes the revolving loan cycle. Logically, the collections provide the cash necessary to repay previous advances from the lender.

    The collateral-based revolving loan is equivalent to cash flow financing because the sales-borrowing-repayment cycle operates continuously. In essence, the system accelerates the cash flow process.

CASH FLOW FINANCING IN ACTION

The collateral-based revolving loan accelerates cash flow. The borrower obtains the immediate use of a major portion of each sales dollar without waiting to collect the accounts receivable from those sales. To illustrate this, we will look at the experience of the Crandall Company, an expanding wholesale operation.

Crandall's growth rate recently led to increasing cash needs that exceeded the bounds of standard bank financing. Consequently, the firm arranged for an accounts-receivable revolving loan from a commercial finance company. The finance company agreed to advance Crandall cash in amounts up to 80% of its eligible accounts receivable.

Table 23–1 tracks the first five days in the operation of the loan.

On day 1, when the revolving loan agreement begins, Crandall's accounts receivable total $300,000. The 80% advance rate provides the firm with $240,000 in borrowing power. Initially, Crandall exercises its option to obtain the full amount of cash available. It uses that cash to retire its bank debt and perhaps to pay some past-due trade credit.

On day 2, after initiating the loan agreement, Crandall generates $50,000 in sales but receives no collections from accounts receivable previously outstanding. Consequently, the firm's total investment in receivables increases to $350,-000, which raises its total borrowing power to $280,000 ($350,000 × 80%).

Crandall again exercises its option and gains an additional $40,000 in cash from the lender. Thus, the sales create new receivables that increase the collateral-based borrowing power available from the lender.

On day 3, Crandall generates no sales. However, the company does receive $40,000 in payments on account from its customers. Since the receivables stand as collateral for the credit consideration, Crandall remits the collections to the lender.

Application of the collections to the firm's outstanding loan balance completes the revolution of the loan. New sales create new borrowing power; collections on account reduce any existing loan balance.

Observe the first three days and measure all of the results that come from the $40,000 in collections. Of course, the firm's total investment in receivables drops to $310,000. Simultaneously, the collections reduce Crandall's total loan balance to $240,000. However, observe that, despite the lack of any new sales, the collections produce $8,000 in new cash capability, or borrowing power, for the firm.

This new borrowing power develops naturally from the characteristics of the revolving loan. The lender advances cash only up to 80% of each sales dollar. However, collections usually represent 100% of each sales dollar. Thus, the collection "overpays" the original advance. The borrower sees the effect of the overpayment in a rise in his borrowing power equal to 20% of the collected amount.

On day 4, Crandall receives no collections but generates $30,000 in new sales. The new sales increase the firm's cash capability by $24,000

TABLE 23-1 Cash Flow Financing

THE CRANDALL COMPANY

Day	Sales	Collections	A/R Balance	Total Cash Capability	Daily Cash Advance	Loan Outstanding	Unused Cash Capability
1	—	—	$300,000	$240,000	$240,000	$240,000	—
2	$50,000	—	350,000	280,000	40,000	280,000	—
3	—	$40,000	310,000	248,000	—	240,000	$ 8,000
4	30,000	—	340,000	272,000	20,000	260,000	12,000
5	—	—	340,000	272,000	5,000	265,000	7,000

($30,000 × 80%). We presume that Crandall's cash needs will absorb $20,000 out of that capability.

This raises another critical point: The borrower using cash flow financing does not have to use the full amount of the cash capability available from the lender. He can use all of it, none of it, or part of it, as his cash needs dictate. Thus, it is easy to see how cash flow financing provides an element of flexibility for the business with fluctuating cash needs. So long as the excess capability exists, the business can control the use of leverage in direct response to its cash needs.

Finally, on day 5, Crandall generates no new sales and receives no new collections. However, at the close of the previous day, the company enjoyed $12,000 in unused cash capability. Crandall obtains $5,000 from that amount on day 5.

Of course, the actual administration of the collateral-based revolving loan is more complex, but the Crandall Company's experience demonstrates the basic concept and suggests some of the potential benefits that can come from cash flow financing. Our illustration also should encourage you to adopt a different perspective of the cash flow process.

A NEW DEFINITION OF CASH FLOW

The collateral-based revolving loan changes the concept of cash flow. No longer is it totally dependent on collections; instead, it becomes primarily dependent on sales. Moreover, it fluctuates on a daily basis depending upon the interrelationship of sales, collections, borrowing power, and the needs of the business.

A straightforward relationship identifies the specific cash flow in a business using every dollar available from the collateral-based revolving loan. Thus, presuming the business has an 80% advance rate, its cash flow becomes 80% of sales plus 20% of collections. That cash flows naturally from the mechanical process that revolves the loan. The borrower obtains up to 80% of any new sales in cash. This is 80% of the cash flow equation.

Subsequently, as indicated in Crandall's experience, collections provide another 20% in cash capability, since they reduce the loan dollar for dollar.

Of course, different advance rates change the cash flow equation. For example, with various advance rates, the cash flow becomes:

Advance Rate	Cash Flow	
70%	70% of sales plus 30% of collections	
75%	75%	25%
80%	80%	20%
85%	85%	15%
90%	90%	10%

Thus, to the extent that you can predict your sales and collections, you can reasonably estimate the cash flow and benefits you might derive from the collateral-based revolving loan.

Note that the business with excess cash capability gains a unique benefit from this financing method. Indeed, it can gain complete control over its cash flow. For example, assume that a business has $320,000 in borrowing power from an 80% advance rate applied to a $400,000 investment in accounts receivable. However, the company only uses an average of $200,000 of that borrowing power, leaving $120,000 in excess or unused cash capability.

In this instance, the company can exercise complete control of its cash flow: It requests cash only when necessary for actual expenditure. It controls its borrowing in direct response to its cash requirements.

FACTORING AND ACCOUNTS-RECEIVABLE FINANCING

Thus far, we have categorized factoring and accounts-receivable financing as analogous forms of cash flow financing. Certainly, either alternative activates the same fundamental concepts. However, three critical characteristics distinguish these two methods:
1. The matter of notification
2. Credit and collection services
3. The element of cost

As we examine the basic distinctions, the advantages and disadvantages of each alternative should become apparent.

The Matter of Notification

Both accounts-receivable financing and factoring rely on the pledge of a firm's receivables to a lender (or factor) to secure a loan. In both, the total cash capability available from that pledge comes from the application of the contractual advance rate to the firm's total eligible accounts receivable. (Some receivables that fall too far past due or whose ultimate collectibility is questionable may receive no consideration at all in the cash capability calculation.)

Also, in both cases, the loan revolves as the lender advances funds against the accounts receivable created by new sales, and as he applies the collections from outstanding accounts against the existing loan balance.

However, the first distinction between the two alternatives arises from the factor's standard practice of *notification*. We can sum up this basic distinction in Cash Flow Concept 73:

73: The matter of notification distinguishes accounts receivable financing from factoring.

Thus, the factor accepts the pledged accounts as collateral. At the same time, however, he directs the borrower's customers to remit payment directly to him, rather than to the borrower.

For example, assume the Best Company factors its accounts receivable. Then, using a $10,000 sale as an example, the factoring process proceeds as follows:

1. Prior to the actual shipment, the Best Company obtains the factor's approval of the sale to the Better Company
2. Subsequent to the shipment, the Best Company issues an invoice to the Better Company as evidence of the sale with the designated terms for payment
3. The Best Company obtains an advance from the factor—up to $8,000—using the Better Company's promise to pay as collateral
4. However, the invoice issued to the Better Company requires remittance directly to the factor

Of course, this summary oversimplifies the factoring process. Moreover, the factor often provides services that exceed well beyond the basic cash advance. But what is important here is that the lender instructs your customers to remit payments directly to him.

In contrast, accounts-receivable financing operates on a *non-notification* basis: The lender accepts the receivables as collateral for the loan but allows the borrower to continue the normal credit and collection process. Of course, the lender receives copies of sales invoices that support the specific pledge. Also, the borrower remits collections on account to the lender for application against the loan balance.

However, barring financial disaster on the part of the borrower, his customers—the debtors whose promises to pay serve as collateral for the loan—remain unaware of the financing relationship. Non-notification preserves the confidence of the financing transaction.

Unfortunately, many businessmen believe notification carries a stigma of financial distress. Consequently, they eliminate the factor as a potential source of credit consideration. However, factoring offers other benefits that can offset the negative effects of this imaginary stigma.

Credit and Collection Services

Credit and collection services are usually included in a factoring arrangement. Remember this as Cash Flow Concept 74:

74: The factor typically supplements cash flow financing with credit and collection services.

The borrower agrees not to extend credit to any customer without the factor's prior approval. Then, as a logical extension of the notification process, the factor also becomes responsible for the collection of the firm's receivables. Any uncollected accounts ultimately become bad-debt losses for the factor, rather than for the borrower.

Of course, not every factoring arrangement includes credit and collection services, but this arrangement eliminates the need for an internal credit and collection service. Instead, it is provided by the factor and his own efficient, experienced staff.

In another direct contrast, the lender who provides accounts-receivable financing contributes little to the borrower's credit and collection effort. The borrower makes the credit decisions and manages the necessary collection effort. He also absorbs any loss from bad debts.

At the same time, the lender may refuse advances against accounts receivable if he considers the collateral value to be questionable. But the decision to extend credit consideration to any customer remains in the hands of the borrower.

The Element of Cost

You incur a borrowing cost when you use accounts-receivable financing or factoring as a source of leverage. If you use the factor's credit and collection services, you pay an additional fee. However, keep in mind Cash Flow Concept 75:

75: Cost distinguishes factoring from accounts-receivable financing.

Lenders who provide cash flow financing typically charge 4% to 7% over the prevailing prime lending rate. The uninitiated often consider such rates to be exorbitant. However, you should recognize two critical facts about that charge.

First, the lender properly charges a firm only for the actual dollars borrowed each day. Thus, a 12% annual interest rate becomes a 1/30 of 1% daily charge. Using $100,000 for one day costs the borrower $33.33.

Since a borrower's cash usage usually fluctuates on a daily basis, the *actual dollar cost* of cash flow financing often falls below comparable bank financing. That holds true even though the bank's stated annual interest charge appears to be significantly lower.

For example, assume that a business foresees a peak need for $150,000 over a thirty-day period. A bank may satisfy that need with a $150,000 loan for thirty days at a 10% annual interest rate. The monthly charge for the bank's funds totals $1,250.

However, the business also recognizes that its actual need for borrowed funds fluctuates from day to day. That need never exceeds $150,000, but it often drops as low as $50,000. Indeed, projections indicate that the average daily cash needs for the month actually total only $100,000.

Thus, the business considers cash flow financing at 12% annual interest rate as a possible alternative to bank financing. Since the system allows the business to control its borrowing in direct response to its daily usage, its *average* loan balance totals only $100,000.

The monthly charge for that average totals $1,000, or $250 below comparable bank financing. Note that the difference becomes larger if we recognize the cost of a bank's standard compensating balance requirement.

Second, even when the actual dollar cost is higher, you might still find cash flow financing preferable to bank financing. That occurs when cash flow financing leads to larger net bottom-line benefits, as discussed under "The Contribution from Flexible Leverage."

The cost of accounts-receivable financing seldom exceeds the daily interest charge. However, in addition to any financing charge, you pay the factor a commission of 1% to 5% out of each sales dollar to compensate for the credit and collection services included in the factoring arrangement.

The specific commission rate paid to a factor arises from many interrelated considerations, such as invoice size, administrative effort, sales volume, and negotiation. However, since it includes credit and collection services, factoring exceeds the cost of accounts-receivable financing.

Of course, the higher cost of factoring should not preclude it from consideration as a source of leverage. The factor's total commissions may be well below the cost of a competent credit and collection effort.

THE CONTRIBUTION FROM FLEXIBLE LEVERAGE

Cash flow financing often leads to net bottom-line benefits that exceed those available from bank financing. This holds true even though the actual dollar costs associated with cash flow financing are higher.

The potential advantage arises from the flexibility of the lending method, and of the lenders who provide it. Compared to other forms of leverage, factoring and accounts-receivable financing both can contribute:

1. More cash capability
2. Expanding cash capability
3. Permanent cash capability

More Cash Capability

In many circumstances, collateral-based revolving loans provide more cash capability to a business than alternative financing methods. Two facts lead to that potential. First, commercial finance companies employ liberal credit criteria, and they are not restricted to normal lending limits. Second, the pledged collateral determines the cash capability available to the borrower. As the total collateral increases, the firm's borrowing power increases.

We use the experience of Marvel Products, Inc., an electronic parts distributor, to demonstrate the benefits. Column 1 in Table 23–2 reflects Marvel's financial structure as it stood at 12/31/79.

This structure shows the following characteristics about Marvel's circumstances:

1. A forty-day average collection period translated the firm's $2,000 daily sales volume into an $80,000 investment in accounts receivable

TABLE 23-2

MARVEL PRODUCTS, INC.

	12/31/79	6/30/80	6/30/80
Cash	$ 20,000	—	$ 40,000
Accounts Receivable	80,000	$160,000	160,000
Inventory	80,000	160,000	160,000
Total Assets	**$180,000**	**$320,000**	**$360,000**
Accounts Payable	$ 80,000	$208,000	$160,000
Bank Loan	40,000	40,000	—
A/R Financing	—	—	128,000
Total Liabilities	$120,000	$248,000	$288,000
Stockholders' Equity	$ 60,000	$ 72,000	$ 72,000
Liabilities and Equity	**$180,000**	**$320,000**	**$360,000**

2. To preclude excessive stock-out costs, Marvel maintains an investment in inventory sufficient for two month's sales.

3. The firm's suppliers allow credit consideration equal to the inventory level necessary for two month's sales

4. Marvel's bank provided an additional $40,000 in cash capability at 12/31/79

These characteristics left Marvel with a satisfactory financial structure. However, increasing demand for electronic parts encouraged Marvel to expand its sales volume. In fact, over the six months following 12/31/79, the firm pushed sales up to $4,000 per day.

Unfortunately, that higher volume devastated Marvel's financial structure. As receivables and inventory increased in line with the higher volume, the firm no longer paid suppliers on time. As shown in Column 2, the firm's effort to observe that policy exhausts its cash reserve.

Not surprisingly, Marvel's higher debt/equity ratio at 6/30/80 precluded additional bank credit consideration. Indeed, the firm's banker demanded repayment of the $40,000 already committed.

Column 3 shows how cash flow financing solved Marvel's problem. Since the firm's total borrowing power comes from the collateral value (80% × $160,-000), Marvel gains the cash adequate to maintain a consistent trade credit record. In addition, the company has excess borrowing power that it uses to expand its cash reserves.

Expanding and Permanent Cash Capability

As suggested by Marvel's experience, the cash capability available from a collateral-based revolving loan expands in direct line with a borrower's growth rate. As sales increase, so does the firm's borrowing power. Indeed, both factoring and accounts-receivable financing can provide the cash necessary to fuel rapid growth.

In addition, cash flow financing can provide permanent cash capability for a business. Remember this as Cash Flow Concept 76:

76: A collateral-based revolving loan can become a permanent source of expanding cash capability for a business.

Each new sale provides new cash capability to offset the natural reduction in that capability through collections. Consequently, the borrower isn't concerned with the cash drain enforced by the maturity of a single-payment note. Also, lenders who provide cash flow financing do not require annual cleanups. But most important, the borrower can concentrate on sales and not worry about financing.

CREDIT CRITERIA

The commercial finance company's credit analysis proceeds in the same general direction as any other lender's. It begins with an evaluation of the applicant's prospects within its industry and in the general economic environment and proceeds to an analysis of the firm's past operating results, present financial condition, and projected cash flow. Finally, it considers the collateral that provides the critical insurance for eventual repayment.

However, the commercial finance company approaches the major portion of any credit analysis from a different perspective than traditional lenders, and often it will approve credit consideration when other lenders might deny it.

Financial Credit Criteria

The financial credit criteria employed by a commerical finance company appear to be remarkably liberal. Thus, neither a high debt/equity ratio nor a low current ratio necessarily eliminates a prospective borrower from credit consideration. Indeed, the commercial finance company may disregard ratio analysis altogether and, instead, concentrate on two basic financial considerations.

First, the business should have reasonable expectations of profitable operations. While this seems obvious, the requirement does not disqualify the business with a recent history of operating losses. Indeed, the favorable elements presented by a business in the midst of a turnaround often justify cash flow financing.

Second, a prospective borrower should demonstrate financial strength measured by *tangible net worth*. This is the difference between a firm's real assets and liabilities. It excludes assets that have no realistic liquidation value: intangible assets such as goodwill, leasehold improvements, and loans to officers. Tangible net worth provides a reasonable estimate of the fundamental financial foundation in a business.

In general terms, the commercial finance company expects a borrower to have a tangible net worth sufficient to absorb an ordinary financial setback without threatening the survival of the firm. Some lenders set a minimum requirement, such as a $50,000 or $100,000 tangible net worth. Others relate the firm's total debt to tangible net worth, with no specific debt/equity ratio automatically requiring a negative credit decision.

Indeed, a liberal flexibility describes the financial criteria that orient the commercial finance company's credit decision.

Cash Flow Credit Criteria

A commercial finance company expects a borrower to have a cash flow satisfactory for normal operations. However, the finance company will include the proposed credit consideration in its examination of the borrower's cash flow balance sheet.

Thus, simulating approval of the cash flow financing, the business must then demonstrate the capacity to meet all obligations in a timely manner: It must show the ability to pay trade creditors within their desigented terms and to meet debt repayment requirements, as well as retire all normal operating expenses on schedule.

Certainly, the business that can't satisfy these requirements, even with the proposed credit consideration, does not have a cash flow satisfactory for normal operations.

Collateral Credit Criteria

Collateral analysis ultimately becomes the pivotal element in the commercial finance company's credit decision. Two logical considerations justify this fact.

First, collateral analysis identifies the potential borrowing power available to the business. Should the borrowing power prove inadequate to satisfy the cash flow credit criteria, the business doesn't qualify for cash flow financing.

Second, the liberal financial and cash flow credit criteria rely strongly on collateral. This pivotal element can be summarized in Cash Flow Concept 77:

77: A commercial finance company's credit decision centers on the fundamental value of the borrower's collateral.

Indeed, the collateral value must be sufficient to offset the lack of financial strength and tight cash flow allowed by the other credit criteria.

Ultimately, the collateral value comes from the creditworthiness and payment habits of the firm's customers. The more likely the customers are to pay for purchases as agreed, the better the quality of the collateral that justifies cash flow financing.

LENDER RELATIONS

The collateral-based revolving loan contract specifies the rights and obligations of the borrower and the lender. In addition, it clearly defines the terms of the borrowing relationship, such as advance rate, credit line, and interest charge.

Consequently, the borrower's personal relationship with the lender has little influence on the cash capability available to the business. This is defined by the contract.

However, this does not diminish the need for a good working relationship with the lender. Because the administrative process associated with cash flow financing typically requires daily contact, the need for a sound relationship actually becomes even more significant.

Open lines of communication provide the foundation for that relationship. When you satisfy the lender's need for information about your business, you allow him to satisfy your need for cash capability. Indeed, open lines of communication ensure a profitable relationship for both parties.

Leasing vs. Leverage

Leasing has become a significant financial tool in modern business. However, many businessmen still view leasing as a mysterious alternative to external financing, and often they are unaware of how it can affect cash flow and earnings. This chapter solves the mystery and introduces a practical approach to leasing.

In Chapter 14, we advised the use of external financing to purchase fixed assets. This practice preserves cash reserves that can help absorb the shock of a financial reverse. But a business can achieve the same objective with a lease agreement.

We will emphasize the similarities and differences between a lease and a standard installment loan agreement and then compare a lease against a leveraged purchase as an alternative path to obtaining the use of fixed assets. This approach focuses on the comparative cash commitments of the two alternatives.

However, we must recognize the deteriorating value of the dollars used to meet lease or installment loan payments over a number of years. Thus, we will illustrate the basic process that measures the *time value of money*.

Of course, the decision to lease or use leverage may result from considerations other than the comparative cash commitments. Consequently, we also review other elements that might enter into the decision process.

Finally, we will discuss the sale and leaseback process, which can become a major reservoir of cash for a business. Indeed, it enables a business to gain cash benefits from the inflationary values locked in its fixed assets.

THE COMMON LEASE AGREEMENT

In format and function, the common long-term machinery and equipment lease differs little from a standard installment loan agreement. The lease imposes a fixed obligation on the business to make scheduled monthly payments for a predetermined period.

Without special provisions, a lease is seldom subject to premature termination. Consequently, as a measure of commitment, it usually imposes the same obligation on a business as an installment loan. At the same time, however, it does not ensure permanent use of the fixed assets. The leasing company (the lessor) retains actual ownership and thus enjoys the benefits that come from the investment tax credit and depreciation process. Moreover, the lessor retains the residual rights to the equipment subsequent to the expiration of the lease. The business leasing the equipment (the lessee) must renew the lease or lose the use of the assets.

Of course, a lease may include an option that allows the lessee to purchase the assets during the term of the lease or at the time it is terminated. However, this option must satisfy restrictive IRS requirements. Consequently, the option to purchase often becomes a secondary consideration in the decision of whether to lease or to purchase.

Alternatively, of course, the business that finances the purchase of fixed assets with an installment loan retains all of the rights of ownership. The lender receives a pledge of the assets to secure his loan, but this pledge expires simultaneously with the final installment loan payment. Naturally, the business also retains the rights to the investment tax credit and depreciation charges that accompany the purchase.

From our perspective, however, the major difference between a lease and a leveraged purchase is found in the comparative cash commitments.

COMPARATIVE CASH COMMITMENTS

The cash commitment of a lease agreement, as opposed to an installment loan, requires no initial cash outlay other than one or two prepaid lease payments. Conversely, a conventional lender may require a 10% to 30% down payment: Thus, a $100,000 fixed-asset acquisition could mean a $10,000 to $30,000 initial cash outlay.

The term of the typical lease agreement also requires a different cash commitment, because the term often exceeds that of an installment loan. For example, a business might obtain a five- or six-year lease to use equipment with a seven-year useful life. In some instances, the term of a lease actually matches the life of the equipment. In contrast, a conventional lender may require repayment of an installment loan in no more than three or four years.

Thus, although the different terms can leave a business with approximately the same annual cash commitments, at least until the shorter-term installment loan is retired, the *total* cash commitment over the full term of a lease usually exceeds that required for a comparable purchase. This is natural, since the lessor incurs a borrowing (or opportunity) cost from the funds used to purchase the leased equipment.

Thus, the lessee's monthly payment must be sufficient to amortize most of the actual cost of the equipment, absorb the financial expenses, and provide a profitable return to the lessee. The total payments necessary to meet those requirements inevitably lead to a larger overall cash commitment than a comparable purchase.

Note that you shouldn't try to compare the financing charge of a lease directly with that of an installment loan. Surprisingly, the financial cost of a lease often appears to be less, but this can be misleading. In addition to the interest income, the lessor obtains the right to the investment tax credit, the depreciation charges, and the residual value of the equipment. Those benefits often become more significant than the interest income derived from a lease, and lead to a lower apparent interest charge.

In any event, the apparent interest is an irrelevant element in the decision process that chooses between a lease or leveraged purchase.

TO LEASE OR TO PURCHASE?

The experience of the Abba Company will demonstrate the differences between a lease and a leveraged purchase.

The Abba Company is contemplating the addition of $50,000 in fixed assets to its production line. The assets will have a ten-year useful life with no residual value at the end of that term. Abba has the capacity to lease the assets or to complete a purchase with the aid of external financing.

The proposed lease requires $9,000 in annual payments for the full ten-year life of the equipment. The lessor requires no other cash outlay. Alternatively, if Abba decides to purchase the equipment, the lender will require an $8,000 initial down payment. The remaining $42,000 will be repayable over seven years. Total annual installment payments will be $8,730. The annual payments include $6,000 in principal and $2,730 in interest.

Two other elements in Abba's circumstance also enter into the analysis.

First, company policy calls for the straight-line depreciation of all fixed assets. The firm loses the benefits that come from accelerated depreciation, but it maintains a simplified accounting process.

Also, Abba presently stands in the 40% marginal tax bracket, and it expects to operate in that bracket throughout the ten-year life of the equipment. Abba's comparative analysis begins with the calculation of the net cash cost associated with each alternative.

The Net Cash Cost of a Lease

A lease payment becomes an operating expense for a business. Consequently, the calculation of the net cash cost of a lease requires proper recognition of the effect that expense has on the lessor's annual income-tax obligation.

In Abba's circumstance, this expense reduces the firm's tax obligation by $3,600 ($9,000 × 40% tax rate). Abba retains that much cash in the business that otherwise would flow out in the form of income-tax payments.

From our perspective, that reduces the net cash cost of Abba's lease as follows:

Annual Lease Payments	$9,000
Less: Reduction in Taxes Payable	(3,600)
Net Cash Cost (annually)	$5,400

Thus, the firm's net lease payments will total $5,400 annually for the ten-year life of the equipment.

Of course, the business in a lower tax bracket realizes a smaller cash benefit from the lease expense. The business in a higher bracket gets a larger benefit. In any circumstance, the calculation procedure doesn't change. Remember this as Cash Flow Concept 78:

78: A lower tax obligation reduces the net cash cost of a lease.

The Net Cash Cost of a Leveraged Purchase

Conceptually, the calculation of the net cash cost of a purchase made with external financing is the same as that applied to a lease. In other words, you gain a reduction in taxes because of the expenses associated with the purchase; then, you offset that reduction against the direct cash expenditures. We can summarize this effect in Cash Flow Concept 79:

79: A lower tax obligation reduces the net cash cost of a purchase.

However, calculating the net cash cost of a leveraged purchase becomes more complicated because you have to recognize the impact of the initial down payment on your cash flow, and note the subsequent effects of

1. The investment tax credit
2. The depreciation expense
3. The interest expense

Table 24–1 demonstrates how these considerations enter into Abba's analysis.

Of course, Abba's actual cash expenditures for the purchase are apparent. Thus, on the day Abba completes the purchase (year 0), it must come up with an $8,000 cash down payment. Then, for the next seven years, Abba's annual installment loan payment totals $8,730.

However, to measure Abba's net cash cost each year, you must calculate

TABLE 24–1 The Net Cash Cost of a Leveraged Purchase

THE ABBA COMPANY

Year	Cash Expenditure	Tax Credit	Interest Effect on Taxes Payable	Depreciation Effect on Taxes Payable	Net Cash Cost
0	$8,000 (a)				$ 8,000
1	8,730 (b)	(5,000)	($1,092)	($2,000)	638
2	8,730 (b)		(1,092)	(2,000)	5,638
3	8,730 (b)		(1,092)	(2,000)	5,638
4	8,730. (b)		(1,092)	(2,000)	5,638
5	8,730 (b)		(1,092)	(2,000)	5,638
6	8,730 (b)		(1,092)	(2,000)	5,638
7	8,730 (b)		(1,092)	(2,000)	5,638
8	—		—	(2,000)	(2,000)
9	—		—	(2,000)	(2,000)
10	—		—	(2,000)	(2,000)
					$36,466

(a) Down payment at time of purchase
(b) Annual cash payments to lender, including $6,000 in principal repayment and $2,730 in interest

the reduction in taxes derived from the acquisition. In the first year, Abba gains a $5,000 reduction in taxes from the 10% investment tax credit earned with the purchase. Remember that a tax credit provides a dollar-for-dollar offset against a firm's income-tax obligation.

Also, for the first seven years after the acquisition, Abba enjoys a $1,092 annual reduction in taxes from the interest expense of the installment loan ($2,730 × 40%). The company also realizes a $2,000 annual reduction in taxes from the $5,000 depreciation expense incurred each year ($5,000 × 40%). Abba obtains that benefit each year for the full ten-year life of the equipment.

Now, note some interesting elements about Abba's net cash costs.

First, the tax credit, coupled with the depreciation and interest expenses, reduces the firm's net cash cost in year 1 to only $638. Indeed, the net cash cost in the first year becomes nominal, and it holds constant for the next six years, until Abba fully repays the installment loan.

Second, over the last three years in the life of the equipment, Abba actually realizes a $2,000 annual cash benefit from the purchase. The company continues to accrue a $5,000 annual depreciation charge, but it incurs no more cash outlay. The $2,000 reduction in taxes translates directly into a higher annual cash flow.

Predictably, the primary difficulty in comparing a lease against a purchase arises from the fluctuations in the annual net cash costs associated with a purchase. This means you must consider the time value of money as an element in the comparative analysis.

THE TIME VALUE OF MONEY

The net cash cost of the leveraged purchase made by the Abba Company totals $36,466. This falls well below the $54,000 total net cash cost that arises from leasing the same equipment. However, that does not necessarily make the purchase the preferable alternative. Our comparison must proceed one step further—to translate the total net cash costs associated with each alternative into current value dollars. In other words, the analysis must properly recognize the time value of money. Remember this as Cash Flow Concept 80:

80: Use present-value dollars to compare the net cash costs of a lease and leveraged purchase.

We introduced one perspective of this concept in Chapter 17, when we illustrated the detrimental effects of inflation on the purchasing power of the dollar. A dollar expended today has more purchasing power than a dollar expended a year from today. And a dollar expended in two years is worth less than a dollar expended in one year.

Fortunately, we can measure that deterioration precisely and translate the nominal value of dollars expended in the future into present-day equivalent dollars. This translation comes from the *discounting* process used by financial analysts.

The logic that leads to discounting the value of dollars expended (or received) in the future comes from the more familiar principle of compounding. This principle presumes that an investment earns a return at some specified rate across a defined time period. At the end of each period, the earned amount is added to the investment. Then, the accumulated balance earns the same return for the next period.

For example, assume that a business invests $1,000 in a project that promises a 10% return, compounded annually. Over four years, the compounding process increases the $1,000 investment to $1,464:

```
Year 1   $1,000 × 1.10 = $1,100
Year 2   $1,100 × 1.10 = $1,210
Year 3   $1,210 × 1.10 = $1,331
Year 4   $1,331 × 1.10 = $1,464
```

Discounting is the exact opposite of compounding. So, to measure the current value of a dollar to be expended (or received) in the future, you merely reverse the compounding process.

For example, assume that a business expects to receive $1,464 from an investment in exactly four years. The business uses a 10% opportunity cost to measure the fundamental value of the funds committed to a project. (Financial analysts employ a theoretical *cost of capital* for a business. Utilizing some opportunity cost, or the prevailing rate of inflation, serves the same basic objective.) Thus, to measure the present value of the $1,464, you use the calculation:

$1,464 ÷ 1.10 = $1,331 = Value at end of three years
$1,331 ÷ 1.10 = $1,210 = Value at end of two years
$1,210 ÷ 1.10 = $1,100 = Value at end of one year
$1,100 ÷ 1.10 = $1,000 = Value today (present value)

The proper comparison of a lease with a leveraged purchase employs the discounting process to measure the net cash costs of each alternative in present-value dollars. The preferable alternative is the one that registers the lower equivalent cost.

PRESENT-VALUE COMPARISON OF NET CASH COST

The Abba Company employed the discounting process to complete the comparative analysis of the lease and leveraged purchase. Using a 10% annual opportunity cost, the company translated the annual net cash costs associated

TABLE 24 – 2 Present-Value Comparison: Lease vs. Leveraged Purchase

THE ABBA COMPANY

Year	Net Cash Cost — Lease	Present Value Cost — Lease	Net Cash Cost — Purchase	Present Value Cost — Purchase
0	—		$8,000	$ 8,000
1	$5,400	$ 4,908	638	579
2	5,400	4,460	5,638	4,656
3	5,400	4,055	5,638	4,234
4	5,400	3,688	5,638	3,850
5	5,400	3,353	5,638	3,501
6	5,400	3,045	5,638	3,179
7	5,400	2,770	5,638	2,892
8	5,400	2,521	(2,000)	(934)
9	5,400	2,289	(2,000)	(848)
10	5,400	2,084	(2,000)	(772)
Total Present Value Costs		**$33,173**		**$28,337**

with each alternative into present-value equivalent dollars. Table 24–2 summarizes that analysis.

Note that the total present value cost of a leveraged purchase falls significantly below that of the lease. Indeed, measured in current dollars, the leveraged purchase costs $4,836 less. In this instance, the comparison clearly favors the purchase.

However, let's alter one major assumption in the case and assume that Abba negotiates annual lease payments of $8,000 rather than $9,000 per year. This reduces the annual net cash cost of the lease to $4,800 ($8,000 × 60%).

The discounting process translates those payments into current dollars worth $29,494. Now, the present-value cost of the lease exceeds that from the purchase by only $1,157. This smaller difference may lose significance when you consider the other potential benefits of a lease.

OTHER DECISION CRITERIA

We know that the decision to lease instead of purchase may not hinge on the current dollar cost of each alternative. This often occurs when a leasing arrangement includes a service agreement. For example, an equipment lease might include a service agreement that reduces the firm's responsibility for maintenance. Instead, the lessor answers that need. The business pays a higher cost to warrant against expensive, time-consuming breakdowns.

In other instances, a lease agreement may proceed beyond the provision for basic maintenance. Thus, a fleet vehicle lease may guarantee the availability of replacement equipment in the event of breakdowns. The same agreement may provide for the temporary use of additional units to help satisfy an unforeseen increase in sales.

Such agreements also shift much of the fleet administrative management, such as insurance, tax records, and cost analyses, to the lessor. This again adds to the cost of the lease, but the higher cost easily may be offset because the firm can reduce its administrative personnel.

In some circumstances, practical financial considerations (other than comparative net cash costs) encourage the use of a lease. For example, a business may lack the cash capability to make the down payment for a purchase. A lease may be the only way to obtain necessary equipment.

Alternatively, a business with adequate cash might use a lease to preserve those reserves. Being able to absorb an unforeseen financial setback may justify the higher cost of a lease.

In still other circumstances, a lease enables a business to preserve financial flexibility. It can use its cash to take advantage of profit opportunities that offset the higher cost of the lease.

In any circumstance, of course, a business must compare the present value cost of a lease against the present value cost of leveraged purchase. But the considerations reviewed here may ultimately become the final decision criterion.

THE SALE AND LEASEBACK ARRANGEMENT

Many businesses derive profitable benefits from a special leasing arrangement called a *sale and leaseback*. Under this arrangement, a business sells one of its assets to a lessor, who leases it back to the firm. The price of the sale typically approximates the market value of the asset.

In essence, a sale and leaseback arrangement enables a business to generate cash from fixed assets that carry an actual value well above that measured by standard accounting principles. The business yields ownership of the assets, while retaining their use, and gains a direct contribution to its cash capability.

For example, assume a business owns equipment with a current market value of $100,000. At the same time, the assets have no accounting value: The depreciation process has reduced the book value of the assets to zero.

To increase its cash capability, the firm sells the assets to a leasing company, simultaneously executing a lease agreement that ensures the future use of the assets. Although the proceeds of the sale are subject to capital-gains taxes, the business gains more than $70,000 in cash after taxes. This can become a significant contribution to the cash capability in many businesses.

Of course, this example does not demonstrate all of the considerations that enter into a sale and leaseback arrangement. Indeed, it only illustrates how a business can free the cash capability locked in its fixed assets. The arrangement ultimately makes sense only if it leads to significant bottom-line benefits.

Leverage from Investors

On occasion, a business may need external financing in excess of that available from institutional lenders. The need could arise from the cash demands set by rapid expansion, or because an unbalanced financial structure precludes institutional credit consideration. Whatever the justification, the sale of an equity interest in the business may become the only source of additional cash capability. We discuss this alternative in this chapter and weigh the advantages and disadvantages of equity financing. We will also discuss the basic instruments of external financing, including common stock, preferred stock, and convertible securities. And finally, we will review its potential sources.

EQUITY AS LEVERAGE

Equity represents the owner's net financial interest in a business. In simplest terms, the difference between assets and liabilities measures the size of that interest. The net equity includes the common stock, capital surplus, and retained earnings represented in the financial structure of the business.

Most businesses begin with 100% of the ownership interest vested in the hands of the founder. Of course, the founder typically tries to maintain complete ownership. However, the cash needs in a business can exceed the contribution available from its creditors. If the owner lacks the financial capacity to meet these needs, he can generate cash by selling some portion of his ownership interest. In other words, he might seek external equity financing.

From the owner's perspective, using external equity financing to increase the firm's cash capability is no different from using credit or borrowed funds. In both cases, the external investor commits his funds to the business in exchange for the promise of some return on that investment in the future. The business then employs those funds in a way that will keep that promise, as well as to increase the return on the original equity investment. The new equity serves as leverage for the old.

However, we should emphasize one major point at the outset. Remember Cash Flow Concept 81:

81: External equity financing has both advantages and disadvantages.

THE ADVANTAGES OF EXTERNAL EQUITY FINANCING

In comparison with leverage, external equity financing as a source of cash capability offers some distinct advantages to a business. For example:

1. It does not require repayment
2. It has no scheduled interest payments
3. It enhances creditworthiness
4. It imposes no personal liability on the original ownership

First, in direct contrast to leverage, a business has no obligation to repay external equity financing on some predetermined date. Indeed, it provides a permanent contribution to the cash capability in the business. The investor naturally anticipates a profitable return from his contribution. However, he expects that return to come from the appreciation in the value of his investment, perhaps enhanced by future dividend payments.

Of course, the business doesn't guarantee any return on the investment at all. Moreover, neither the lack of price appreciation nor the failure to receive dividends allows the investor to withdraw his cash contribution. Indeed, the investor makes a permanent contribution to the cash capability in the business.

The investor may anticipate some compensation in the form of dividend payments. But realizing that return depends directly upon the success of the operation. Dividends and price appreciation of the investment both remain a hope, not a promise.

In another contrast with leverage, external equity financing from the sale of common stock imposes no fixed charges on the business. The business does not irrevocably commit any portion of its future earnings to compensate the external investor.

However, external equity financing from the sale of preferred stock or convertible bonds *does* impose fixed charges on the firm. The elimination of the fixed-charge obligations comes only from the sale of common stock.

External equity financing also enhances the creditworthiness of a business.

This benefit comes from the increase in financial strength generally represented by a higher net worth. Thus, as the business increases the size of its equity base with the aid of external financing, it becomes a more attractive risk for its creditors. Ultimately, it can expand its cash capability beyond the amount contributed by the external investors.

The first column in Table 25–1 shows the balance sheet of a business that has exhausted its potential for additional credit consideration. Using a fundamental credit criterion, the firm's $1 million in liabilities and $250,000 in equity translate into a four-to-one debt/equity ratio. Certainly, that exceeds the limits set by most creditors.

Now, in the second column, observe the benefit that comes from raising $250,000 in cash from the external equity financing.

Presuming all of the cash reduces the firm's liabilities, that total drops to $750,000, while the firm's equity account rises to $500,000. The interrelated effects leave the business with a 1.5-to-1 debt/equity ratio. This new relationship should justify additional credit consideration.

Indeed, the business can obtain $250,000 in additional cash capability from creditors without exceeding the two-to-one debt/equity relationship, the critical benchmark for many lenders. Thus, each dollar invested in the firm translates in this instance into a potential two-dollar increase in cash capability. Certainly, that enhances the direct cash contribution that comes from external equity financing.

Another advantage of equity financing is that using the sale of equity to increase cash capability doesn't affect the personal financial liability imposed on the original owners. When a closely held corporation, one owned by one or a few stockholders, incurs institutional debt, the lender usually requires the personal guaranty of the individual(s) who controls a majority of the outstanding stock. Naturally, that guaranty encourages the proper disposition of the cash advanced to the corporation. Of course, each time the business increases its institutional debt, the owner also increases his total personal liability for the firm's financial obligations.

External financing has no effect on the original stockholders' personal financial liability. The new investor accepts the risk of loss in exchange for a potential substantial return on his investment. Should the business collapse, he loses his investment. He cannot look to the founders for recovery.

TABLE 25–1 How External Equity Financing Enhances Creditworthiness

Total Assets	$1,250,000	$1,250,000
Total Liabilities	1,000,000	750,000
Stockholders' Equity	250,000	500,000
Equity and Liabilities	$1,250,000	$1,250,000
Debt/Equity Ratio	4 to 1	1.5 to 1

THE DISADVANTAGES OF EXTERNAL EQUITY FINANCING

Before you decide to use external equity financing to expand your cash capability, you should recognize some potential disadvantages. For example:

1. It dilutes ownership control
2. It is difficult to obtain
3. It costs more than debt
4. It becomes inflexible financing

The first disadvantage is usually the most apparent to the entrepreneurial businessman. Selling a portion of his business to external investors obviously dilutes his right of ownership. At the same time, he loses some management control.

Thus, when he decides to sell an interest in his business, the businessman confronts the prospect of splitting future profits with outsiders. This can become a psychological burden to the man who has labored, worried, and risked his financial wherewithal to build a business. Indeed, the prospect of sharing the future earnings often becomes the obstacle that eliminates external equity financing from consideration as a source of cash capability.

Similarly, along with their equity interest, external investors usually expect a voice in corporate affairs. That voice may express itself only in the form of representation on the firm's board of directors, or it may be raised in day-to-day operations. Naturally, the volume of the voice increases according to the proportion of ownership assumed by the investors.

Of course, the original owner can retain controlling interest in the business, but he cannot ignore the legal rights of the minority shareholders. External interference that begins as a nuisance often becomes a severe management problem.

The problem becomes even more severe because of the difficulty the small or medium-size business has in obtaining external equity financing. The number of equity financing sources is limited. Moreover, the business reluctant to yield a significant ownership position will find the potential limited even more.

Thus, an external investor seldom will make a major cash commitment for a 5% interest in a business. However, his interest increases as the prospective proportion of ownership increases. Consequently, the business that seeks external equity financing usually will be successful only if the investor obtains a significant fraction of the total ownership. Of course, as the size of that fraction increases, so does the probability of interference from the new investors. The businessman must confront one disadvantage or the other.

High cost can become another major disadvantage of external equity financing. This may appear to contradict our assertion that the lack of fixed-debt service is an advantage of external equity financing. However, a successful operation eventually incurs more cost from external equity financing than from comparable amounts of leverage. That cost comes from two sources.

First, as we have mentioned, selling an interest in a business invites interference from the external investors. Not only does this become a management problem, it also can become an operating expense for the business.

Part of the expense arises from the commitment of management time to nonproductive concerns. Communication may be necessary, but it often becomes a time-consuming expense. And this expense increases in proportion to the external investors' efforts to influence the firm's actual management. The interference soon translates into a material expense.

Second, the investors' justifiable expectation of dividends on their investment can become a perpetual rising expense for a business. The successful business must pay a portion of its earnings to investors in the form of cash dividends. The amount paid typically increases as the business becomes more successful. Unlike debt service, dividends continue—and grow—over the life of the firm.

Moreover, a dollar paid out as a dividend is more expensive than a dollar paid out as interest expense on debt. Interest payments are tax deductible, while dividends flow out of after-tax earnings. Thus, the cost of external equity financing is even more expensive than it appears at first glance.

Another disadvantage is that external equity financing is the least flexible source of cash capability. Once it is obtained, it cannot be used arbitrarily to repurchase the investor's interest. Indeed, any repurchase ultimately negotiated becomes an expensive proposition.

In contrast, a business usually has the option to prepay debt. Of course, early payment of some fixed debt may involve a prepayment penalty. However, the penalty will seem modest compared to the premium commanded by an external investor for the repurchase of his stock.

Of course, inflexibility may not disqualify external equity financing from consideration as a source of cash capability in a business. But before proceeding with any effort to obtain leverage from investors, consider the advantages and disadvantages.

EQUITY INSTRUMENTS

Equity financing can take a variety of different forms. In fact, the variations are limited only by the imaginations of the businessmen in need of equity financing and the investors who provide it.

Nevertheless, the more familiar equity financing instruments fall into three major categories:

1. Common stock
2. Preferred stock
3. Convertible securities

Of course, you shouldn't employ any of these instruments without measuring the legal and financial ramifications. Indeed, proper consideration of any external equity financing requires professional advice.

Common Stock

Most external equity financing comes from the sale of common stock. A share of common stock represents the fundamental unit of ownership in a business. Thus, the business that sells common stock to an external investor yields some ownership interest to him.

As a simple example, assume that an investor purchases 100 shares of common stock in a corporation that has 1,000 total shares outstanding. The investor obtains a 10% ownership interest in the business. This interest automatically provides the investor with some significant rights.

The stockholder obtains the rights to the net income in the business in proportion to his pro rata ownership. Of course, the earnings may not be paid out but, instead, retained in the business to finance future operations. Nevertheless, when they are distributed, the stockholder is legally entitled to his share.

A common stockholder also receives the right to cast a vote on certain company matters, such as the election of the board of directors. Of course, each share of stock entitles the investor to one vote. Consequently, the more shares held by an investor, the more influence he exerts.

A common stockholder also receives a privileged position in terms of his rights to buy any new stock issued by the corporation. This *preemptive right* gives him the first option to purchase any new shares.

The preemptive right ensures that management cannot subvert the position of present stockholders by selling shares to other investors without offering them to the existing ownership. This protects the stockholder against unfair dilution of his ownership interest.

Preferred Stock

Preferred stock remains an alternative to common stock as an instrument for external equity financing. However, certain undesirable characteristics reduce its potential value as a source of funds for a small business.

First, preferred stock provides no ownership interest in the firm. The investor receives the right to a predetermined, fixed dividend, but he obtains no residual ownership in the business.

Second, while the sale of preferred stock preserves the existing ownership's position, the dividends payable again come out of after-tax earnings, which makes it substantially more expensive than debt.

Thus, preferred stock may be attractive to both the business and the investor only when it is issued as a convertible security.

Convertible Securities

In contrast to straight preferred stock, convertible securities can become useful instruments for external equity financing. A convertible security, either a bond or a share of preferred stock (designated as convertible when issued), can be converted into common stock at the option of the holder. Thus, it offers the investor two complementary advantages.

First, he receives a predetermined, fixed income on his investment, either in interest payments or in preferred dividends. At the same time, when the business prospers, he can convert his holdings into common shares at a predetermined conversion ratio. Thus, he can maintain his position as a debtor or become an owner.

Convertible securities also offer a significant advantage to the business. The business obtains the investor's cash capability without yielding any management control. Convertible securities seldom carry voting rights until formally transformed into common stock.

Of course, as the business achieves its objectives, holders of convertible securities will exercise their options to obtain common stock. However, that conversion eliminates the requirement for interest or preferred dividend payments. Indeed, convertible securities may offer a realistic alternative that enables a business to balance the advantages and disadvantages of external equity financing.

SOURCES OF EXTERNAL EQUITY FINANCING

The decision to use external equity financing often proves difficult for the entrepreneurial businessman. However, making that decision may be less difficult than searching for that financing. Indeed, few sources of external equity financing are available to the small business. Usually, the business is limited to the potential equity investment from

1. Informal (noninstitutional) sources
2. Suppliers or customers
3. Venture-capital companies
4. Small-business investment companies

Informal Sources

Rarely can a young, small business obtain external equity financing from institutional sources. Instead, the businessman most often must turn to informal sources—to friends, relatives, or business acquaintances.

From one perspective, obtaining equity financing from informal sources can be beneficial. Personal relationships can overcome some of the problems that arise from investor interference in the business. Moreover, the informal source may accept a smaller ownership position than that normally accepted by institutional lenders.

From another perspective, using personal relationships to generate external equity financing can lead to problems. Should the business ultimately fail, the investor's loss may sour the personal relationship. At best, the relationship will suffer severe stress.

In any event, the availability of external equity financing from informal sources is a matter of circumstance. The businessman who has no contact or personal relationships with investors will find himself shut out from this source. Nevertheless, you should begin your search for external equity financing close to home. The further you proceed from that base, the more difficult the search becomes.

Suppliers and Customers

On occasion, the business that demonstrates extraordinary promise can obtain equity financing from major customers or suppliers. Of course, the proper circumstance must exist to justify that investment.

The major customer of a small business might commit equity financing to ensure a dependable source of supply for a necessary element in its production line. The equity interest encourages preferred service. Alternatively, a major supplier might venture an investment in a growing concern to ensure the demand for its product. Helping the customer grow with an injection of cash ultimately helps the supplier expand his own operation.

In either circumstance, of course, both sources of external equity financing expect a profitable return on their investment as the business prospers.

Venture-Capital Companies

With the exception of small-business investment companies, venture-capital companies offer little potential as a source of external equity financing for most businesses because they have such restrictive selection requirements.

Most venture-capital companies invest only in businesses that display established credentials, exceptional prospects, and extraordinary management ability. Moreover, the venture-capital company must foresee a realistic potential for a substantial return on its investment, usually from a public offering of stock. A business with modest prospects, however satisfactory to the ownership, will receive little aid from most of these companies.

Small-Business Investment Companies

Among venture-capital concerns, the Small Business Investment Company (SBIC) typically is more accessible to the business in need of external equity financing. Indeed, SBIC's are unique among privately organized venture-capital companies.

The distinction arises from the source of the bulk of the funds SBIC's have for investment. As entities licensed and regulated by the Small Business Administration, SBIC's have access to long-term federal loans as a source of cash for venture-capital investments. Not surprisingly, SBIC's operate under some restrictions set by the Small Business Administration. However, these restrictions typically favor the business seeking financial aid. First, an SBIC seldom makes a direct equity investment in a business. Instead, the equity financing usually comes in the form of convertible bonds. Of course, the business pays interest to the SBIC until conversion. But the initial commitment in the form of debt also preserves the potential for repayment. The original ownership ultimately may preserve its equity position.

Second, the SBIC cannot obtain more than a 49% interest in a customer. While that substantial interest may require active participation in major management decisions, it still leaves final control of the business in the hands of the original owners.

Third, as regulated institutions, SBIC's have limits on the amount of funds they can commit to any single operation. Many also have relatively low investment limits, such as $50,000 to $200,000. Consequently, they must seek the bona fide small business as a prospect for investment.

Certainly, SBIC's hope to profit from their investments, but their operating limitations force them to adopt a more realistic view of the term required for that return.

Leverage: Comparative Analysis

The comparative criteria that should encourage the use of one form of leverage over another can be confusing. When should a business employ trade credit in preference to institutional leverage? What can make a bank loan more desirable than leverage from the trade? When does a collateral-based revolving loan become most appropriate for a business?

Unfortunately, no single answer exists for any of these questions. Indeed, a specific form of leverage that benefits one business may prove detrimental to another. However, some common considerations should enter into the leverage decision process. We review those considerations in this chapter. Some have been discussed previously; others are new. Taken together, they should alleviate some of the confusion that surrounds the comparative analysis of the alternative forms of leverage. Of course, our discussion will not necessarily make the leverage decision process a simple task, but it should provide an adequate foundation.

We will not always observe the esoteric principles of classic financial management, because the principles appropriate for the industrial giant may not answer the special needs of the smaller, entrepreneurial business. You should temper these criteria with the demands set by your own business requirements. Indeed, you must adapt principle to circumstance.

COMPARATIVE CRITERIA

We will separate the major comparative criteria of the alternative forms of leverage into five categories:

1. Availability
2. Profitability
3. Reliability
4. Flexibility
5. Risk

Of course, this list does not exhaust the considerations that should be weighed before employing leverage or deciding which kind of leverage to choose. Nevertheless, these are the major categories. But keep in mind the critical point of our illustration, summarized in Cash Flow Concept 82:

82: Complete comparative analysis should precede the employment of any leverage in a business.

Availability

The form of any debt employed in a business should be appropriate for the purpose. Thus, a business seeking funds to finance a temporary increase in inventory will not consider leasing as a realistic source of leverage. Neither is a collateral-based revolving loan the appropriate method of financing the purchase of fixed assets. Recognizing the need to match the form of the leverage to the purpose it serves inevitably reduces the number of alternatives that enter into the comparative analysis.

Of course, the lenders' standard credit criteria also may reduce the sources of leverage available to a business. Thus, the business with a high debt/equity ratio may not be eligible for bank credit consideration. Similarly, the business that lacks an investment in accounts receivable usually can discount the commercial finance company as a potential source of leverage.

A business also should consider the *acceptability* of the alternative forms of leverage. For example, management may consider external equity financing to be an undesirable alternative in any circumstance. Or a business may not use leasing as a matter of financial policy. Or the stigma associated with notification may eliminate factoring as an acceptable source of leverage.

Eliminating both the unavailable and unacceptable sources of leverage can quickly narrow the list of candidates for external financing.

Profitability

A business often employs leverage to solve a cash flow problem. In such instances, the solution takes precedence over profitability as a borrowing objective. More often, however, a business obtains leverage because the additional cash capability opens the door to higher profits. Logically, the business in that circumstance should use the source of leverage that ultimately provides the largest contribution to its earnings.

However, many businessmen approach this management objective from the wrong perspective: They concentrate on the comparative costs of the alternative forms of leverage and decide that the least costly must be the most profitable. Unfortunately, this approach can lead to a false conclusion. Instead, remember Cash Flow Concept 83:

83: Leverage profitability analysis concentrates on the *net* bottom-line benefits available from the alternative source of external financing.

This emphasis recognizes that leverage with a higher apparent cost ultimately may be most profitable for the firm.

Assume that a business needs external financing up to $100,000 over the next six months. However, the maximum need occurs only five days out of each month, or a total of thirty days out of the total six-month period. Cash requirements fluctuate during the other twenty-five days each month, but they average $50,000 per day.

The business has eliminated all but two sources of leverage. It can obtain a $100,000 single-payment bank loan at an 8% annualized rate for the full six-month period, or it can obtain an accounts-receivable revolving loan that carries a 12% annual charge.

Of course, a straightforward comparison of the annual interest charges makes the bank loan the preferable alternative. However, the business that uses accounts-receivable financing borrows only to meet its actual daily cash requirements. Then, it pays a daily rate (1/365 of the annual rate) for the funds actually employed.

Now, let's compare the *actual dollar cost* of bank financing with accounts-receivable financing:

Cost of Bank Financing	
$100,000 at 8% for six months	$4,000
Cost of A/R Financing	
$100,000 at .033% per day for 30 days	$ 990
$50,000 at .033% per day for 150 days	$2,475
	$3,465
Advantage from A/R Financing	$ 535

Repeat the experience for another six months and the net bottom-line benefits from accounts-receivable financing becomes over $1,000 higher! Also, this example doesn't consider the other costs that may arise from bank borrowing. Thus, the advantage gained from accounts-receivable financing may become even larger.

In other circumstances, comparative leverage analysis may find a relatively expensive lease more desirable because it leaves funds free for a profitable investment in inventory. Or one source of leverage may promise a higher line of credit than another, again leading to higher net bottom-line benefits. Always proceed beyond the simple comparison of direct costs. Indeed, the leverage that costs more may be worth more.

Reliability

Leverage contributes cash capability to a business. The borrower employs that capability to increase its investment in accounts receivable, inventory, or fixed assets. Any unanticipated withdrawal of the lender's contribution can leave the business with a severe cash flow problem. Consequently, comparative leverage analysis should include an estimate of the reliability of the prospective lenders. The estimate measures the potential for sudden withdrawal of the lender's credit consideration.

Of course, reliability is seldom a concern when the leverage obtained is an installment loan. So long as the borrower meets the repayment schedule set in the installment note, the lender must honor the original agreement.

However, lender reliability becomes a larger concern for the business that uses a revolving loan or anticipates the renewal or extension of a single-payment note. In either circumstance, continuation of the credit consideration is to some extent subject to the discretion of the lender: The lender can extend it or end it.

The borrower's estimate of the lender's reliability should proceed on two levels: one financial, the other personal.

The borrower should be certain that the lender has the financial capacity to continue the credit consideration. Is the lender subject to excessive strain in a tight money period? Does the lender have the financial strength to guarantee the cash advances anticipated from a revolving loan agreement? The business relying on those funds needs affirmative assurances in both instances. Of course, special expertise is necessary to evaluate financial institutions, but raising the questions with prospective lenders will usually provide satisfactory responses.

The businessman must estimate the reliability of the lending officer handling his firm's account. That officer, as a member of a loan committee, has a major influence on the lender's credit decision. In essence, he becomes the firm's representative on the loan committee. Thus, the business should seek a strong, reliable representative to ensure that credit decisions are not subject to the whims of an anonymous committee.

Personal relationships often have a strong influence on the quality and quantity of consideration a business receives from its creditors. They should never be taken for granted.

Flexibility

Lender flexibility means the capacity to adapt to the fluctuating needs of a business operating in a volatile economic environment.

Among other elements, the analyst should measure the lender's flexibility by its repayment requirements, its restrictive covenants, and its potential for expanded credit consideration.

In response to changing circumstances, a flexible lender readily alters the repayment requirements established by an original agreement. Thus, should the purpose that called for a single-payment loan remain unfulfilled, the lender provides an extension beyond the regular due date. Alternatively, should installment loan payments become a burden, the flexible lender develops a revised repayment schedule that fits the firm's actual cash flow. Of course, the revolving loan provides the maximum flexibility for a borrower: The business employs and repays cash capability in direct response to its own needs.

The tighter the restrictive covenants in a loan agreement, the less flexible the lender. Indeed, the borrower may become bound by rigid restrictions that exclude the potential for numerous profitable business opportunities.

A business should estimate each lender's potential response to the expanding cash requirements of a successful operation. A growing business needs increasing, not decreasing, amounts of cash, and it should not lock itself into an inflexible source of leverage that restricts that potential for growth. Indeed, an inflexible lender can hamper the success of any operation.

Risk

We define risk narrowly here as the potential for default that arises from the inability to meet repayment obligations as agreed. A business naturally should exclude any form of leverage that raises the risk too high. Of course, because of future uncertainty, a business often finds it difficult to measure the risk of default. However, some estimate of that risk can develop from a look at the firm's sales stability (or predictability), financial condition, and profitability.

Of course, the relationship between sales stability and the risk of default is apparent. The more stable (predictable) the sales volume in a business, the less risk of default from any form of leverage.

In a broad sense, sales stability is directly related to the industry in which the business operates. The less subject that industry is to technological and economic disruptions, the more predictable the sales volume of a business becomes. From a narrower perspective, a business must recognize its position within the industry. The more secure that position, the more predictable the sales. That, in turn, reduces the risk of default.

Thus, a business operating in the volatile electronics industry might avoid fixed-debt requirements in favor of short-term debt that can be paid quickly from liquidating accounts receivable and inventory. Alternatively, a wholesale grocer can accept fixed-debt obligations, secure that his business will remain relatively stable whatever the state of the economy.

The characteristics of the firm's financial structure also affect the risk associated with leverage. The borrower should assess his financial condition no less rigorously than he would a prospective lender's. In many instances, a lender will approve credit consideration that the business would be ill-advised to accept. The business must assess both the potential profitability and the potential dangers that come with any credit consideration.

Finally, a business should not accept debt without considering the level of profitability that will be necessary to meet the interest and amortization requirements. While this may seem obvious, many borrowers assume debt in an effort to turn a losing operation into a profitable one. From a positive perspective, this decision may provide the cash capability necessary to achieve that objective. The borrower should recognize that such debt ultimately can become a burden for the marginal operation. The interest and repayment requirements can leave the business deeper in a financial hole than before.

The risk of default depends on the types of leverage being considered. An installment loan, for example, imposes fixed obligations on the business. Without lender flexibility, financial setbacks cannot relieve the firm from its obligations. Indeed, fixed-debt requirements compound other financial problems.

Alternatively, single-payment or revolving loans actually may impose less financial risk on a business. This holds true so long as the business maintains the collateral adequate to liquidate that debt. The business may not prosper, but the potential transformation of the collateral into cash reduces the risk of default.

Remember, even though a comparative analysis of the various forms of leverage may be tedious and time-consuming, it can reduce the potential for cash flow problems and increase your earnings. You will be assured that you have chosen the proper kind of leverage for your needs, and that you have chosen it wisely.

In this section, we will introduce some concepts that will help you unite the complex cash flow considerations with a comprehensive approach to positive cash flow management.

Chapter 27 emphasizes the specific business objectives that should ultimately orient the management effort. Indeed, the cash flow manager justifiably may violate some basic management principles if that violation serves the firm's primary objectives.

In Chapter 28, we will look at cash resource management, which seeks the proper balance between the sources and uses of the cash capability employed in a business. Maintaining that balance significantly reduces the potential for cash flow problems.

Chapter 29, introduces the single, essential tool necessary for positive cash flow

PART SIX

Positive Cash Flow Management

management in any circumstance—the cash flow budget. This budget can enable you to foresee and eliminate most of the problems that can disrupt the cash flow in your business. Moreover, it is the fundamental key for deriving the maximum benefits held in the cash flow concepts that we have discussed throughout the book.

27

Management Perspectives

Maximum cash generation is usually the primary objective of the cash flow manager. This objective proceeds from the assumption that a business benefits from any action designed to improve its cash flow. However, cash flow management is not an isolated task in the operation of a business. Indeed, it interrelates with every aspect of it. Consequently, any management effort must first serve the basic objectives of the business, even though those objectives may *conflict* with the idea of maximum cash generation. We can summarize this in Cash Flow Concept 84:

84: The cash flow manager must orient his effort toward the fundamental objectives of the firm.

This chapter considers the major implications this requirement raises for the cash flow manager. Specifically, we discuss the appropriate cash flow management perspectives when the primary objectives of a business become:

1. Survival
2. Profitability
3. Growth
4. Maximum earnings

Of course, a business often works toward several objectives simultaneously, and in fact, it can aim toward all four. The priorities may vary, but they ultimately remain compatible with one another. At the same time, a business should identify one primary objective to orient management decisions.

Management perspectives should be flexible enough to adjust to the constant changes that confront the business operating in a volatile economic environment. But, at any given time, those perspectives should contribute to the primary objective of the business.

PERSPECTIVES FOR SURVIVAL

Survival becomes the primary objective for the business suffering financial distress of any degree. The temporary inability to pay all obligations promptly measures one level of distress. So long as creditors accept deferred payments, the problem may pose little threat to the survival of the business. Of course, the threat increases if the term of the deferred payments falls too far past due. Suppliers may cease shipments of replacement inventory, and without a product to sell, the business will quickly fail.

The threat becomes even more severe when suppliers seek recourse by forcing a business into bankruptcy. Although suppliers seldom recover significant amounts from bankrupt concerns, the threat often forces many businesses into voluntary bankruptcy actions. In either circumstance, the bankrupt business rarely returns to active operations.

The most immediate threat to the survival of a business occurs when it cannot meet payroll requirements. Indeed, the employee who isn't paid on Friday won't return to work on Monday. Certainly, suppliers accept deferred payments more readily than employees.

From the cash flow manager's perspective, the desire for survival encourages the original objective of cash flow management—maximum cash generation. Thus, the manager seeks to convert the firm's investment in receivables and inventory into cash as rapidly as possible. Moreover, he seeks that objective even though it temporarily damages sales and profits. Obviously, if the business doesn't survive the short term, long-term prospects become irrelevant.

The desire for survival again raises the specter of risk as an element in the operation of a business. Even if a business is not faced with any immediate threat to its continued operations, risk should be a relevant consideration in management decisions. This means that the desire for growth and profitability may become secondary if achieving either objective threatens the survival of the firm.

Certainly, a measure of risk is involved in every business operation. But the size of the risk should be commensurate with the size of the potential reward. An imbalance in favor of risk can lead to the ultimate demise of a business.

PERSPECTIVES FOR PROFITABILITY

The higher the profits a business generates, the more successful it is. However, the drive for higher profits often raises higher levels of risks. Indeed, as the firm stretches for a more rapid increase in earnings, it inevitably risks its survival.

This encourages many businessmen to accept a "reasonable" level of profits. The business earns less, but it is more likely to survive.

The business that seeks a reasonable, satisfactory level of profits isn't necessarily eliminating growth or maximum profits as natural business objectives. Instead, it may be building those objectives into the foundation for long-term stability.

Of course, no standard definition identifies the satisfactory level of earnings. A proportionate increase of 5%, 10%, or 15% over the previous year's results may be satisfactory to some businesses. Others may look for a specific dollar increase in earnings each year. Still others may measure the return as a percentage of their anticipated sales volume. Of course, however defined, the satisfactory earnings level recognizes two facts of business life.

First, in any circumstance, earnings must be sufficient to offset the detrimental effects of inflation. The business that fails to match the rate of inflation falls behind, even though it registers an apparent increase in profits. Indeed, a business actually needs to generate earnings that grow more rapidly than inflation. This arises from the exaggerated influence inflation has on the firm's investment in current assets.

Second, the business sets its satisfactory earnings level in line with some measure, however imprecise, of the risk associated with its operations. Thus, it will not chase earnings if that effort would impose risk beyond the acceptable level. Again, this recognizes that the size of the risk and the potential return in any operation tend to increase proportionately.

The cash flow manager who seeks satisfactory earnings without inordinate risk adjusts his activities accordingly. His cash management decisions seek to preserve the financial integrity of the business without seriously impairing its desired earnings level. He will not risk a gap in the firm's cash flow in exchange for an extra dollar of earnings beyond the desired level. Neither will he allow an overinvestment in receivables or inventory merely because they promise more rapid growth. Indeed, he constantly seeks a balance between profitability and the security that comes from a healthy cash position.

PERSPECTIVES FOR GROWTH

Rapid expansion often orients the drive of the ambitious entrepreneur. He measures success not in terms of profitability, but by this year's sales volume, and inevitably, he either accepts or ignores the risk that is a natural companion to accelerated growth.

We have demonstrated that rapid growth is accompanied by a need for external financing that actually expands more rapidly than a firm's sales volume. Indeed, the limit on the financing available to a business becomes the primary restriction on its maximum growth potential. At the same time, as a business increases the use of external financing relative to equity, it raises the risk of a major financial setback. Broad swings in operating results naturally accompany the use of higher degrees of leverage.

The cash flow manager serving the growth objective adjusts his approach accordingly. He first discounts the value held in excess cash reserves that provide insurance for survival. A business cannot grow without committing itself to a rising investment in inventory and accounts receivable, even at the expense of its cash reserves.

Next, he designs a credit and collection policy that encourages sales, even at the expense of carrying a larger investment in receivables. Indeed, the growth-oriented business may suffer a lower profit margin per sales dollar because of the carrying costs involved in its investment in receivables and inventory.

Finally, the cash flow manager in the rapidly growing business cannot overlook the use of leverage. Indeed, leverage is the single necessity for the expanding concern. The business can accept lower earnings and higher risks, but without expanding its use of borrowed funds, it will not continue to grow.

PERSPECTIVES FOR MAXIMUM EARNINGS

A business might ignore all other objectives in its pursuit of maximum earnings. The businessman who selects this objective is less concerned with growth than with an immediate increase in earnings (although the two typically are interrelated). He also blinds himself to much of the risk involved in the drive toward maximum profitability.

In this case, the cash flow manager must allow profitability to take precedence over the desire for efficient cash flow. Thus, a more liberal credit policy that increases earnings might be acceptable, even though it absorbs cash reserves. Similarly, the business might add to that strain by expanding its investment in inventory in the pursuit of profitability.

Of course, the desire for every last dollar of profits should not push the firm toward a cash flow disaster. Sound business sense recognizes the practical limits on any objective. At the same time, the cash flow manager must recognize and accept the higher risk of a cash flow problem that naturally rises when a business selects maximum profitability over liquidity as its primary objective.

Cash Resource Management

While day-to-day cash flow management should remain your primary focus, you should also recognize the need to maintain the proper balance among the sources and uses of cash capability. Failure to maintain that balance can lead to cash flow problems. Consequently, this chapter discusses the fundamental elements of *cash resource* management.

First, we introduce the primary objectives of cash resource management, and then review the process that provides the analytical basis for it. This analysis isolates the significant interrelationship of source and use of the cash capability employed by a business. Identification and control of this interrelationship is essential for the proper maintenance of a balanced financial structure. That balance, in turn, helps to ensure the smooth operation of the daily cash flow cycle.

THE OBJECTIVES OF CASH RESOURCE MANAGEMENT

Cash resource management adopts a comprehensive view of a business's cash receipts and outlays. From this broad perspective, the effort focuses on

1. The *source* of cash capability
2. The *use* of cash capability
3. The interrelationship of both

The basic objective of cash resource management is to use the cash capability employed in a business to reflect the characteristics of each source.

As an example, remember our discussion of leverage management, which emphasized the need to match the form of any debt to the purpose it serves. Thus, a business should not use a short-term, single-payment note to finance the purchase of fixed assets. Nor should it employ a five-year installment loan to finance a temporary increase in inventory.

The broad perspective of this same principle provides the foundation for cash resource management. We can summarize this in Cash Flow Concept 85:

85: Positive cash flow management properly matches the source and use of any cash capability employed in a business.

Cash Resource Analysis

Cash resource analysis concentrates on the changes that occur in a business's financial structure between two time periods. Properly categorized, the changes represent the source and disposition of the net cash capability gained by the business over that period.

To illustrate the analytic process, we use two consecutive fiscal year-end balance sheets of the Parker Company, a small valve manufacturer. The first step in the analysis, summarized in Table 28–1, isolates the increase or decrease in each balance sheet account (except cash) from one year to the next.

The next step places the net change in each account into one of two categories. Each change translates into either a source or use of cash capability in the business.

A business gains an increase in its cash capability from
1. A decrease in assets (other than cash)
2. An increase in liabilities
3. An increase in stockholders' equity

TABLE 28–1 Comparative Fiscal Year-End Balance Sheets

THE PARKER COMPANY

	12/31/79	12/31/80	Changes
Cash	$100,000	$ 75,000	
Accounts Receivable	110,000	170,000	60,000
Inventory	160,000	195,000	35,000
Fixed Assets (net)	60,000	250,000	190,000
Prepaid Expenses	20,000	10,000	(10,000)
Total Assets	**$450,000**	**$700,000**	
Accounts Payable	$100,000	$220,000	120,000
Other Liabilities	30,000	20,000	(10,000)
Long-Term Debt	100,000	200,000	100,000
Total Liabilities	$230,000	$440,000	
Stockholders' Equity	$220,000	$260,000	40,000
Liabilities and Equity	**$450,000**	**$700,000**	

Alternatively, a business employs cash capability to
   1. Increase assets
   2. Decrease liabilities
   3. Decrease stockholders' equity

Table 28–2 illustrates a format that facilitates this phase of the analysis and provides a concise picture of the disposition of the net cash capability available to the business.

The Parker Company ended 12/31/79 with $100,000 in cash reserves. Changes in its financial structure produced an additional $270,000 in cash capability. An increase in credit consideration in the form of accounts payable and long-term debt provided $220,000 of that added capability. Also, Parker enjoyed another $40,000 contribution from an increase in stockholders' equity, presumably from profitable operations during the year (although a part of that increase might have come from the sale of common stock).

Finally, a net reduction in prepaid expenses translated into a $10,000 increase in total available cash capability. A reduction in prepaid expenses as a source of cash capability may be questionable, yet, conceptually, the liquidation of any asset (except cash) becomes additional cash capability for the business.

In this instance, the liquidation of the prepaid expenses lowers the actual cash expended for operations during the year ending 12/31/80. The business is merely regaining the cash capability used in the previous period to pay the expenses in advance.

The $10,000 reduction in prepaid expenses raises the total cash capability

TABLE 28–2 Cash Resource Analysis

THE PARKER COMPANY

Beginning Cash Reserves (12/31/79)	$100,000
Sources of Cash Capability:	
1. Reduction in prepaid expenses	$ 10,000
2. Increase in accounts payable	120,000
3. Increase in long-term debt	100,000
4. Increase in stockholders' equity	40,000
Total Sources of Cash Capability	$370,000
Uses of Cash Capability:	
1. Increase in accounts receivable	$ 60,000
2. Increase in inventory	35,000
3. Increase in net fixed assets	190,000
4. Decrease in other liabilities	10,000
Total Uses	($295,000)
Ending Cash Reserves (12/31/80)	**$ 75,000**

available to the company to $370,000. Had the company held all other elements of its financial structure constant, the 12/31/80 balance sheet would have included $370,000 in cash reserves. Instead, the company decided to employ the bulk of that capability for other purposes. In fact, other changes in the financial structure absorbed $295,000 of the $370,000 total.

The major part of the cash capability contributed to a $190,000 increase in net fixed assets. An additional $95,000 supported an increase in Parker's investment in accounts receivable and inventory. Finally, it managed a $10,000 reduction in other liabilities, ending 12/31/80 with $75,000 in cash reserves.

Again, Table 28–2 summarizes the net cash capability that flowed from changes in the company's financial structure, as well as the ultimate disposition of that capability. This disposition also is reflected directly in the financial structure.

The final step in cash resource analysis is less precise than the first two. In fact, it requires no direct calculation. Instead, you complete the analysis with a critical assessment of the relationship between the sources and uses of cash capability represented by the changes in financial structure. This assessment compares the source of the cash capability to the disposition of that capability, and it operates according to two fundamental principles:

1. The cash capability devoted to permanent assets should come from an increase in stockholders' equity or long-term debt
2. The cash capability devoted to current assets may come from an increase in accounts payable or other short-term liabilities

Thus, a business should not use trade credit as the source of cash capability to finance the purchase of fixed assets. The business that makes that mistake invites a cash flow problem, since the trade credit comes due almost immediately. Indeed, permanent assets should have the support of a permanent source of cash capability.

Alternatively, so long as the business maintains prompt payment habits, trade credit may be the appropriate source of cash capability to finance an increase in receivables or inventory. Again, cash resource management seeks the proper match between the sources and uses of cash capability in the business. Of course, a business also may use fixed sources—long-term debt and equity— to support its permanent, minimum investment in current assets. This, too, represents a proper match.

Finally, the business must recognize the ultimate effect of the interrelationships on its cash reserves. If other sources are exhausted, the decision to use cash capability for any purpose naturally absorbs some of these reserves.

Referring to Table 28–2, note that the Parker Company has some cause for concern. It increased its net investment in fixed assets between 12/31/79 and 12/31/80 by $190,000. Yet stockholders' equity and long-term debt registered an increase of only $140,000. Thus, $50,000 out of the cash capability devoted to the fixed assets had to come from other sources. In this instance, accounts payable increased by $120,000, while Parker's investment in receivables and inventory rose by only $95,000. Consequently, Parker used $25,000 in supplier credit consideration as a source of cash for the fixed assets. Another $25,000 came from a reduction in cash reserve.

Certainly, the Parker Company remains in a relatively healthy financial position. At the same time, improperly matching the sources and the uses of cash capability has reduced the company's financial flexibility. Another increase in current assets may impose an additional drain on cash reserves that will reduce that flexibility even further.

Use the Parker Company's case as a reminder of the need to interrelate periodically the sources and uses of cash capability.

The Cash Flow Budget

The cash flow budget provides the signals that spur the positive management actions necessary to fill any impending gaps in the cash flow cycle. Indeed, it becomes the focal point of your cash flow management effort. The importance of the cash flow budget can be summed up in Cash Flow Concept 86:

86: A cash flow budget is the single, indispensible tool for positive cash flow management.

This chapter reviews the basic concepts that orient the development of a cash flow budget. First, we reestablish the critical distinction between financial and cash transactions in a business. Understanding that distinction is an essential precedent for the cash budgeting process. Then, we follow the logical path that develops into a cash flow budget. This can help you avoid the unhappy surprise that comes from an unforeseen gap in your cash flow.

As a natural complement to the cash flow budgeting process, we also identify a straightforward approach that helps identify the minimum operating cash balance appropriate for a business. Certainly, the size of that balance varies among businesses, but the analytic approach that identifies the proper operating balance fits almost any circumstance.

271

FINANCIAL AND CASH TRANSACTIONS

A manufacturer or wholesaler seldom generates a sale directly in exchange for cash. Instead, he trades his product for his customer's promise to pay for the purchase in accordance with his designated selling terms. Similarly, a business typically purchases inventory on the same basis. Thus, cash payment usually follows the actual purchase by thirty days.

Unfortunately, the basic accounting process does not distinguish between financial and cash transactions. Thus, on the seller's side, a financial transaction requires a record of the sale on the day it occurs, even though no cash actually changes hands. The buyer's side similarly records a purchase (although not necessarily an expense), and at the same time records an increase in inventory and accounts payable. But the financial transaction has no immediate effect on either business's cash reserves.

Some businessmen find this confusing because the accrual accounting system requires balance sheet entries reflecting the exchange of cash that completes a financial transaction. The business incurs no expense at the time of the transaction, even though cash flows out of the business on paper.

We know that financial accounting enables a business to measure its financial performance by properly matching its revenues and expenses as they occur. At the same time, however, accrual accounting does not provide the proper picture of the cash flow through a business. This picture comes from the record of cash receipts and payments that register the actual exchange of cash.

The exchange of cash completes a business transaction: It represents either a customer's payment for a purchase or a business's final fulfillment of its own obligations. The record of cash receipts and disbursements, then, reflects the actual cash flow into and out of a business. Indeed, that record provides the proper picture of the cash flow, whether or not the *financial* transactions coincide with the *cash* transactions. Thus, positive cash flow management clearly distinguishes between financial and cash transactions.

THE CASH FLOW BUDGETING PROCESS

A cash flow budget projects the cash receipts and disbursements anticipated in the normal course of business. However, that budget proceeds beyond the simple summation of the year's upcoming activity. Indeed, it projects the actual time that cash will flow into and out of the business. Our illustration projects that flow on a monthly basis, but note that you could also project a weekly or even a daily cash flow.

The precision of the budget depends on the characteristics of the business coupled with a reasonable estimate of its cash capability. The larger that capability, of course, the more cushion the business has to absorb an unforeseen fluctuation in cash collections. This will become more apparent as we review the procedures that make up the basic budgeting process.

Many businessmen shy away from cash flow budgeting because they think it is too esoteric or complex. However, the process can easily be broken down into five distinct, straightforward steps:

1. Forecasting sales
2. Projecting cash receipts
3. Projecting cash disbursements
4. Interrelating cash receipts and cash disbursements
5. Filling the gaps

In our discussion of each step, concentrate on the fundamental simplicity of the budgeting process. You will find that even a haphazard effort can provide important benefits for your business.

The Sales Forecast

Any financial plan must begin with a sales forecast. Of course, the planner recognizes the uncertainty inherent in that forecast. Actual sales rarely equate exactly with the forecast. Variables in the economy, the industry, and the company preclude absolute predictability.

Nevertheless, the lack of precision does not eliminate the need or value of the forecast. Even an intuitive effort, such as using the previous year's volume, adjusted for inflation, provides an adequate basis for the development of a cash flow budget. Moreover, that effort will enable the business to anticipate most major cash flow problems. Of course, the more accurate your forecast, the better your cash flow budget. We can sum up the value of this forecast in Cash Flow Concept 87:

87: The sales forecast is the cornerstone of the cash flow budget.

As the starting point for the budget, we will use the sales forecast developed by the Prudent Company, a specialty paper wholesaler with a history of sound financial planning. For the first six months of its upcoming fiscal year, the company projects the following monthly sales volume (in $1,000's):

Jan	Feb	Mar	Apr	May	June
$200	$250	$400	$500	$300	$200

This forecast provides the basis for the next two steps in the budgeting process.

Projecting Cash Receipts

The cash flow budget recognizes that the primary source of cash flow into a business comes not from sales (unless the sales are for cash), but from the collection of accounts receivable. Of course, a business may supplement that cash flow with external financing, but the basic budget predicts the need for that potential supplement. Consequently, this step of the process does not look beyond the anticipated flow from collections.

The Prudent Company relies on historical experience to project the cash flow into the business over the first six months of the upcoming year. This history indicates that the company collects its receivables according to the following pattern:

1. 70% in the month immediately following the sale
2. 20% in the second month following the sale
3. 10% in the third month following the sale

Anticipating that the historical collection pattern will extend into the future, the Prudent Company projects its cash flow for the next six months, as shown in Table 29–1. (The company's actual sales for the three months immediately preceding the projection period totaled $200,000 in each month.)

From this pattern, the company anticipates $200,000 in collections in January. Those collections represent 70% of December's sales, 20% of November's sales, and 10% of October's sales. Of course, collections equal to monthly sales are not the common circumstance for the Prudent Company. Indeed, a look at the projections for March indicates sales of $400,000 for the month, but collections from previous sales of only $235,000. This shows that collections come from the prior months' sales, not the current month's.

If your sales *and* average collection period remain constant from month to month, your cash flow into your business will match your sales volume. Thus, a business with a $1,000 in daily sales and a consistent forty-day average collection period generates sales of $30,000 per month and matches that with collections from previous sales. Certainly, that simplifies the cash flow budgeting process.

Projecting Cash Disbursements

Most cash disbursements in a business fall into one of three basic categories. Thus, a business expends cash to (1) pay for purchases, (2) pay operating expenses, and (3) retire debts. In most circumstances, a business can project the expenditures required in each category with reasonable accuracy.

Of course, the repayment of any scheduled debt obligation stands as a certain cash expenditure. However, using its sales forecast, a business makes purchase and operating expense commitments that also become relatively certain cash expenditure requirements. Indeed, it usually must expend the cash appropriated for those purposes, even though actual sales in a month fall below the level forecasted.

Note that depreciation does not appear in a firm's projected cash disbursements. Remember, depreciation is a noncash expense, so it is not part of the cash flow budget.

Let's again use the Prudent Company's circumstance to demonstrate the elements that enter into a projection of monthly cash expenditures. The projection reflects additional characteristics about Prudent's business:

1. Cost of goods sold averages 60% of sales.
2. Prudent purchases the inventory for each month's forecasted sales volume one month in advance: That is, the firm purchases the stock for March sales in February.

TABLE 29-1 Projecting Cash Receipts

THE PRUDENT COMPANY

	October	November	December	January	February	March	April	May	June
Sales (actual for first three months; the rest are forecasted)	200	200	200	200	250	400	500	300	200
Collections:									
First Month at 70%	—	—	—	140	140	175	280	350	210
Second Month at 20%	—	—	—	40	40	40	50	80	100
Third Month at 10%	—	—	—	20	20	20	20	25	40
Total Cash Inflow from Receipts				**200**	**200**	**235**	**350**	**455**	**350**

3. Suppliers allow Prudent thirty days to pay for its purchases; consequently, the firm pays for all inventory in the month following the actual purchase.
4. Monthly cash operating expenses average 30% of sales.
5. Prudent has $10,000 in monthly debt-service requirements.

Using the sales forecast as the starting point, Table 29–2 projects the Prudent Company's cash expenditures for the six-month period.

In January, Prudent must pay $120,000 for inventory purchased in December. The company purchased that amount based on the January sales forecast. Cash operating expenses (30% of sales) in January will total $60,000. That, coupled with the $10,000 fixed-debt payment, increases the company's total cash needs for the month to $190,000.

Repeating the projection process for the next six months, we find that Prudent's monthly cash expenditures peak at $460,000 in April, then drop back to $190,000 in June. This fluctuation reflects a seasonal demand for Prudent's products in the spring.

The next step interrelates the two cash flow projections and measures the net effect those flows will have on the company's cash reserves each month.

Interrelating the Cash Flows

Table 29–3 interrelates the two cash flow projections and isolates the resulting net effect on the Prudent Company's cash reserves. This identifies the specific months in which the company can expect a net increase or decrease in cash.

We see a $10,000 net increase in cash projected in January. However, over the next three months, cash expenditures exceed anticipated cash collections by a cumulative total of $280,000. Alternatively, in the final two months of the forecast period, Prudent generates healthy cash surpluses. This follows naturally from the collection of the receivables due from the seasonal peak in sales.

TABLE 29–2 Projecting Cash Expenditures

THE PRUDENT COMPANY (in $1,000s)

	January	February	March	April	May	June
Sales	$200	$250	$400	$500	$300	$200
Payments:						
Purchases (60% of sales)	120	150	240	300	180	120
Operating Expenses (30% of sales)	60	75	120	150	90	60
Debt Service	10	10	10	10	10	10
Total Cash Payments	**$190**	**$235**	**$370**	**$460**	**$280**	**$190**

TABLE 29-3 Interrelating Cash Collections with Cash Expenditures

THE PRUDENT COMPANY (in $1,000s)

	January	February	March	April	May	June
Projected Cash Collections	$200	$200	$235	$350	$455	$350
Projected Cash Expenditures	(190)	(235)	(370)	(460)	(280)	(190)
Net Effect on Cash Reserves	**+10**	**(35)**	**(135)**	**(110)**	**+175**	**+160**

Now, we will use the information in Table 29-3 to project the Prudent Company's need for external financing to offset the impending imbalance in its cash flow.

Filling the Gaps

The final step in the cash flow budgeting process interrelates the Prudent Company's cash reserves with the monthly net inflow or outflow of cash.

Of course, there is little cause for concern so long as the net cash outflow in any month doesn't indicate a drain of the company's cash reserves below some practical minimum. However, if any monthly drain drops operating reserves below the minimum, the company must seek external financing to fill the gap. Or, alternatively, it can execute the positive management action necessary to avoid the gap, by reducing the investment in receivables or inventory, or using some other cash flow action tool.

Again using the Prudent Company as the focal point, we will note three additional facts about its circumstances:

1. Prudent will open the six-month period with a $100,000 cash reserve
2. It has a $300,000 revolving line of bank credit
3. Company policy requires $100,000 in cash as the minimum operating balance necessary to begin any month

Table 29-4 interrelates these facts with the previous projections to identify the potential gaps in Prudent's cash flow over the forecast period. The projection also specifies the extent to which Prudent must use its line of credit to satisfy its cash operating constraints.

Prudent has no cash flow problem projected in January. In fact, the net $10,000 gain enables the company to enter February with $110,000 in cash reserves. However, in February, Prudent feels the first effects of the seasonal increase in sales on its cash reserves. While the $35,000 net cash drain in that month doesn't create a problem, it does mean that the company must use $25,000 of its revolving line to satisfy its minimum cash operating constraint.

The $135,000 net cash drain projected in March emphasizes the critical justification for the cash flow budgeting process. Indeed, failure to foresee that deficit in the absence of a cash flow budget would have left Prudent with a severe

TABLE 29–4 Filling the Gaps in the Cash Flow Budget

THE PRUDENT COMPANY (in $1,000s)

	January	February	March	April	May	June
Beginning Cash	$100	$110	$100	$100	$100	$100
Net Change	+10	(35)	(135)	(110)	+175	+160
Ending Cash (without borrowing)	110	75	(35)	(10)	275	260
Borrowing	—	25	135	110	(175)	(95)
Ending Cash	110	100	100	100	100	165
Cumulative Borrowing	—	$ 25	$160	$270	$ 95	—

cash flow problem. Instead, Prudent will anticipate the problem and use an additional $135,000 of its credit line to maintain the $100,000 minimum operating balance.

Prudent borrows another $110,000 in April to reach a peak usage of its external financing of $270,000. Then, the positive cash flow in the following two months of the projection enables the company to repay its debt and end June with a comfortable $165,000 in cash reserves.

Although many businesses enjoy a more regular cash flow than is apparent in Prudent's seasonal business, the cash flow budget remains valid and, indeed, indispensable.

CASH FLOW ACTION TOOLS

The Prudent Company fills the gap in its projected cash flow with the aid of external financing. This is the obvious answer to any cash flow financing. However, the cash flow budget may serve as the signal to initiate other positive actions that will eliminate a problem without the aid of external financing.

For example, you might fill the gap with the cash that flows from a reduction in your investment in accounts receivable. Indeed, a more restrictive credit policy may generate the cash that eliminates the need for external financing.

Similar logic applies to an investment in inventory. Item analysis may indicate that the business can achieve its projected volume with less inventory. Lowering that investment again frees funds that can fill the gap in the cash flow budget.

In the extreme circumstance, the solution to a projected deficit cash flow might come from less desirable, although nonetheless necessary, management decisions. For example, a business might use trade credit as the source of the external financing. This means that the business decides to defer payment to suppliers beyond their designated terms. This solves the cash flow problem but it risks the business's credit rating.

Alternatively, the solution might come from a lower sales volume. That is, the business might find that it can avoid a deficit cash flow only by lowering its expectations. Indeed, holding expansion in check often becomes a rational alternative to a cash flow problem. In any circumstance, whatever management actions you take, you must first identify the potential problem. This is the critical contribution that comes from the cash flow budget.

CASH SAFETY STOCK

We have often drawn assumptions that set the minimum level of cash a business needs for normal operations. Thus, we should review a basic approach that helps identify that minimum level of operating cash.

From one perspective, you can view those cash reserves as you view your investment in inventory. In other words, your cash reserves should be sufficient to meet daily cash expenditures. To that basic inventory, you should add some cash safety stock to absorb any unforeseen expenditure requirements. Finally, should the potential exist, you might carry an additional investment in cash sufficient to take advantage of profitable business opportunities that require cash.

However, here we focus on the method that determines the practical minimum cash balance necessary for normal operations, including the appropriate safety stock. You identify that balance from a straightforward analysis of your own historical experience: You merely calculate your *average daily cash expenditures* over recent months. Then, recognizing the special characteristics of your business, you estimate the appropriate cash reserves as a specific number of days' average cash outflow.

For example, assume that your business made $180,000 in cash expenditures in each of the last three months. Thus, using a thirty-day month as the basis for analysis, your average daily cash outflow comes from the calculation:

$$\text{Average Daily Cash Expenditure} = \frac{\text{Monthly Cash Expenditure}}{30} = \frac{\$180,000}{30} = \$6,000$$

The business expends an average of $6,000 in cash per day. However, unless you are certain that daily cash collections will equal or exceed daily cash expenditures, you must carry some cash safety stock—cash equivalent to several days' expenditures—to decrease the risk of not meeting all obligations on time.

You can identify that balance with another simple calculation. Thus, relying on the example above, a business might determine that cash sufficient to meet six days' average expenditures is sufficient for normal operations. In that event, the minimum required balance is found as:

$$\text{Average Daily Expenditure} \times \text{Days Cash Required} = \text{Minimum Operating Balance}$$

$$\$6,000 \times 6 = \$36,000$$

In this instance, anytime the balances drop below $36,000, the manager should use an action tool appropriate to regain that minimum level.

Unfortunately, the number of days' cash required varies with the circumstance. You must identify that number by considering (1) the predictability of cash inflows, (2) the flexibility in cash expenditures, and (3) the availability of external financing.

First, the certainty associated with your cash collections exerts a direct influence on the days' cash expenditures required for your reserves. The more certain the collection rate, the fewer days' expenditures required as a minimum balance. Alternatively, an erratic collection rate calls for a larger cash reserve. Without the larger reserve, the business with unpredictable collections increases the risk of a cash flow problem—the inability to meet all obligations promptly.

The flexibility of projected cash expenditures also influences the size of a business's cash reserves. If you can defer supplier payments without losing discounts or impairing future credit consideration, you can reduce the minimum operating balance necessary for your business. If you lack that flexibility, a larger minimum balance may be necessary to preserve your financial integrity.

Finally, the pivotal factor that affects the size of a minimum operating cash balance is a business's immediate access to additional external financing. The business with immediate access to additional financing can absorb the risk normally associated with lower operating balances. In such instances, the failure to receive anticipated collections is offset easily with perhaps no more than a phone call that draws on a line of credit.

Logically, the business without the privilege for an immediate cash advance from some external financing source must employ larger minimum cash balances. In any event, the prudent businessman recognizes the need to carry the appropriate cash safety stock necessary to absorb an unforeseen disruption in his cash flow. Safety stock reduces the risk of a cash flow problem.

Accelerated Depreciation. A depreciation method that writes off the cost of an asset at a faster rate than the write-off under the straight-line method; the accelerated write-off increases the cash benefits from depreciation in the early years of an asset's life.

Accounts Payable. Amounts due for purchases made on credit.

Accounts Receivable. A claim against a debtor for merchandise sold or services rendered in exchange for the customer's promise to pay.

Accounts-Receivable Revolving Loan (A/R/R/L). A unique borrowing method that employs the firm's accounts receivable as collateral for a continuous revolving loan arrangement.

Accounts-Receivable Turnover. The net credit sales during a specific period divided by the average accounts receivable due from trade debtors; evaluates the quality of the accounts by relating the average total outstanding to the volume of credit sales.

Accrual Accounting. An accounting method that recognizes sales when made and expenses when incurred, regardless of when the cash transactions actually occur.

Acquisition Cost. The cost a business incurs from purchasing inventory, distinct from actual product costs, such as ordering costs.

Advance Rate. A percentage measure of the loan value relative to the accounting value of an asset pledged as collateral for credit consideration.

Aged Analysis of Accounts Receivable. A report showing how long accounts receivable have been outstanding; it identifies the receivables not past due and those past due by, for example, one month, two months.

Annual Cash Flow. The total of a firm's net income plus depreciation; the total measures the net incremental cash generated by operations over the course of a year.

Asset Turnover. The ratio of total sales to total assets; a measure of the efficiency of asset utilization.

Average Collection Period. The average number of days each credit sales dollar remains outstanding; a qualitative indicator of the collectibility of a firm's accounts receivable.

Average Investment Period. The length of time each dollar remains in inventory before a sale converts it into cash or accounts receivable.

Average Payable Period. The average length of time a business employs each dollar of trade credit consideration.

Bad-Debt Write-Off. The loss incurred when an open-account sale proves to be uncollectible.

Balance Sheet. A financial statement that indicates what the firm owns and how those assets are financed in the form of liabilities and ownership interest.

Break-Even Analysis. An analytic technique for studying the relationships among fixed costs, variable costs, and profits.

Break-Even Cash Flow. The level of operations where total cash expenses equal total cash revenue.

Break-Even Point. The volume of sales in a business where total costs equal total revenue.

Carrying Costs. Financial or operational expenses incurred from a firm's investment in assets.

Cash Accounting. An accounting method that recognizes sales and expenses only when the cash transactions actually occur.

Cash Capability. The total that comes from adding the firm's cash reserves to any available but unemployed credit consideration.

Cash Conversion Period. The time lapse between the customer's decision to purchase a product and the date the payment for the purchase becomes cash available for reinvestment.

Cash Flow Cycle. The natural flow of cash through the operations in a business: cash to inventory to accounts receivable to cash.

Cash Insurance. See *Credit Insurance*.

Collection Period. See *Average Collection Period*.

Common Stock. A document that represents ownership in a corporation.

Compensating Balance. A required minimum checking-account balance that a firm must maintain as partial consideration for a loan from a commercial bank.

Component Management. The management effort that concentrates on control of the firm's investment in assets.

Contribution Margin. Excess of sales price over variable expenses; an important element in break-even analysis.

Cost of Goods Sold. The cost associated with units sold during a specific time period.

Credit Insurance. A unique form of insurance that indemnifies the firm for material losses because of accounts receivable that become uncollectible.

Credit Policy. The guidelines used in the decision process that approves or disapproves of an open-account sale.

Current Ratio. Current assets divided by current liabilities; a measure of a firm's liquidity.

Days' Sales in Inventory. See *Average Investment Period.*

Debt/Equity Ratio. The ratio of the total debt to the total equity employed in a business.

Depreciation. A deduction of part of the cost of an asset from income in each year of the asset's useful life.

EBIT. Earnings before interest and taxes.

Economic Ordering Quantity (EOQ). The optimum (least cost) quantity of inventory that should be ordered.

Equity. See *Stockholders' Equity.*

Factoring. Selling accounts receivable to a finance company or bank.

FIFO Accounting. A system of writing off inventory into cost of goods sold; items purchased first are written off first; referred to as *first in, first out.*

Financial Structure. The firm's balance sheet.

Fixed Assets. Relatively permanent assets used in the operation of a business.

Fixed-Asset Turnover. The result obtained by dividing the firm's sales volume by its investment in fixed assets; a measure of the efficiency in employing those assets.

Fixed Costs. Operating costs that remain constant regardless of the firm's sales volume; an important element in break-even analysis.

Float. The amount of funds represented in checks that have been written but are still in process and have not yet been collected.

FYE. Fiscal year end.

Gross Profit Margin. Total sales minus total cost of goods sold.

Growth Stock. That portion of the firm's investment in inventory designed to satisfy an anticipated increase in sales.

Income Statement. A financial statement that measures the profitability of the firm over a period of time; all expenses are subtracted from sales to arrive at net income.

Indemnification. The principle of insurance that compensates a policyholder for incurred losses.

Inventory. Goods, purchased or manufactured, held by a business for sale.

Inventory/Sales Ratio. The proportional relationship between a firm's investment in inventory and its monthly sales volume; a criterion for controlling the firm's investment in inventory.

Inventory Turnover Rate. The cost of goods sold for a period divided by the firm's average investment in inventory; a measure of inventory management efficiency.

Investment. The funds a business invests in accounts receivable, inventory, and fixed assets.

Investment Tax Credit. A specified percentage of the purchase cost of a new fixed asset that a business can deduct as a credit against its income-tax liability.

Invoice. A detailed list of goods shipped or services rendered, with an account of all charges due from the customer; the bill that evidences a sale.

Item Analysis. The technique that isolates the turnover rate associated with the specific items that make up the inventory in a business.

Leverage. The ratio between the total debt and the total assets employed in a business.

LIFO Accounting. A system of writing off inventory into cost of goods sold; items purchased last are written off first; referred to as *last-in, first-out.*

Line of Credit. An arrangement whereby a financial institution commits itself to lend up to a specified amount of funds during a specified period.

Liquidity. The ability of a business to meet obligations in a timely manner.

Lock-Box Plan. A procedure used to speed up collections and reduce float; customers mail payments directly to a post office box designated and serviced by the firm's bank.

Non-Notification. Part of a lending arrangement whereby a business obtains a loan secured by accounts receivable; however, the lender does not notify debtors that receivables are pledged to secure the loan.

Notification. A procedure often employed when a borrower pledges accounts receivable to secure a loan; the lender advises the debtors that their promises to pay secure the credit consideration.

Open-Account Sale. A sale made in exchange for the purchaser's promise to pay on a later date; however, no promissory note is involved.

Opportunity Costs. Earnings that might have been obtained if a productive asset, service, or capacity had been applied to some alternative use.

Overinvestment. Any cash committed to excess investment in accounts receivable, inventory, or fixed assets; or, extra assets unnecessary for the firm's level of operations.

Physical Count. The actual count of the items held in the firm's inventory.

Preferred Stock. A hybrid security combining some of the characteristics of both common stock and debt.

Purchase Order. The document or advice that enters an order for the purchase of merchandise or services.

Quantity Discounts. Price reductions obtained by purchasing goods in larger lots.

Receivables/Sales Ratio. The proportional relationship between a firm's investment in accounts receivable and its monthly sales volume; a criterion for controlling the firm's investment in accounts receivable.

Return on Assets (ROA). Earnings divided by average total assets; a profitability ratio.

Return on Investment (ROI). Earnings divided by average total assets; same as return on

assets. A measure of the firm's operating efficiency.

Safety Stock. Inventory held by a firm in excess of anticipated requirements to protect against unforeseen shortages.

Sales/Fixed-Asset Ratio. See *Fixed-Asset Turnover.*

Selling Terms. The length of time a seller allows for payment of purchases made on credit; often includes discounts allowed for early payment.

Stockholders' Equity. The total of common stock and all retained earnings.

Stock-Out Cost. The opportunity cost that results from the inability to satisfy customer demand because of insufficient inventory; the firm loses the profit from a potential sale.

Straight-Line Depreciation. A method of depreciation that takes the depreciable cost of an asset and divides it by its useful life to determine the annual depreciation expense; straight-line depreciation creates a uniform expense every year an asset is depreciated.

Structural Management. The management perspective that seeks to maintain the proper balance among the elements that make up the financial structure in a business.

Tangible Net Worth. The book value of a business less any intangible assets; the value of the corporeal assets.

Tight Money. A term used to indicate time periods in which financing may be difficult to obtain and interest rates may be unusually high by normal standards.

Trade Credit. Interbusiness debt that arises from credit sales; recorded as an account receivable by the seller and as an account payable by the buyer.

Trade Discount. A deduction in the list price of goods allowed by a seller in return for payment within a specified time; for example, 2% ten, net thirty-day terms allow a 2% discount from the list price if paid within ten days.

Variable Cost. A cost that is uniform per unit, but that fluctuates in total in direct proportion to changes in the related total activity or volume; an important element in break-even analysis.

Wire Transfer. Transfer of funds through the electronic network that unites the banking system.

Index